The Troubles of Journalism

A Critical Look at What's Right and Wrong With the Press

LEA'S COMMUNICATION SERIES
Jennings Bryant/Dolf Zillmann, General Editors

For a complete list of titles in LEA's Communication Series, please contact Lawrence Erlbaum Associates, Publishers, at www.erlbaum.com.

The Troubles of Journalism

A Critical Look at What's Right and Wrong With the Press

Third Edition

William A. Hachten

LAWRENCE ERLBAUM ASSOCIATES, PUBLISHERS

2005   Mahwah, New Jersey   London

Lawrence Erlbaum Associates, Inc., Publishers
10 Industrial Avenue
Mahwah, New Jersey 07430

Cover design by Kathryn Houghtaling Lacey

Library of Congress Cataloging-in-Publication Data

The Troubles of Journalism: a Critical Look at What's Right
    and Wrong With the Press, Third Edition, by William A. Hachten
        p. cm.
Includes bibliographical references and index.
ISBN 0-8058-5166-6 (cloth : alk. paper)
ISBN 0-8058-5167-4 (pbk. : alk. paper)

Copyright information for this volume can be obtained by contact-
ing the library of congress

Books published by Lawrence Erlbaum Associates are printed on acid-
free paper, and their bindings are chosen for strength and durability.

Printed in the United States of America
10   9   8   7   6   5   4   3   2   1

Contents

Preface To Third Edition

The second edition of *The Troubles of Journalism* came out in early 2001 before the seismic events of September 11th and subsequent upheavals in American life. The U.S. news media, in what critics considered their finest hour, magnificently reported this historic event.

Confronted with a war on terrorism, the American press now has a slightly different and perhaps more serious perception of itself and how it should serve the American public. Some matters that before were considered important are no longer so pressing; in other ways, the news media probably have changed little—certainly less than media critics had hoped.

Since 9/11, the nation has been "at war" with terrorism but Americans cannot agree what kind of war and who indeed are the enemies of America and other Western nations. Some say the enemy is Islamic fascism or totalitarianism, but others here and in Europe are not so sure. Does this amorphous and vague "war" constitute a very real threat to American lives or is it more of a threat to the American way of life and its freedoms (including press freedom), constitutional protections, and our values because of the ways the war has been conducted?

These are some of the matters the press must deal with in this asymmetrical war against an elusive and shadowy opponent. One journalist probably overstated the challenges of defending the "homeland" when he said, "Now we are all war corespondents."

In the months after Sept. 11, 2001, the news media responded to three historic, interrelated challenges—the 9/11 terrorist attacks on New York City and Washington DC, a prolonged war against the Taliban in Afghanistan, and a full-scale war against Iraq with its continuing and unresolved aftermath. The pluses and minuses of uneven media performance since 9/11 need to be analyzed.

Other significant recent challenges to the media have involved (a) continuing mergers and consolidation of media ownership; (b) new concerns about press credibility and bias, as exemplified by *The New York Times'* ordeal over Jayson Blair; (c) the expanding and controversial role of cable news channels; (d) the growing impact role of news and comment on the Internet; and (e) continuing globalization and controversy over the role of American media in international communications.

To do justice to these recent "troubles" of the news media, important additions and modifications have been made in every chapter of this revised edition.

Preface

The human understanding is like a false mirror, which, receiving rays irregularly, distorts and discolors the nature of things by mingling its own nature with it.

—Francis Bacon (1620)

During the early 1930s when I was a youngster in Huntington Park, California, I would hear the cry of newspaper boys walking through the neighborhood, sometimes at night, hawking the *Los Angeles Herald Express* or the *Los Angeles Times,* calling out EXTRA! EXTRA! to announce some breaking news story, such as FDR's first election, that required a special edition—an Extra!—to get the news out faster.

Soon, news "bulletins" on radio supplemented and in time replaced the newspaper extra. During World War II, we listened to radio for breaking news but with wartime constraints, the time element of major battles and other war-time events was vague and often several days old. Newspapers were still important, but so were newsreels, which in darkened movie theaters provided motion pictures of distant events—Hitler haranguing Nazi crowds in Germany, the abdication of King Edward VIII, but the immediacy of the newspaper Extra was not there.

During the 1936 presidential campaign, I can remember my family huddling around our radio set listening to ex-President Herbert Hoover addressing the Republican Convention. We were all Republicans and hoped that the GOP would nominate Hoover to take on FDR again as in 1932. This was a forlorn hope. My uncle was an International News Service (INS) reporter in Washington, DC and an admirer of Hoover. I later rejected my uncle's politics but not his work. He was my role model for a career in newspapering and later, journalism education.

When I studied journalism at Stanford University in 1947, the curriculum still required students to learn to set type by hand, using the California Job Case. Some weekly papers, despite the widespread use of Linotype machines, were still doing it the old way.

During my newspaper days from 1948 to 1956, daily papers were still being put together much as they had been for the previous 75 years—local news stories were written on typewriters (preferably Underwood or Royal Standard), "wire" or telegraph news stories came clattering in on Associated Press or United Press teletypes. News stories, after being funneled through the city and news desks and then to the copy desk for close editing and headlines, were set in type by Linotype operators. Then galleys of lead body-type and headlines were "made up" on page forms; stereotype mats and lead castings were made and transferred to a rotary press, which printed out the newspapers.

In those days, there was a sense of romance and excitement about working on newspapers that appealed to idealistic young people who wanted to change or improve the world, or at least have fun and interesting jobs, despite the obvious reality that salaries were meager and the hours long. (When he retired, John Chancellor of *NBC News* recalled that when he began as a young reporter on the *Chicago Sun- Times* in 1948, the management didn't know it but he was having so much fun that he would have worked for nothing!) Then, few worried about the future because there was a certain amount of social prestige and cachet in just being a newspaperman. Then (and now), journalists were always interesting and stimulating people to be around.

World War II had produced its journalistic heros—Ernie Pyle, Edward R. Murrow, Hal Boyle, Eric Sevareid, and others. Still in its salad days, radio news was much admired and relied upon. One of its early giants, Eric Sevareid, later commented that he was in the broadcast end of the news business, not the news end of the broadcasting business, as he would later be. As will be seen, that was an important difference.

Much has changed of course since I had my first newspaper job in 1948 at the Santa Paula (California) *Daily Chronicle* (circulation 3,000 but now defunct.) I later worked as a reporter for the *Long Beach Press Telegram* and as a copy editor for the *Santa Monica Outlook, Los Angeles Examiner,* and the *Minneapolis Star.* As a newspaperman and later, journalism educator, I have been dazzled by the changes, for better or worse, that have occurred over the last 50 years.

Some of those changes were technological—new cold type production methods and computer terminals revolutionized the news room and the backshop. Computerized high-speed data transfers assisted by communication satellites greatly accelerated the speed and volume of news and photos. The old-time newspaper city room with its clattering typewriters and its floors strewn with copy paper and galley proofs began to look more like an insurance company office—rugs on the floor, reporters and editors quietly peering into computer terminals, and perhaps Muzak playing in the background.

Changes in daily newspaper journalism, however, have been overshadowed in the past 50 years by the impact of television. In many diverse ways, television news has remade, glamorized, and expanded the reach and impact of daily journalism. But at the same time, the television screen has also distorted, trivialized, and, in many ways, corrupted the news business.

Many of the changes in American journalism—economic, social, cultural, and technological—seem mostly related to what television has done *for* and *to* journalism and to society. We have seen how television continues to modify and transform the Olympic Games (away from sport to entertainment) as well as our national political conventions, which no longer choose candidates but merely crown them. The earlier ethic of the near-anonymous reporter has given way to "celebrity" journalists appearing on television news and talk shows and commanding huge salaries and large lecture fees. Added to this media mix has been the more recent phenomena of 24-hour cable news shows, "talk radio," with it combative commentators, and in the background, the informative and acerbic din of the interactive Internet.

This book looks at these and other criticisms and evaluates some of the changes in journalism, both positive and negative, and suggests what they may have meant for this nation and indeed for the world at large because American journalism—its methods and its standards—has markedly influenced the way many millions overseas receive news and view their world.

As the new century began, deeper and more disturbing concerns about a perceived crisis in the practice of journalism have surfaced. Media critic, Howard Kurtz (1998), of *The Washington Post,* said the crisis has three essential elements:

> First, a crisis of confidence. Journalists no longer see journalism as the business they got into and are worried about the erosion of fundamental values. Second, a crisis of credibility. More and more people do not believe journalists, don't trust journalists, and think we put our spin on the news. Third, a crisis of tabloidism. The whole business has channel-surfed lately, from Marv Albert to Diana to the nanny trial to O. J. and back again. We are complicit, in varying degrees, in the paparazzi phenomenon. (p. 46)

(More recently, media concern with the Lacy Peterson murder trial and the rape trial of Kobe Bryant have pushed aside news about Iraq.)

Another prominent press critic, Tom Rosenstiel, said of contemporary journalism that

> What is going on in the so-called serious press is a crisis of conviction, a philosophical collapse in the belief in the importance of journalism and the importance of news. When supposedly responsible news organizations stop pursuit of the best obtainable version of the truth and reproduce rumor and gossip, they are shedding long-standing principles. The same is true when they fill space with sensational celebrity news to the exclusion of significant matters. (cited in Kurtz, 1998, p. 47)

Moreover, there is a growing concern among newspeople and many in the public that media organizations today are more concerned about making money than they are in providing the news of the day as completely and accurately as possible.

I share these views and acknowledge a personal bias; I believe that serious public-affairs journalism is an important resource of American public life that should be nurtured and shielded from the various influences, both commercial and cultural, that have been marginalizing and trivializing serious news. This volume is an inquiry into the causes of the malaise that seems to grip the news business today.

The mirror has often been used as a metaphor (as well as a name) for the daily newspaper; two of the largest, the defunct *New York Daily Mirror* and the flourishing *Daily Mirror* of London, were sensationalist tabloids. Today there is a sense that the bright, shiny mirror of American journalism has acquired some serious cracks, becoming at times a distorted mirror. One astute journalist, Kenneth Walsh (1996) wrote: "The media are no longer seen as society's truth-sayers. In holding up a mirror to America, journalists too often have filtered out the good and embellished the bad, resulting in a distorted image" (p. 281). I suggest that sometimes our admirable press, as a "false mirror," like Francis Bacon's human understanding, "distorts and discolors the nature of things" by bringing at times its own preconceptions and biases to bear in reporting the news.

This book is based on a 50-year involvement with newspapers and journalism education. My colleagues and students, particularly during my 30 years at the University of Wisconsin-Madison, have helped to educate me about the press. My thanks to Professor James Scotton for his editing suggestions. I alone am responsible for any errors and wrong-headed opinions in this book.

—*William A. Hachten*

Introduction

Most journalism is not about facts but about the interpretation of what seem to be facts.

—Walter Lippmann (1922)

As the 21st century begins, it hardly needs repeating that journalism and mass communication play a central role in modern society. Over time, our newspapers, magazines, radio, television, cable, videocassettes, computers, and movies have been demanding more and more of our attention and leisure time. The media markedly affect our politics, sports, recreation, education, and in general and profoundly, our culture and our perception and understanding of the world around us.

We rely on news media during times of crisis, as on September 11, 2001, when journalists responded quickly and professionally. The horrifying details of the terrorist attacks on New York's World Trade Center and the Pentagon in Washington, DC were quickly conveyed by global television in vivid color to every corner of the world. Supplemented by radio, the Internet, and print, much of the world received virtually the same video and reports as Americans.

Although the news media may lack coercive power (a newspaper cannot draft you and send you off to a foreign war or put you in jail), their influence and pervasiveness are beyond doubt. Yet there are wide disagreements and conflicting views about just how, for better or worse, we are influenced by media in general, and by journalism in particular.

The media, in their diverse, ubiquitous manifestations, are everywhere. As Pember (1992) wrote:

> Perhaps no nation in the history of mankind has enjoyed a communication system equal to the one that currently exists in the United States. It must be regarded as one of the technological marvels of the modern world. It is a multi-faceted system of interpersonal and mass communication elements, and some parts of the network touch virtually everyone in the nation. (p. v)

THE IMPORTANCE OF NEWS

Much of the essential and useful information we require for our personal lives and livelihoods comes from the news media. Our economy, our government, and our society would have great difficulty functioning without the continuing flow of news and information—the lifeblood of our body politic. An open, democratic society without independent news media is impossible to imagine.

Many Americans have a strong need for, and attachment to, news and use a variety of news sources at least several times a week. About half of the people in the United States say they get most of their news from television. Much of the public believes that news is either very or somewhat useful to them in making practical decisions. Even more believe it would matter if they could not get news for a week.

Journalism or what is often called the *news business*—the gathering, the processing, and delivery of important and interesting information and developments by newspapers, magazines, or broadcast media—is inextricably entangled in that giant, whirling entity often referred to as "the media."

Journalism, of course, is concerned with news, which is somewhat different from information, because of its public nature. Michael Schudson (1995) believes that news is a form of culture that he terms "public knowledge," and defines as "this modern, omnipresent brand of shared knowing" (p. 3). Many millions of Americans pay close attention on a daily basis to the news.

James Fallows (1996) argued that the real purpose of journalism (and news) is to satisfy both the general desire for current information and its meaning. "People want to know the details but they also want to see what the details add up to. Journalism exists to answer questions like, 'What is really going on?' and 'Why is this happening?'" (p. 134).

By definition, news reports should be accurate and objective in order to be believed or to be credible. Objectivity means that a news story should be free of a reporter's feelings or opinions and should be based on verifiable facts. Careful verification of a news story is essential because that report should be so convincing that there can be no argument about its truth or accuracy.

In explaining the meaning or importance of any event, a journalist runs the risk of being considered biased or partial, hence, the need to be fair and evenhanded. (Many readers consider news "biased" if it conflicts with their own views; objectivity, it has been said, is in the eye of the beholder.) Objectivity and fairness may be difficult, if not impossible, goals to achieve but it is essential that the journalists try. News provides perspective by telling the public what is considered important and significant and what is not. Page location and size of headlines can indicate this; any story placed on the right-hand column of page one of a metropolitan newspaper is considered important, usually what an editor considers that day's major story. Most of the time, the first item on a television or audio newscast is considered of prime interest. The news, on whatever medium, is not all the news available but only a small selection of it.

Fallows (1996) pointed out that

> During times of scandal our media abandon the pretense of maintaining perspective, and in times without scandal, it hopes for a scandal to come. The financial press does the same thing waiting for the next big takeover deal. The foreign affairs press does so waiting for the next big international disaster. All of them are too busy looking for what is "urgent" to do the daily chore of telling us what is important and why. (p. 134)

This illustrates a long-standing contradiction and dilemma for daily journalism. News should also provide placement in time by not only reporting what is happening, but explaining to us the background or the history of a particular story. When genocidal warfare breaks out suddenly in Kosovo or Rwanda, the press should tell us the background and details of similar tragic instances in that land and elsewhere. News should also point out the similarities and differences in events because many events are important because they fit a certain pattern and as such have added significance. When an airliner explodes in midair, people want to know about similar catastrophes of recent years.

News is not usually a discrete, singular event, although television news often gives that impression. Most news is a process with a recent past, present, and future; hence, the importance of giving background and context to a story as well as providing follow-up stories. Also news is said to be a "liquid," not a "solid."

Much news can be interesting and diverting but may also be important mainly because many people find it useful. A crisis in the Middle East can mean that gasoline will be more expensive at the pump. Other examples: Next Tuesday is election day and polls are open from 8 a.m. to 8 p.m. Here are the candidates.... Here is the weather forecast for today. Business sections of newspapers are replete with useful information about changes in markets and the shifting prices of investments and commodities. For stockholders, news may be quite useful in reporting crime or malfeasance by corporations. Sports pages provide scores. Scores and scores of scores.

In more abstract terms, Harold Lasswell (1971) wrote that the communication process (including serious journalism) in society performs three broad functions: (a) surveillance of the environment, disclosing threats and opportunities affecting the value positions of the community and of the component parts within it; (b) correlation of the components of society in making a response to the environment; and (c) transmission of the social inheritance to the next generation. According to Lasswell, in democratic societies, rational choices depend on enlightenment, which in turn depends on communication; and especially on the equivalence of attention among the leaders, the experts, and the rank and file. A workable goal of democratic society is equivalent enlightenment among expert, leader, and laymen. If, for example, the president, leading scientists, and the public disagree over the potential threat of global warming, then the society has a problem.

News, as useful public knowledge, is usually distinct from rumor, titillation, diversion, gossip, and particularly scandal, although any of these elements may contain kernels of news and unfortunately often become involved in news stories. News has a long and fascinating history; one man's news is another man's titillation, entertainment, propaganda, or diversion.

Nonetheless, news in whatever form seems essential for any society. Gossip, or just idle talk or rumors about the private affairs of others, is not without purpose and seems to be a human requirement; inquiring minds really do want to know. Gossip is all mixed up with and an integral part of journalism and always has been. Much of what is considered news is also gossip, that is, idle talk and rumors, often about the private affairs of others. A large portion of news in a newspaper concerns human interest stories, interviews, items about personalities or celebrities, and so forth. This is true of serious publications as well as tabloids.

Anthropologists and evolutionary psychologists tell us that gossiping is not only a very human activity but is perhaps central to social relationships. At whatever level, at the family, in the workplace, or the broader community, we require and seek out information about other people, in order to adjust our relationships with each other. This includes people close to us as well as distant public figures and celebrities of all kinds.

Robin Dunbar (1996) wrote:

> Most of us would rather hear about the doings of the great and the not-so-good than about the intricacies of economic processes or the march of science. It is a curious fact that our much-vaunted capacity for language seems to be mainly used for exchanging information on social matters; we seem to be obsessed with gossiping about one another. Even the design of our minds seems to reinforce this. Language makes us members of a community, providing us with the opportunity to share knowledge and experience in a way no other species can do. (p. 7)

A central problem for serious journalism is how to manage gossip as news, how to keep it from overwhelming the significant news that must be reported. Often important stories are rife with gossip and titillation, as in the prolonged Clinton–Lewinsky scandal; what separates the serious from the trivial media is the way these stories are reported. Continued and repetitious coverage with emphasis on salacious details of a scandalous story is often an indicator of bad journalism. The excessive and prolonged attention to the death of Princess Diana was a case in point. Media attention often creates celebrities who then become life-long "newsworthy" persons. Charles Lindbergh was a notable example of the 1920s and 1930s. For several decades, there has been a continuing interest in any morsel of news or gossip about the Kennedy family. One sociologist's definition of news as "organized gossip" is not far off the mark.

What kinds of news do people want to read about? A Pew Research Center for the People and the Press (1996) survey found that crime, the local community, and health were the news subjects that most interest the American public. Culture and the arts, news about famous people, and business and financial news were the least interesting of 14 subjects tested. Other topics of interest were: sports (4th place); local government (5th place); science and technology (6th place); religion (7th place); political news (8th place); international news (9th place); and entertainment (10th place).

Of course, there are marked differences between, say, listeners to National Public Radio (NPR) or C-SPAN and those who watch MTV and tabloid, tell-all television shows. The former are less interested in crime news whereas the latter follow news about crime very closely.

STORIES OF HIGH INTEREST

Other surveys conducted over 5 years by the Pew Research Center for the People and the Press (1997) found that relatively few serious news stories attract the attention of adult Americans, except those that deal with national calamities or the use of American military force. Only one in four Americans (25%) followed the average story closely. Of 480 stories reported over 5 years, the survey found that most attention went to natural or man-made disasters, such as the Challenger spacecraft explosion, and stories about wars and terrorism involving American citizens. Most notably, only 5% of Americans paid very close attention in late 1991 to news about the outbreak of civil war in Yugoslavia.

But when serious news hits home, audiences soar. Seventy-nine million Americans were watching news on broadcast and cable television during prime time on Sept. 11, 2001.Three days later, 39.4 million viewers tuned in to television news coverage.

And yet, the public also has a taste for trivia. In early 1990, for example, when only 21% of Americans were following the historic fall of Communist regimes in Eastern Europe, 74% of Americans had "heard a lot recently" about the Teenage Mutant Ninja Turtles, 78% knew about the recall of Perrier water, and 76% could name President George H. W. Bush's least favorite vegetable—broccoli.

Sometimes an event of no apparent importance takes on a media life of its own and becomes a consuming passion for many millions of people for weeks or even months on end. In early 2000, no one could have predicted that the plight of a 6-year-old Cuban boy, Elian Gonzalez, who was washed ashore in Florida in November 1999 after his mother drowned, would become the center of a media-driven custody controversy involving Cuban exiles in Miami, Fidel Castro, the immigration service, other legal bodies, and various politicians. This prolonged media event, a cross between a Cold-War skirmish and a soap opera, enthralled many people and dismayed many others but it was undeniably news.

In a broad sense, the term *media* encompasses most of commercial entertainment—movies, popular music, television, radio, books, and video programming as well as print journalism and broadcast news. But more often, media are separated into the *entertainment media* and the *news media* and that is a distinction I cover in later chapters. News media, or simply "the press," is used to designate newspapers, journals, news magazines, and those aspects of electronic organizations primarily involved with news and information of public interest and concern. But I quickly add that the intermixing and overlapping of news and entertainment and/or sensationalism is a central concern about today's journalism. Along with this is a trend for opinions and predictions to replace facts, particularly in political reporting.

Increasingly, the media, and sadly some serious journalism and some of its best-known practitioners have become ensnared in the various orbiting worlds of advertising, publicity, public relations, promotion, and that pervasive commercial activity, marketing. In modern America, apparently, no organization is too proud or pure to refrain from trying to market or sell its ideas, its by-products, its people. The aim is to "brand" your name or product so that everyone recognizes it. The serious news media, which are mainly, but not exclusively, concerned with public affairs news, can at times pursue the same stories and share the news values of trivial or entertainment-oriented media. Even worse, the serious news media can, at times, emulate the trash journalism as typified by the supermarket tabloids and various television magazine shows.

Today, even the best and most responsible of news media are often a mix of hard news, self-help, and lifestyle stories, news about celebrities and pop culture, and some scandal and crime news. The editor's goal is to maintain a balance between the important and the fascinating but yet trivial. That essential balance is easier to achieve on daily newspapers than in broadcasting because print media have much larger news holes than the network television news's usual 21 minutes to tell everything. (A *news hole* is the space left over after advertising, comics, features, etc., have been allocated.) A newspaper can follow an ongoing scandal story, such as the Kobe Bryant trial, but still have room for many other stories.

After all, from its beginnings, the press has sought to entertain its readers. Even today, a great many people will be interested in or diverted by an entertaining story. (The press is still not too far removed from Hearst's 19th-century definition of real news: a story whose headline causes a reader to first stagger back in disbelief and then to rush to buy the paper and read all the shocking details.)

Further, due to pressures for profit-making or just economic survival, some news media and their journalists are facing an identity crisis—they are becoming increasingly involved in the entertainment business. *Infotainment* is a pejorative term used to describe the mixing of news and titillation that is so widespread today, (Historians may argue that the press has always sought to profit by seeking the greatest possible audience with content as low or enticing as necessary. Perhaps so but not all the press.)

NEWSPEOPLE'S NAMES MAKE NEWS

A trend in recent years is that some journalists, from network anchors to television talk-show regulars, have become highly-paid celebrities whose names appear in gossip columns and who command large speaking fees. Peter Jennings commands a multimillion dollar salary not because he is a good journalist, which he is, but because his familiar face and delivery attracts a large audience to his *ABC Evening News* show and that means big bucks in advertising revenue.

Many in journalism are distressed by this trend. The journalist as celebrity, it is argued, has undermined press standards and fueled public animosity toward the press. The identity, if not the soul, of American journalism, appears to be threatened. At times, it seems that the news media have made Faustian bargains with the devil in order to increase their circulations, audience sizes, corporate profits, and, in the case of individual journalists, to maximize their personal wealth. For a few "stars," journalism is a very lucrative career. The best newspapers and magazines, as well as broadcast outlets, have always been in business to make money and indeed must prosper in order to survive in the marketplace. But critics detect a recent willingness to unduly compromise journalistic standards to increase monetary gain. In the past, there were always some news organizations for whom public service was a higher calling than merely making money. Today, that seems to be the case less often.

DISAPPEARING FIRE WALL

Public communication today appears to be marked by a kind of Manichaean struggle—a battle between good and evil propensities of journalists and their masters. There is a sense that public affairs journalism has become seriously tainted by the emphasis on profitability at the expense of public service.

Veteran newsmen say there used to be a "fire wall" located at responsible news organizations—such as *The New York Times, The Washington Post, Time, Newsweek,* and *CBS News*, and a few other media—between serious news reporting and mere sensationalism and entertainment. Some feel that wall has almost disappeared or at least has too frequently been breached in the competitive scramble for audiences, circulations, and profits. This scramble has been exacerbated by the intense competition provided by 24-hour cable news outlets, talk radio, and increased use of the Internet to spread rumors and dubious assertions as well as news.

Certain kinds of lurid stories come along that seem to cause some of the most reputable news organizations to forget the fire wall and compete with the "bottom feeders" (i.e., supermarket tabloids) for juicy tidbits about the travails of some celebrity or public figure well-known to television viewers. Examples come along too regularly—the Amy Fisher trial, the Menendez brothers trial, the Tonya Harding–Nancy Kerrigan episode, the JonBenet Ramsey murder, Chandra Levy's disappearance, the Lacy Peterson murder case, and accusations against Michael Jackson, among others.

Perhaps, the prime example of recent journalistic waywardness was the way the press reported the prolonged murder trial of O. J. Simpson, the story that had everything—a brutal double murder, a well-known athletic celebrity, spousal abuse, celebrity lawyers, racial overtones, and a prolonged, televised trial. During election campaigns, scurrilous and often unfounded rumors make their way into the news cycle of even the most responsible media.

These trends toward the trivialization of content and decline of serious news reporting are seen as somehow related to the consolidation of newspapers, magazines, television, and radio stations into bigger and more pervasive media conglomerates with great economic power and influence both here and overseas. Well-regarded news organizations such as *Time* magazine, the three networks, Cable News Network (CNN), and a long string of once-prestigious daily newspapers such as *The Louisville Courier Journal,* and *The Des Moines Register,* have been swallowed up by media mergers into giant conglomerates. In these multibillion-dollar operations, news organizations devoted to serious journalism represent only a small fraction of a media giant dedicated to maximizing profits from highly profitable entertainment divisions. How have such organizational changes affected the quality and integrity of serious journalism?

For these and other reasons to be discussed later, the American public has become increasingly annoyed and dissatisfied with the news media. Public opinion polls show widespread scorn and dislike of much popular culture, the media, and of journalists in general. High-profile journalists such as Diane Sawyer, Sam Donaldson, Barbara Walters, and Dan Rather, among others, have been singled out at times for failing to meet the standards of public affairs journalism. The highly competitive cable news channels have spawned such popular but controversial commentators as Chris Mathews, Bill O'Reilly, and Greta Van Susteren.

Public dismay or unhappiness with the media is often confused—and confusing. When the media are under attack, one should ask which medium or media personalities are being singled out—your local daily newspaper, Tom Brokaw on *NBC News*, Russ Limbaugh on talk radio, shouting anchors on *Crossfire* or smart-aleck comments in *Newsweek*? Equally unclear is what aspects of the media are undergoing scrutiny—charges of violence or sex in the entertainment media or biased opinions and distortions in the news media? Critical readers and viewers usually treat "The Media" as a monolith, forgetting that "media" is a plural noun (although the usage is changing) that refers to a complex and multifaceted activity composed of many diverse elements.

Widespread distrust and suspicion of the press exists across the political spectrum from the far left to the far right and among many political moderates. A few critics such as James Fallows believe the press' cynical distortions of political reporting are undermining American democracy. Such accusations go to the heart of public unease with the news media.

The public itself, however, is not blameless. The usual comeback of criticized media has long been, "we're just giving the public what it wants." In a sense that is true, and a major failing of the public is that too few people are adequately concerned and informed about the serious issues and problems facing the nation. People under 30 years of age read less in general and are not reading many daily newspapers; recently a dramatic drop in watching news on network television occurred among this group.

Many young people get their political news, especially during presidential campaigns, not from serious media, but from entertainment sources such as "The Daily Show With John Stewart" (Comedy Central), Music Television (MTV), late-night television comedians, Jay Leno and David Letterman, and from talk radio's call-in shows. There is an obvious need to develop a more attentive and critical audience for serious news.

The crisis in journalism may be related to the reality that we are becoming an increasingly polarized society—a small, affluent, and well-educated upper class that attends to news and public information and the swelling bottom 85% of our population (especially those under 30) that reads less and pays less and less attention to public information, opting instead for pop culture and entertainment. The news media themselves reflect these schisms.

I agree with Stephen Hess (1996) that the United States is a "one nation with two media" society, especially in the case of foreign news. Hess wrote:

> Our society is awash in specialized information, available to those who have the time, interest, money, and education to take advantage of it. The other society encompasses the vast majority of Americans, who devote limited attention to subjects far removed from their necessary concerns. They are content to turn to the top stories of television networks' evening news programs and their community's daily newspaper for their information. (p. 5)

Another cultural fault line, reflected in the media, turns on such issues as abortion, gay marriages, religious fundamentalism, school prayers, and so forth.

These distinctions are central in understanding the strengths and weaknesses of American journalism.

THREE MODES OF DAILY JOURNALISM

This analysis may be helped if we consider that the press often seems to operate under three different modes in covering the day-to-day news. Mode one is a routine, normal news day when no one major story or "blockbuster" dominates the news. The better newspapers will cover a variety of stories, perhaps even reporting foreign news and highlighting a few features or "soft news" stories. Television will do likewise, probably stressing stories of self-help, medical news, personal advice, or human interest.

Mode two is when a story of major significance breaks: the mysterious explosion of an airliner, results of a presidential election, outbreak of war overseas, or the assassination of a major world leader. (A good recent example was the capture of Saddam Hussein in December 2003) Both print and broadcasting will throw all their resources into covering these stories. Evening television may devote an entire program to the story—excluding most or all of the other news. The *New York Times* may give the story four or five full pages. This mode usually shows U.S. journalism at its best.

Mode three is when a major scandal or sensational story of high and continuing interest such as the O. J. Simpson case, the JonBenet Ramsey murder, or even the air crash death of John Kennedy, Jr., takes over the news spotlight. The most sensational story of the late 1990s, the scandal involving President Clinton with Monica Lewinsky, also had major implications for public affairs and created serious dilemmas for the news media. Television news will respond to stories appearing first in tabloids and pick up the story even while decrying such journalism. Often, the coverage of the coverage becomes a compelling story as well. This mode shows the national media at their worst due to the unseemly scramble over tidbits of news about the continuing scandal. It is worth noting that the current unhappiness with news media and journalists comes during a period of rapid technological change in news communication and entertainment media and their economic underpinnings as well as in a period of societal change. Media—movies, television, pop music, videos, cassettes, CD-ROMs, DVDs, and computer-generated exchanges such as the Internet—are the main conveyor belts of our vast popular culture, mostly generated in America, that have been sweeping the world, for better or worse. As noted, American journalism in all of its forms is a small but important part of that cultural flow. The old distinction between foreign and domestic news, especially since 9/11, has all but disappeared as well.

Change brought on by electronic media, especially the Internet, as well as computer-assisted information transfers, threatens the viability of traditional ways of reporting the news yet offers promising new ways of disseminating information.

The focus in this book is on serious news coverage, primarily American journalism, and how news is gathered, edited, and disseminated here and abroad. Although faced with such recent disturbing trends as tabloidization, mixing of facts and opinion, lowering of standards, and trivialization, as well as media consolidation and commercialization to increase profitability, American journalism is still arguably the most informative and most free anywhere and is an influential and significant source of news for news organizations of other nations.

A great advantage of the free and independent journalism Americans have enjoyed is its ability to correct its own excesses through the process of self-criticism. American journalism has had a long tradition of self-examination throughout the 20th century—from Will Irwin to A. J. Liebling to various journalism reviews and a current bumper crop of astute critics, several of whom are quoted here. Some newspapers have ombudsmen who act as representatives of the public in responding to complaints about media performance.

Many within the field of journalism are concerned about its shortcomings and want to see changes made. So if it will recognize its faults (some say U.S. journalism is in denial), U.S. journalism can potentially correct and improve itself. Recently, a good deal of self-criticism has been going on within U.S. journalism, a reassuring sign. The power of embarrassment and shame to convince journalistic peers to mend their ways should not be underestimated. There are some indications that media criticism has been bringing results. Perhaps, this volume can contribute to that debate.

CHAPTER

1

Best News Media
in the World?

There is much to criticize about the press, but not before recognizing a ringing truth: the best of the American press is an extraordinary daily example of industry, honesty, conscience, and courage, driven by a desire to inform and interest readers.

—Ben Bradlee

A major news event can occur unexpectedly somewhere in the world at any moment—the explosion of a jet airliner in midair, a terrorist bombing of an American military facility, the assassination of a world leader, an outbreak of war in the Middle East, a major oil spill in a ecologically sensitive region.

On hearing about an important news story, millions of Americans then turn to their television sets or radio to learn more—to CNN perhaps, or to an all-news radio station for the first details from the Associated Press (AP) or Reuters or from broadcast reporters. The evening network news shows will give a fuller picture and one of the networks—ABC on Ted Koppel's *Nightline,* or maybe NBC or CBS may put together a special report later that evening. The news will also be available on cable networks and the Internet.

The next morning more complete stories with additional details will appear in more than 1,500 daily newspapers and hundreds of radio and television stations will recap the story with more developments. If the story is big enough, if it "has legs"—of continuing interest—*The New York Times* may devote three or four inside pages to more details, related stories, and news photos. Other major dailies may do the same.

Within a week, the news magazines—*Time, Newsweek,* and *U.S News and World Report*—will publish their own versions, complete with cover stories, more background, and commentary.

If an event is important enough, aware Americans will know the basic essentials—"Terrorists bomb U.S. military housing in Saudi Arabia,"—within 24 hours, and the "news junkies" and interested specialists among us will know a great deal more.

The quintessential "big story" of recent memory, of course, was the terrorist attacks of September 11, 2001. After the collapse of The World Trade Center's twin towers, the scarring of the Pentagon in Washington, DC, the crash of four airliners, and about 3000 lives lost, Americans (and others in the West) no longer felt safe from the threats of a dangerous world beyond our borders. Damage from the 9/11 events was estimated to be about $350 billion. The United States promptly embarked on a war against terrorism.

News coverage of 9/11 was comprehensive and magnificent. In New York and Washington, journalists covered a local story of grave national and international import. Global color television, nonstop and constantly updated, carried unfolding details to every corner of the world. Supplemented by radio, print, the Internet, and cell phone, much of the world saw the same video and news reports as Americans. Nielsen Media Research reported an American audience of 79.5 million watching television news in prime time on 9/11. The Internet audience (which is international) was huge as well. The number of page views that CNN.com normally receives on an average day is 14 million. On 9/11, the number of page views on CNN.com jumped to l62.4 million. Moreover, the vast audience approved of the way both the U.S. government and the media had responded. According to a Pew Research Poll, 89% of the public felt the media had done a good or excellent job in covering the attacks; professional journalists agreed.

Another Pew poll taken in October 2001 found that the terrorist attacks and war in Afghanistan had created a new internationalist sentiment among the U.S. public. And support for assertive U.S. leadership had grown. These dramatic opinion shifts as well as greatly expanded media coverage of international news did not, however, persist.

Even on slow news days, such extensive communication of so much news and information, driven by high-speed computer systems, communication satellite networks, and various databases, is commonplace today. Many Americans will pay little attention and will not be much impressed, but to some of us, such an impressive journalistic performance can be dazzling. For when it is good, modern journalism is very good indeed—as any careful examination of the annual Pulitzer prizes, DuPont–Columbia awards, National Magazine awards, and Peabody awards should remind us. Probably no newspaper covers the day's news as well and as thoroughly as does *The New York Times,* which received six of its 89 Pulitzer prizes for its 9/11 coverage. Rivals that may outperform the *Times* at times (and they often do) would be other major U.S. dailies such as *The Washington Post, The Los Angeles Times,* and *The Wall Street Journal.*

There are many good newspapers, of course, in other open, democratic societies, many of which serve their readers well. Newspapers are edited for the interests and concerns of their own readers in their own cultures, so comparisons of papers across national boundaries are often interesting but probably pointless.

NATIONAL MEDIA SET AGENDA

These four daily papers just mentioned plus *Time, Newsweek, U.S. News,* and the television networks—ABC, NBC, CBS, and CNN—plus National Public Radio (NPR)—are often referred to as the national media, and to a large extent they set the news agenda for other media across America. The national media decide what is major or important news in New York City and Washington, DC, and that will be considered, or at least noted, in Pocatello and Peoria, because electronic news, as well as AP news, reaches almost every community.

This nationalizing of the American press took place over several decades. News magazines and nationwide radio news were well established before World War II. A national television news system took on real importance after the 30-minute format took over in 1963. The highly successful *60 Minutes* appeared in 1968 and *Nightline* in 1979, becoming important supplements to the evening news and imitated later by lesser broadcast news magazines. In 1970, educational and noncommerical radio licensees formed NPR and out of it came two superior daily news programs, *All Things Considered* and *Morning Edition.* C-SPAN also started in 1979 and CNN in 1980. In the 1990s, other cable channels from NBC and Fox became players, while more and more of the public turned to the Internet for late-breaking news as well as sports results.

Due to facsimile and satellite publication, several major newspapers, *The Wall Street Journal, The New York Times,* and *U.S.A. Today* are now available to many millions through home delivery, by same-day mail, or on newsstands almost everywhere in the nation. Today, an American interested in significant news has almost the same access to these national media as anyone in New York City or Washington, DC.

In this sense, *national* has two meanings. These media are available across the country and they provide news and information of national, not of local or parochial, interest. This agenda-setting function of the national media flies in the face of the reality that most news is local, as the perusal of page one of any small daily newspaper or local television news show will attest. People are most interested in what happens close to home, whatever seems to most directly affect their own lives. A small airplane crash at a nearby airport is a bigger story than a jet going down with 250 aboard in Europe.

But for important news from distant places, the national media decide what is significant or at least highly interesting, and regional and local media generally take heed. The national media also gather and edit foreign news.

The dissemination of that news is assisted greatly by the AP, the cooperative news service owned by U.S. press and broadcast outlets, which is instantly available to almost every daily paper and most broadcasters. Reuters and the news syndicates of The New York Times, The Washington Post, and The Los Angeles Times Companies supplement the AP's round-the-clock coverage. News video reports on television and cable networks are often syndicated or cooperatively shared with local broadcasters in much the same way. United Press International (UPI) is no longer able to compete with AP and Reuters.

Televised news has evolved as an elaborate process of gathering and disseminating news and video from domestic and foreign organizations. For many millions, a television set and perhaps a car radio may be their only source of news. A major reason for the steady decline of afternoon newspapers in big cities was that the papers' midday deadlines enabled the evening television news shows to offer major stories breaking too late to be reported by those papers.

Although declining in audiences and profits, the three networks news shows, identified for many years with ABC's Peter Jennings, NBC's Tom Brokaw, and CBS's Dan Rather, usually maintain professional standards. Until 1996, Jennings' report was considered the best; ABC's news resources, especially in foreign news, were superior, and Jennings was seemingly less tempted than CBS or NBC to present more entertainment-oriented and trivial features at the expense of hard news. More recently, NBC has topped the ratings and CBS has made something of a comeback. But essentially the highly competitive networks stay fairly close together in the size of their audiences as well as their popular appeal and choice of news content.

Broadcast media and print media each have different strengths in reporting major news stories. For epochal events from the opening attacks of the

Iraq War to the election returns of a presidential contest, network television can command the nation's attention for hours on end.

Television news, both network and cable, easily switches locales to bring information and comments from a variety of sources; at times, widely scattered reporters or experts can be brought together electronically to report or engage in group discussions—all of which we take for granted. Through video and spoken reports, television viewers get the headlines and the first available facts. (However, the number of news bureaus maintained abroad by television networks has markedly declined. More on this later).

Newspapers and news magazines, however, have the space and the time to provide more stories in greater detail and background and offer greater analysis than broadcasting. Moreover, print media are much better on follow-up stories to inform the public about what really happened during, say, the air war over Kosovo and Serbia and its complex aftermath.

NEW CATEGORIES OF NEWS

This book is critical of some current journalistic practices, so it is important to realize that in many ways the news media today are better than they have ever been. Forty years ago, most newspapers considered the news was covered adequately if they reported some news of government affairs and politics, a smattering of foreign news, local crime and disaster stories, some business news, and sports. In addition, light and human-interest features to divert and entertain were often included.

In recent years, this same subject mix is still being covered but in much more detail and depth. For journalism is very much a part of the information explosion and news media now have far larger amounts of news available. More importantly, the definitions of what is news have been greatly expanded to include news and developments about science, medical research, reviews of movies, the arts and popular culture, the entertainment business, a wide range of social problems, education, legal affairs, information technology and the computer revolution, personal health, nutrition, and many more stories of the business and financial world here and abroad. Much of this expanded reporting is done by specialists with professional training in their fields. (These expanded news categories are distinct from the gossip, trivia, and celebrity-oriented sensationalistic stories that have also proliferated.)

A recent study of media during the last 20 years found that the current news media are producing fewer stories about what happened today than 20 years ago, and are devoting less coverage to government and foreign affairs. More prevalent now are features on lifestyle, human interest, personal health, crime, entertainment, scandal, and celebrities. Why the shift? The Cold War was over, and technology, medical science, and the environment took on new importance. This broader newspaper and broadcast coverage is supplemented by a plethora of specialized magazines, journals, and books that deal with such topics in a more leisurely and detailed manner.

But during the first 2 years of the war on terrorism, the media were full of news of the wars in Aghanistan and Iraq as well as domestic stories about homeland security and various efforts of government and business—particularly the airlines and airports—to protect the nation against terrorist attacks.

Any person living anywhere in America who is determined to be well-informed and be on top of the news can do so by owning a television set with cable, subscribing to a national newspaper such as *The New York Times* or *The Wall Street Journal*, listening to NPR, selectively watching CNN and C-SPAN, and subscribing to several magazines such as *Newsweek, Harper's The New Republic, The New Yorker, The Atlantic, Foreign Affairs,* or *The Economist*, plus getting a good state or regional daily newspaper.

Further, our hypothetical news junkies can gain access to a lot more news and information (as well as rumor and conjecture), if they also own a computer with a modem to scan the news and information available from online services such as America Online, Google, Yahoo, CNN, MSNBC, Slate, or the interactive editions of hundreds of newspapers on the World Wide Web, as well as hundreds of "bloggers" offering opinions, criticism, and tirades about the news (see chap. 12, this volume).

At this time of media bashing, it is well to remember that a lot of good reporting still gets done by newspapers. Phillips (1996) commented:

> Anyone with an hour for a Nexis computer search can come up with 50 courageous exposés of special interests buying congressional favors, lobbies run amok, the plight of the Middle Class and such in *The New York Times, The Washington Post, The Wall Street Journal, The Chicago Tribune, The Philadelphia Inquirer, The Los Angeles Times, and The Boston Globe.* The ghost of Lincoln Steffens is not gone from the nation's newsrooms. (p. 8)

The leading newspapers employ an impressive number of investigative reporters. Press critic, Ben Bagdikian, commented that newspapers are much better today than they were 40 years ago and report a great deal more news than before. But, he added, newspapers now need to be better because much more and varied information is required to cope with today's complex and changing world. Further, many Americans today are better educated and desire, indeed require, more sophisticated and specialized news for their lives and their jobs. (But it is interesting to note that a great fraction of Americans do not vote or stay informed about salient issues in national or global affairs.)

As always, what some people consider to be very important news does not get reported. Most news is mainly of local or parochial interest and does not make it beyond city or state borders. Sometimes, major stories, such as the savings and loan scandals of the 1980s, will be reported in some national media but fail to make an impression on other media and hence, do not attract the attention of the public in general.

Further, despite the availability of so much news each day, long-standing space and time constraints still persist. ABC, CBS, and NBC have only 21 minutes each evening for their major newscasts. Sometimes a major breaking story, such as the TWA Flight 800 disaster, will take the entire 21 minutes; no other news gets reported on that broadcast. Radio's on-the-hour-news broadcasts usually last 5 minutes or less. Many daily newspapers have small news holes for the day's news after all the retail advertisements, features, comics, advice columns, classifieds, stock market reports, and sports have been allocated. Most people probably devote less than 1 hour per day to news from various media.

Journalism, as that proverbial "watchman on the hill," keeps its eyes open and sees more because news gatherers can penetrate almost all corners of the world, but not always. Between 1928 and 1938, an estimated 10 to 20 million people were killed or starved to death in the Soviet Union as a result of Stalin's brutal and disastrous policies, but little news about this horror reached American readers. Similarly, in the early 1960s, little was reported about the 20 to 30 million Chinese who perished during Mao's Great Leap Forward. Today, it is less likely that an autocratic regime could hide calamities of such proportions from the global media's scrutiny.

To better understand what is ahead, we need to provide a concise overview of the American press as it exists today.

THE "MIGHTY WURLITZER" OF U.S. JOURNALISM

The two main arms of U.S. journalism today, print media and electronic media, are divided as well into three main approaches:

1. The "new news" of daily journalism as exemplified by the daily newspaper, evening television news, 24-hour cable news, or radio's "on-the-hour-news" with the latest from AP; plus proliferating and Internet sources;

2. weekly or periodical journalism as typified by *Time* and other news magazines as well as the better television discussion shows such as *Meet the Press, Washington Week in Review; Face the Nation,* and *This Week with George Stephanopoulos;*
3. commentary or opinion journalism in various periodicals; *The New Republic, Nation, Foreign Affairs, Atlantic,* and Sunday editions of some dailies, as well as books.

Naturally, the expectations for objectivity, balance, and impartiality are much higher for daily journalism, which reports the first version of events, than for the more leisurely weekly and opinion publications or the talk shows of weekend television. Daily journalism also has room for editorial comment and interpretation but the expectation is that comment and predictions should be clearly identified and separated from hard or just-appearing news. (However, some critics say that more opinion and assertion is appearing in straight news stories.)

The Print Media

Daily Newspapers. Although viewed by some as a twilight industry, the daily newspaper is still the most effective means of supplying large amounts of serious late-breaking news to the American public. A total of about 1,500 dailies are published—roughly 40% in the morning and 60% in the afternoon—with a total circulation of about 63 million. Almost all metropolitan papers come out in the morning to better compete with television. Circulations vary widely. Fifteen dailies have a circulation of more than 500,000, whereas more than 1,129 dailies have circulations under 25,000 and are primarily concerned with serving small cities and communities.

The backbone and intellectual leadership of daily journalism comes from the 40 to 45 dailies each with circulations of more than 250,000 and includes all those considered the best plus a number of mediocre or fading dailies. A recent survey by the *Columbia Journalism Review* of 150 daily newspaper editors produced the following rankings for what they considered to be America's 21 best daily newspapers:

1. *New York Times;* 2. *Washington Post;* 3. *Wall Street Journal;* 4. *Los Angeles Times;* 5. *Dallas Morning News;* 6. *Chicago Tribune;* 6. *Boston Globe;* 8. *San Jose Mercury News;* 9. *St. Petersburg Times;* 10. *The Sun* (of Baltimore); 11. *Philadelphia Inquirer;* 12. *The Oregonian;* 13. *USA Today;* 14. *Seattle Times;* 15. *Newsday;* 16. *Raleigh News & Observer;* 17. *Miami Her-*

*ald; 18. Star Tribune (*of Minneapolis*); 19. Atlanta Journal-Constitution; 20. Orange County Register (*of Santa Anna, CA ; *21, Sacramento Bee.* ("America's Best," 1999)

From this elite group, the largest and presumably the most influential dailies include: The *Wall Street Journal* (daily circulation about 1.82 million) is primarily a business publication but is noted for its excellent news coverage and fine writing on nonbusiness topics. Owner is the Dow Jones Co., which has 14 other papers.

USA Today (circulation about 2 million) is also distributed nationally and is owned by the Gannett Co., which has 74 dailies and a total daily circulation of more than 6.6 million. The paper has had mixed reviews but is considered to be improving and is carrying more hard news.

The New York Times has a Sunday circulation about 1.7 million, of which about 200,000 comes from its national edition. Although undergoing marked changes in recent years, the *Times* is still considered as the nation's most influential newspaper and targets an elite readership. The paper is prosperous despite (and because of) its staff of 1,200 journalists.

As mentioned, the large circulations of *The Wall Street Journal, USA Today, and The New York Times* are due in part to their national distribution; facsimile newspaper pages are sent via satellite to regional printing plants around the nation.

The Los Angeles Times is one of the notable success stories in U.S. journalism, changing in the past 40 years from a parochial, partisan paper into the finest newspaper west of the eastern seaboard. (In March 2000, the paper and the Times Mirror Company were purchased by the Tribune Company of Chicago.)

The Washington Post is highly regarded and wields great influence in the political vortex of the nation's capital. The Washington Post Company also owns *Newsweek* as well as broadcast and cable properties. The paper competes head-to-head with the *New York Times* on major stories in Washington but targets the greater Washington area for readers.

The New York Times, The Washington Post, The Los Angeles Times, and *The Wall Street Journal* all maintain significant numbers of their own reporters in key capitals overseas. In truth, concern about the global economy and political instability of the world beyond our shores and the willingness to report foreign news is one of the hallmarks of a great news medium. Much of this outstanding reporting finds its way to other dailies through syndication. (The major broadcasters, ABC, NBC, and NBC, have been providing less coverage of foreign news.)

Another major newspaper group is Knight-Ridder Inc., with 29 papers enjoying a circulation of 4,136,770. Highly regarded among its properties are *The Miami Herald, The Charlotte Observer, San Jose Mercury News,* and *The Philadelphia Inquirer,* each an outstanding daily with great influence in its city and suburbs. For $1.65 billion, Knight-Ridder acquired two big additions, *The Kansas City Star,* circulation 291,000, and *The Fort Worth Star-Telegram,* circulation 240,000, from the Disney Company in April 1997.

Finally, Newhouse Newspapers includes 26 dailies with a circulation of 2,960,360, including *The Oregonian.* Newhouse also owns *The New Yorker,* and the Conde Nast magazines.

Weekly Newspapers.   At the other end of the circulation scales are the 7,400 to 7,500 weekly newspapers that average about 7,500 subscribers each. Total circulation of these publications, so important in many small communities, is around 55 million, more than double the mid-1960's total. Although often small and unimposing, these papers are close to their readers and often serve their communities well. Local news dominates these papers (Strentz & Keel, 1995).

Magazines.   Certainly the most diverse and perhaps the most changing yet resilient of the media have been magazines, of which there are about 4,000 published, up from 2,500 in the mid-1980s. Many newly-launched magazines fail.

Comparatively few magazines are mainly concerned with journalism and news but overall magazines contribute tremendous amounts of diverse information and entertainment available to the public. As noted later, U.S. magazines are increasingly popular overseas.

Leading news magazines and their approximate circulations are: *Time* (4.1 million); *Newsweek* (3.2 million), and *U.S. News and World Report* (2.3 million). Business magazines such as *Money* (2.2 million), *Business Week* (900,000), and *Fortune* and *Forbes* (each about 770,000), contribute to the public affairs news as do, of course, *The Atlantic, Harper's* and *The New Yorker.*

Though modest in circulations, opinion journals such as the *New Republic, Nation, Weekly Standard,* and *National Review* have a disproportionate influence on politicians, opinion makers, and intellectuals, particularly in Washington, DC and New York City.

Books.   Over 50,000 new book titles are published annually in the United States and a significant number contribute directly to the swirling cauldron of journalism. Ever since Theodore H. White wrote *The Making of the President, 1960*, after John Kennedy defeated Richard Nixon, journalists have been writing numerous books on national politics and public affairs. Of interest here is that journalists have been writing books critical of media performance. Among important recent efforts have been *Breaking the News*, by James Fallows; *Hot Air: All Talk, All the Time* and *Spin Cycle*, both by Howard Kurtz; *Feeding the Beast,* by Kenneth T. Walsh; *Don't Shoot the Messenger,* by Bruce Sanford; *Warp Speed,* by Bill Kovach and Tom Rosenstiel; *What the People Know,* by Richard Reeves; *The News About the News,* by Leonard Downie and Robert Kaiser; and *Bias,* by Bernard Goldberg.

Electronic Media

Radio. Radio is ubiquitous and was for most of the 20th century. Receiving sets are everywhere—in almost every car, scattered around the house, and carried by young people and joggers. There are over 500 million sets in America. The nation is served by 8,454 radio stations, of which 3,764 are AM stations and 4,690 are FM stations. About 70% of the audience listens to FM. Many big-city radio stations today are quite profitable. Hard hit by the advent of television, radio was slow in finding a new niche. It no longer seeks its previous mass audience and offers instead narrow formats in various kinds of music and news, plus a smattering of network programming, especially in news. Radio's survival has offered additional proof that older media are supplemented by new media, not replaced by them.

Radio's journalistic contributions appear to consist mainly of brief newscasts stressing local and regional news, as well as headlines and brief reports on national and foreign events. As mentioned, two shining exceptions are National Public Radio's *"Morning Edition"* and *"All Things Considered,"* heard nationwide on public stations. These programs make important contributions to the reporting and analysis of public affairs. Another facet of the medium, "talk radio," which is typified by the highly successful *The Rush Limbaugh Show* (with many imitators), has become politically significant because of the outspoken political and social commentary (mostly conservative) spewing out of radio stations.

Television. A good deal is written about television news and its ups and downs. More than 1,290 commercial licenses have been granted by the Federal Communications Commission (FCC). Of these, about half are VHF, with a far-reaching signal, and half are UHF stations, more numerous and limited in reach. Viewers have access to about 350 noncommercial or public television stations. More than 400 commercial stations are independents, not affiliated with the four major networks—CBS, ABC, NBC, and Fox. (Two fledgling networks, UPN and WB, are trying to break into prime time.) Television markets vary widely, from New York City with about 7 million television households, all the way to Alpena, Michigan, with just 15,600 households with television sets (Strentz & Keel, 1995).

Cable channels such as CNN, Fox News Channel, and MSNBC have become important outlets for both news and public-affairs programming. Cable audiences are much smaller than those of broadcast television except during major breaking stories. Most Americans are aware of television's importance as a news medium. If at any time there are rumors of a disaster or other ominous event, people will first turn on their television sets or, if away from home, their radios. But today they are more likely today to find the breaking news on a cable station rather than a broadcast outlet.

Public television stations contribute to broadcast journalism primarily through the *News Hour with Jim Lehrer* and documentary news programs such as *Frontline, Nova,* and *The American Experience.* With the exception of CBS' *60 Minutes*, news documentaries or news magazines on commercial networks rarely reach the journalistic quality of those on the Public Broadcasting System (PBS).

Another important contributor is C-SPAN, the nonprofit cable channel created to report on the legislative process in the U.S. Congress. In addition, it provides television coverage, without comment or interpretation, of a wide variety of meetings, conferences, or seminars, all of which have some involvement with public affairs. C-SPAN has a small but devoted group of listeners who care about public affairs. The Internet has been rapidly growing in importance as a medium for news as computer users have been increasing at exponential rates; broadcast and print news organizations all seem to now have their outlets in cyberspace. (See chap. 12, this volume, for more on jounalistic aspects of the Internet.)

As mentioned, we are largely concerned with the so-called national media, all of whom have the capability of reaching most of the nation—either directly on indirectly. There are, of course, other important regional news media—in Chicago, Boston, Philadelphia, Detroit, Los Angeles, San Francisco, Seattle, Phoenix, Houston, Dallas, Miami, Denver, Atlanta, and numerous other urban areas but the national media have an agenda-setting capability and influence extending beyond their locales. These national media have overlapping audiences and reach the movers and shakers of the American establishment—leaders in government, politics, social affairs, business, and academia, especially along the eastern seaboard from Boston to Atlanta and throughout the midwest and west coast.

But despite the size and scope of the news media, the reality is that the great majority of Americans are not being reached by serious journalism. Whether the U.S. news media are the best in the world may be a pointless argument; a more important question is "Are they are as good as they should be or could be?" Nonetheless, as will be seen in chapter 2, the impact of American journalism on the world has been significant.

2

Global Impact of American Media

Mankind has become one, but not steadfastly one as communities or nations used to be, nor united through years of mutual experience … nor yet through a common language, but surpassing all barriers, through international broadcasting and printing.

—Alexander Solzhenitsyn

Most Americans who keep up with the news are unaware of the influence and reach of American journalism beyond the borders of their nation. During the past 50 years, the U.S. news media, in doing their basic job of reporting the news for local audiences, have participated in and helped shape a world that is economically more interdependent while becoming, since the end of the Cold War, more politically fractured and threatening.

In addition to American-generated news in print and broadcasting, our movies, pop music, television programs, and lifestyles have penetrated the minds and cultures of European and non-Western people with tremendous impact. With results both positive and negative, transnational communication is evolving toward a single, integrated global communication system that espouses free, independent journalism as well as favoring market economies and Western popular culture. As will be seen, the current wave of major media mergers can be viewed in part as corporate strategies to compete better for overseas markets and profits in both entertainment and news.

The enhanced ability of Western journalism (Britain and other industrialized democracies contribute as well) to report quickly and fully on global crises and trends enables leaders of nation states, the United Nations, and business and nongovernmental organizations to respond to such challenges. News media can and do alert nations to a kaleidoscope of such dangers as environmental disasters, changing facets of terrorism, human rights clashes, economic trends and crises, and incipient political crises whether in Bosnia, Central Africa, Chechnya, or Kosovo.

GLOBALIZATION AND MEDIA

The rapid integration of the world's economy, loosely called "globalization," has been facilitated by an information revolution driven by communication technologies that provide a "nervous system" for the globe. Globalization is a broad and inexact word for an array of widespread changes in politics, economics, trade, finance, lifestyles, and cultures. How people feel about globalization depends a lot on where they live and what they do. To its many critics, globalization is trendy and controversial. They see the world becoming a consumer colony of America, led by McDonald's, Nike, Coke, and the vast mass culture output of Hollywood. In recent years, much of the world's economy has become integrated; direct foreign investment has grown five times as fast as domestic investment. But globalization is more than buying and selling:; some see it as a profound interchange of cultures—a communication revolution that is dissolving the sense of boundaries, our national identities, and how we view the world. (Hachten & Scotton, 2002)

Deregulation of telecommunications and computerization have been called the parents of media globalization. Three technologies—computers, satellites, and digitalization—have converged to form a global network that covers the earth as completely as the atmosphere. The era of globalization is based on falling telecommunications costs, thanks to microchips, satellites, fiber optics, and the Internet. Popular culture products of the West have been increasingly flowing around the world. Is the world beginning to share a common pop culture? Critics differ about what happens when cultures meet; rather than fight, they often blend.

Frederick Tipson (1999) noted "More like a thin but sticky acid, this cosmopolitan culture of networks and information media seems to overlay rather than supplant the cultures it interacts with." (p. 12) When cultures receive outside influences, they ignore some and adopt others, and soon begin to transform these influences.

Critics of media globalization castigate it for the centralization of media power and heavy commercialism, which is related to the decline of public broadcasting as well as public service standards for broadcasting. Press critics of globalization have other concerns: the news media, they argue, become increasingly submerged and neglected inside vast entertainment conglomerates seeking entertainment profits.

Others see globalization in a more positive light. Many more millions of people than ever before now have access to news and information, especially in China and India. Globalization means multitudes now have many newfound choices: how they will spend their leisure time; what they will watch and read; and what to buy with newly acquired personal income from rapidly rising standards of living. Anthropologist James Watson wrote in 1999, "They lives of Chinese villagers I know are infinitely better off now than 30 years ago. China has become more open because of the demands of ordinary people. They *want* to become part of the modern world—I would say that globalism is the major force for democracy in China. People want refrigerators, stereos, CD players." (cited in Hachten & Scotton, 2002, p. 4)

The primacy of the issue of globalization reminds us of the extent to which most of us now think and act globally—as a matter of course. Yet there is a dark side of the issues. Many millions in the poor and "failed" nations that do not participate in the global economy resent and despise the West. That anger has given vent to terrorism directed particularly toward the United States.

GLOBAL NEWS SYSTEMS

It has been said with some but not much exaggeration that an American's right to know is the world's right to know. For any news story that gets into the American news, media can and often does flow rapidly around the world and can appear in local media anywhere if it gets by the various gatekeepers that select and reject the news of the day.

Since the end of the Cold War and the demise of Communist news systems in the Soviet Union and other Eastern bloc nations, the American approach to international news, based on independent and wide-roving journalists free to report (at least in theory) whatever they want and wherever they wish, has gained influence and acceptance. English is the dominant language of global news just as it is of computers and the Internet. Global news gathering is now more cooperative and less confrontational than it was in the Cold War days, and more countries are now open to foreign journalists.

Autocratic regimes still exist, of course, and many often restrict their own journalists, as well as foreign reporters, while trying to control the news, but they have not been as successful as they once were. Despite press controls in such currently authoritarian states as Indonesia, China, Iran, Cuba, and Algeria, the news does get out sooner or later.

This global news system, although largely American, is greatly enhanced by such British media as the BBC World Service (mainly shortwave radio) and BBC World Television (a recent competitor to CNN International), Reuters news agency, *The Financial Times, The Economist,* and the long tradition of foreign coverage in several elite newspapers such as *The Guardian, Times of London, Sunday Times, The Independent,* and *Daily Telegraph.* Reuters Television, (successor to Visnews) and Associated Press Television News (APTN), daily gather and distribute video news packages to television stations all over the world.

Among U.S. daily newspapers, most of the foreign reporting, some of high quality, comes from just seven publications—*The New York Times, The Washington Post, The Los Angeles Times, The Wall Street Journal, The Chicago Tribune, The Christian Science Monitor,* and *The Baltimore Sun*—which all maintain overseas news bureaus. (The Tribune Co. now owns *The Los Angeles Times* and *The Baltimore Sun.*) These papers, whose total daily circulation is about 11 million, represent only about 20% of newspaper circulation of all U.S. dailies. Companies controlling 80% of daily newspaper circulation have been making little effort to produce sustained international coverage.

A survey of foreign bureaus of major U.S. dailies in 2002 found *The New York Times* had 40 reporters in 26 bureaus; *The Washington Post* had 20 reporters in 26 bureaus; and *The Los Angeles Times* had 21 reporters in 26 bureaus. Knight Ridder papers had 14 reporters in 14 bureaus and *USA Today* had had 4 reporters in four bureaus. Regional papers with five or more bureaus included *The Chicago Tribune* (10), *Newsday* (5), *Dallas News* (5), *The Baltimore Sun* (5) and *The Boston Globe* (5).

Before the 9/11 events, an increase in overseas coverage had been due to the expanded interest in business and financial news—one aspect of the expanding global economy. This explains the 100 staffers for *The Wall Street Journal,* with its business focus and overseas editions in Asia and Europe. Reuters and Bridge News (formerly Knight-Ridder financial news) have hundreds of overseas staffers to report its specialized economics news. Bloomberg News, another financial news service, have 226 reporters in 62 countries (Arnett, 1998).

Most U.S. dailies rely on the Associated Press's widespread correspondents for news from abroad. AP is probably the single most important agency that collects and distributes news globally. By the agency's count, more than 1 billion people have daily access to AP news. To collect foreign news abroad, AP maintains 95 bureaus in 93 countries staffed by 400 full-time foreign correspondents. Like Reuters, its closest competitor, AP uses an extensive network of leased satellites circuits, submarine cables, and radio transmissions, and even the Internet, to supply newspapers and broadcasters with up-to-the-minute news around the world, 24 hours a day. AP broadcast services are used by 6,000 radio and television stations. Three key centers—New York, London, and Tokyo—channel the millions of words and pictures daily to both U.S. and foreign subscribers.

The New York Times, The Washington Post, and *The Los Angles Times* syndicate their foreign news stories thereby extending the impact of U.S. journalism overseas. The New York Times News Service sends more than 50,000 words daily to 550 clients, of which more than 130 are newspapers abroad. Its close competitor is the Los Angeles Times/Washington Post News Service, which transmits about 60,000 words daily to 50 nations or about 600 newspapers, half outside the United States.

Sad to say, television networks have been closing many of their expensive foreign outposts, saying news can be reported by central hubs. In 2003, ABC had only six bureaus, less than half what it had in the 1980s; NBC had only six bureaus, down from 13 in the 1980s; CBS was down from 10 bureaus to only six. CNN bucked the trend; in 2003, it had 28 foreign bureaus, only four less than it had in the 1980s (Fleeson, 2003). (More on this trend in chap. 6, this volume.)

Time, Newsweek, and *U.S. News and World Report* have long maintained substantial bureaus overseas in major news capitals but numbers of staffers have been shrinking as well in recent years and the magazines carry less foreign news than in earlier years.

Since 1980, CNN has added a new dimension to global television journalism—the ability to broadcast news around the clock via satellite, aided by cable, to millions of television sets in foreign nations as well as to the United States. Broadcast news from ABC, NBC, and CBS is also found on foreign cable and satellite systems but in less quantity.

U.S. global journalism is augmented by two important U.S.-owned daily newspapers: *The International Herald Tribune,* published in Paris, now owned completely by *The New York Times.* The papers carries stories and features from New York in addition to reports generated by a staff of 40 in Paris. *The International Herald Tribune,* a marvel of newspaper distribution, sold (in 2002) about 245,000 copies 6 days a week in 164 countries (in Europe alone sales number about 135,000) and is printed by plants in London, the Hague, Marseilles, Rome, Zurich, Singapore, Hong Kong, and Miami. Although still an American paper in outlook and content, it has acquired an important non-American readership. Nearly half its readers are an elite group of European internationalists—businessmen, diplomats, and journalists fluent in English. *The International Herald Tribune* is perhaps the first newspaper to publish the same edition simultaneously for distribution to all continents.

The Asian Wall Street Journal covers a 16-country, 6,000 square-mile business beat from Manila to Karachi. Averaging about 12 pages an issue and roughly one third the size of the domestic edition, the paper tries for the same mix of authoritative business and political news, a risky effort for a region with so little press freedom. *The Wall Street Journal Europe*, written and edited in Brussels and printed in the Netherlands, had a circulation of 95,000 in 2003.

American magazines are influential abroad as well. Two international-ized versions of *Time* and *Newsweek*—in English—are widely read globally. Among non-news U.S. magazines, Hearst publishes *Cosmopolitan, Esquire, Good Housekeeping,* and *Popular Mechanics* in 14 languages in 80 nations. The Russian language edition of *Cosmopolitan* carried 110 pages of ads and sold 225,000 copies. A long-time overseas success is *Reader's Digest*, which has 47 international editions in 18 languages, cir-culating 13 million copies a month overseas. Many millions reading the *Digest* overseas are unaware that it is an American magazine.

Major Effects of Global News

The increasing capability to broadcast and publish news globally has changed our world as well as our perceptions of our world. Some effects have been global or geopolitical in nature, others are more media related, and some are felt mainly by individuals. (Several of the following topics are expanded later in this book.)

Triumph of Western Journalism. Since the fall of the Communist "second world," the Western concept of journalism has become the domi-nant model around the world and is widely emulated. Non-Western na-tions have adopted not only the gadgets and technology of the U.S. press and broadcasting but also its practices, norms, ethical standards, and ide-ology. Journalists abroad increasingly seek editorial autonomy and free-dom from government interference. These journalists of many nations aspire to the professional values of fairness, objectivity, and responsibil-ity as well as the so-called "checking effect," that is, the role of the press as a watchdog and critic of government and authority. They want to report the news as they perceive it, not as their government wants it reported. And there is evidence that in the Middle East, there is a growing Arab acceptance of American news, which has become more widely available in the region (Fakhreddine, 2003).

Electronic Execution of Communism.   Today many experts agree that news and popular culture from the West contributed to the demise of the USSR and Communist regimes in Eastern Europe. Western media, including Voice of America, BBC World Service, and Radio Free Europe, provided news not otherwise available and delivered the forbidden fruit of Western movies, videocassettes, rock music, lifestyles, as well as promises for a better life—democracy, market economies, and a higher standard of living. Western mass communication, by going over, under, and around the Iron Curtain, played a significant role in raising expectations and breaking the Communists' monopoly on their own news and pop culture.

Some observers believe the breakup of the Communist system began with the successes of the Solidarity trade union in Poland. There the Communists' monopoly on information was broken in two ways: the rise of alternative newspapers challenging the government and supporting Solidarity goals; and second, a triangular flow of news among the alternative newspapers inside Poland, foreign reporters, and international broadcasters. It worked this way: Foreign journalists reported news of Solidarity to their Western media; this news was beamed back to Poland via international shortwave radio, particularly BBC, Deutsche Welle, and Radio Free Europe; these stories were then picked up by Polish listeners and by the alternative papers inside Poland. Western media suggested that political change was possible, that times were changing, and that the world was watching. Potential demonstrators in other nations saw that the unthinkable was indeed possible. Thus events in East Berlin, Budapest, Prague, and Bucharest reinforced each other.

Mass Culture (Usually)Accepted.   In recent decades, Western mass media have also conditioned much of the world to use the media for entertainment and leisure. (Political indoctrination by the media has been mostly rejected, at least currently, by peoples everywhere, including even China, the last great Communist nation.) Ever-growing audiences appear to accept and enjoy the movies, television, and even the ever-present commercials. Parents everywhere find it difficult to prevent the influence on their children of the most powerful engine of mass education the West has yet produced—commercial advertising.

The pervasiveness of entertainment in Western media has become a controversial issue and often the target of anti-American sentiments. American cultural hegemony is said to be cracking, as evidenced by American televison programs which had dominated prime time viewing for decades in Europe and Asia and are now being consigned to the late-night slots. U.S. hit shows like *CSI* and *Judging Amy*, which would be expected to be popular abroad are being relegated to weekend and after-11 p.m. showing (Gabler, 2003).

However, as Neal Gabler notes, movies, not television shows, are the truly potent examples of our cultural imperialism. In 2003, they continued to take in about 80% of the film industry's worldwide revenue. Even in France, where sensitivity to alleged American bullying and cultural arrogance may be stronger than anywhere, Hollywood movies continue to account for 50% to 70% of French box office receipts every year (Gabler, 2003).

Global Audiences Growing.   Each year, many more millions of people are drawn into the global audience mainly through competing satellite and cable services of television as well as shortwave radio, which carry news as well as entertainment. With satellite dishes and antennas proliferating everywhere, even in the face of governmental opposition, the populous lands of Asia, particularly China and India, are flocking to join the global village.

Since the Tiananmen Square crisis, China has felt the impact of heightened international communications. Western television networks—CNN, ABC, NBC, CBS, and BBC—carried words and pictures of the 1989 Beijing uprising to the world, while Voice of America and BBC reached hundreds of millions of rural Chinese with their Chinese language newscasts. After the crackdown on demonstrators when all Chinese media were brought under party control, shortwave radio continued to report news into China.

Since then, China has been facing a quieter but more serious challenge in the form of hundreds of thousands of satellite dishes. Millions of Chinese people can hook in via satellite to global television programs bypassing the Communist Party commissars. Some believe the information revolution threatens to supplant China's Communist Revolution, which was long sustained by the now crumbling government monopoly on news and propaganda. Besides shortwave radio, fax machines are widely available in private homes and direct-dial international phones and computers with modems are multiplying as well, enabling many Chinese to use e-mail and interactive news sources on the Internet. In 2003, it was estimated that 78 million Chinese had access to the Internet and 250 million Chinese had cell phones.

In China and throughout Asia, television programming via communication satellites has been flooding in—Star TV in Hong Kong, HBO Asia, CNN, ESPN, MTV Asia, BBC World—bringing news, information, and entertainment to many millions for the first time. Some Asian nations welcome satellite television but others see it as a threat to their cultural identity and political stability.

Governments across the former Third World have tried to suppress global television with mixed success. Satellite services may be discouraged but educated Chinese can still get world news from BBC and VOA on shortwave radio. Governments are finding it nearly impossible to stop people from taking their news and entertainment from the skies. Dishes are easily put together from imported kits, which are growing smaller, cheaper, and more powerful. During the Afghanistan and Iraq wars, news from various Arab television services, led by Al-Jazeera from Qatar, provided war news to Arab audiences usually shielded from foreign news by their own governments.

In Iran, the government has long tried to maintain a monopoly over news. But Iranians eager for independent information criticizing their rulers have found a reliable source of news—Persian language satellite television stations, based in Los Angeles, where there is a large community of Iranians.

Vast Audiences for Global Events.   Great events—the terrorist attacks of 9/11 or the quadrennial Olympic games—can attract huge shares of the global audience. An estimated 2 billion people watched a Live Aid rock concert to help starving people in Africa. About 3.5 billion people watched some of the 1996 Olympics in Atlanta. Those games were probably watched by more people in China than anywhere else because more than 900 million Chinese had access to television sets, and three channels broadcast events all day long.

Some of the effects of expanded global news communication have subtle political and diplomatic effects.

History is Accelerated.   Nations and peoples react faster to important news because global television information moves so quickly and widely. War breaks out in the Middle East and the price of gas at the pump goes up immediately around the world. The 9/11 attacks immediately affected U.S. and world financial markets adversely. A bomb explodes in an airliner and security measures tighten in airports everywhere. Actions that would have been taken later are taken sooner, thus speeding up the pace of change—and of history.

The Whole World Is Watching.   The reality that many millions around the world can watch on television as tanks rumble across national borders, or as troops storm ashore on an African coast, or as police fire on peaceful protestors, can give heightened consequences to a televised news report. For example, an amateur's camcorder tape of Los Angeles policemen beating Rodney King set off repercussions lasting for years. Vivid and dramatic video of several years of the tragic civil war in Bosnia, Croatia, and then Kosovo seared the world's conscience and had political consequences. Ditto for Tiananmen Square; The Chinese Communist regime won the battle of ruthlessly squashing the demonstrators but lost greatly in the global court of public opinion for its abuses of human rights.

Diplomacy Has Changed.   Foreign relations and the ways that nations react to each other are affected by public (and world) opinion, now often quickly formed by global communication. The editor of *Foreign Affairs* expressed concern about the dramatic increase in live television reporting of international crises. James F. Hoge (1994) wrote:

> These capabilities of modern media to be immediate, sensational and pervasive are unsettling the conduct of foreign affairs.... The technology that makes possible real-time, global coverage is truly revolutionary. Today's correspondents employ lap-top computers, wireless telephones that transmit directly to satellites and mobile satellite dishes to broadcast vivid pictures and commentary from the scenes of tragedy and disorder without the transmission delays, political obstructions or military censorship of old. (pp. 136–137)

Nonstop global coverage by CNN and its new rivals, BBC World, and others, does provide the opportunity to constantly monitor news events and disseminate timely diplomatic information. However, Hoge (1994) believes politicians are more concerned than elated by global, real-time broadcasting. "They worry about a 'loss of control' and decry the absence of quiet time to deliberate choices, reach private agreements and mold the public's understanding" (p. 137).

Autocrats Lose.   An authoritarian regime can no longer control and censor the news as completely as in the past. Shortwave radio, fax, direct-distance telephone, the Internet, and Comsats carrying CNN International or BBC World have changed all that and have blunted the power of censorship. The Chernobyl disaster in the USSR showed the impossibility of keeping a nation's bad news from its own people and from the outside world. During times of crisis, dictators can no longer seal their borders and completely control information. The news will get out sooner or later.

Surrogate Media for Fettered Peoples.   U.S. and other Western news media now provide news and information for people who are captives of their own governments. By publicizing human rights violations, torture, and political imprisonments, outside media often help victims to survive by reminding the outside world of the victims' plight. It has been argued that a famine never occurs in a nation with a free press because the press by reporting incipient food shortages, will bring pressures on its government to act before people begin dying. During a famine in autocratic Ethiopia, the people endured suffering for many months as the world largely ignored their plight. But after dramatic BBC video reports appeared on the NBC evening news program night after night, Americans were galvanized to support relief efforts generously.

Reporting Pariah Nations.   The Western media's persistent reporting about pariah states, such as South Africa under apartheid, or Iran or North Korea, can often help facilitate political change. Such reporting forms world opinion, which, in turn, can lead to actions by concerned nations. Persistent American and European press reporting of the civil war in Bosnia and the growing evidence of genocide by Bosnian Serbs undoubtedly pushed the Clinton Administration and NATO to intervene and impose a military truce. After the bombing war over Kosovo and Serbia, Milosevic was an outcast leader whose days were numbered.

Effects of No News.   Sometimes the failure to report major news events can have unexpected political consequences. Because Western journalists were largely barred from reporting the prolonged war in Afghanistan between Soviet forces and Afghan rebels, the impact of that major event on the world's awareness was minimized. In past years, numerous small wars and insurrections in Africa—Congo, Sierra Leone, Angola, Sudan, and Algeria—have passed largely unnoticed because the world's news media could not, or would not, report them. The prolonged war between Iran and Iraq was largely ignored because both sides barred Western reporters; yet the conflict lasted for years and had major significance.

Terrorism: News or Theater?   Global television, which is capable of bringing the world together to share a common grief, such as the death of a president, or a global celebration, as during Neil Armstrong's walk on the moon, can also be manipulated to shock and terrify the world. Terrorism is still very much with us although the forms keep changing: plane bombings, hijackings, political kidnappings, assassinations, civilian bombings, and more recently, suicide bombings of prominent buildings or groups of people. Such acts are perpetrated, some feel, to capture time and space on the world's media. Terrorism has been called "propaganda of the deed"—violent criminal acts, usually against innocent people, performed by desperate people seeking a worldwide forum for their grievances. Terrorists have learned a lesson of this media age: Television news can be manipulated into becoming the final link between terrorist groups and their audiences, and as with sensational crimes, the more outrageous and heinous the act, the greater attention the media will give it.

Yet, terrorism is news and poses worrisome questions for broadcast journalists: Does television coverage encourage and aid the terrorists' cause? Is censorship of such dramatic events ever desirable? Most journalists agree that terrorist acts are news and must be reported. Most believe that self-censorship is undesirable and usually not feasible. Reporting of terrorism is complicated in regions such as Palestine, where terrorists are viewed as martyrs or freedom fighters.

"Revolution" by Personalized Media.   The spreading information revolution, characterized by personal computers, desktop publishing, CDs, VCRs, the Internet, and the World Wide Web, have turned individuals into influential communicators—even revolutionaries—who can reach out to others abroad. The implications of the Internet for international journalism and terrorism are just beginning to be realized. Hachten (1999) quoted Peter Lewis, who wrote:

> Today, political dissidents of all nationalities are discovering a homeland in the worldwide web of communication known as cyberspace.... Today, many human rights advocates are exploring an even more powerful medium (than fax) the computer web called Internet, as a way of defying censorship. (p. 65)

But there is a dark side: Osama bin Laden has utilized the Internet to communicate with his Al Quaeda network around the world.

Copycat Effects.   With global news so pervasive, a particular act or occurrence can be imitated elsewhere. A terrorist's car bombing in one country, widely shown on television, is repeated 3,000 miles away. Somali clansmen defied U.S. soldiers in Mogadishu and a few days later, Haitian thugs were encouraged to stage a near riot as U.S. troops tried to land at Port-au-Prince, causing U.S. forces to withdraw.

Economic and financial considerations undergird the transnational news system that has expanded so much in recent years.

Profit-Driven Media.   The fact that money was to be made has fueled the rapid expansion of international news and mass culture. INTELSAT, the communication satellite consortium that was such a crucial early component in extending the reach of global news, grew so quickly because of the profitability of a more efficient and cost-effective way to make international telephone calls. For whatever their shortcomings, the new media barons, as typified by Rupert Murdoch, have been entrepreneurs who are risk takers and innovators. Of course, news media have followed (and profited from) the expanding economy as it has become increasingly globalized.

Globalization of Advertising and Public Relations.   The two persuasive arms of Western mass communication, advertising and public relations (PR), have become globalized along with journalism. Here again, the Anglo-American model, speaking English, is the pacesetter. Although often criticized, advertising and PR are necessary and inevitable components of market economies and open democratic societies. Moreover, advertising and PR often make news themselves and are an integral part of marketing.

DILEMMAS OF GLOBAL TV NEWS

If all politics is local, then it also may be true that all news is local, although most of the best journalists believe that foreign news is important and that the news media should carry more of it. Yet, U.S. daily journalism and that of other nations is clearly marked by provincialism. Unless there is a compelling story of global impact, most newspapers and broadcasters stress local news. Dennis (1992) reported that InterMedia published a global survey, A Day in the Life of TV News, that measured country-by-country uses of domestic and foreign news on one day. The study found that 85% of television news on Middle East television was about the Middle East, 92% of Latin-American television news was about Latin America, 80% of news on Eastern European television was about Eastern Europe, 78% of news on Japanese television was about Japan, and so on. The study illustrated the parochialism of news in most countries of the world.

A comparative study of television network news in Japan and the United States over 7 months found 1,121 reports from the United States on Japanese television and only 92 from Japan on American television. U.S. Ambassador, Walter Mondale, commented, "I thought our trade imbalance with Japan was bad, but now I see that the news imbalance is even worse" (cited in Hess, 1996, p. 10). This confirms the impression that most people abroad know more about Americans than American do about foreigners. As we have seen in this chapter, the flow of news and mass culture throughout the world has had a variety of important effects on our global community. Some of those effects have been due to the success of CNN. CNN became the first 24-hour cable news network widely received in many foreign lands. In times of crisis such as the Gulf and Iraq wars, CNN attracted news viewers away from the evening news shows of ABC, CBS, and NBC. When a big story breaks, CNN often is the first to report it and stays with the story. As a result, ABC, NBC, and CBS have become even more reluctant to interrupt scheduled network programs with news bulletins or extended reporting.

From its beginning, CNN supplied television news to many foreign broadcast services, homes, and hotels via cable and direct broadcast satellites in many nations. CNN has provided independent Western news to many millions of people overseas, who previously had received only government-controlled information. CNN has had its great and not-so-great moments: live and global coverage of the Gulf War versus CNN's gavel-to-gavel coverage of the O. J. Simpson criminal trial, thus abdicating for many months its self-proclaimed major role in reporting foreign news. When crisis news is lacking, CNN gets low marks on its programming and low ratings as well. However, during the 1999 bombing war over Serbia and Kosovo and the terror attacks of 9/11, CNN greatly expanded its audience both at home and abroad.

Technologically speaking, however, CNN is a major innovation because of its ability to interconnect so many video sources, newsrooms, and foreign ministries to television sets in so many remote places in the world. In this way, CNN has certainly influenced diplomacy; coverage of a crisis in North Korea or Chechnya alerts not only other journalists but diplomats everywhere tune in to get the latest.

A television news channel of true global reach was an innovation whose time had come, and CNN now has its imitators and competitors. In 1991, the BBC started its own World Service Television, now called BBC World. By 1997, BBC World had started to challenge the dominance of CNN International, which, according to CNN company figures, reaches 113 million homes in 210 countries and territories outside the United States. CNN's domestic services reaches another 71 million homes.

BBC World Service (radio) and BBC World (television) are now widely heard on U.S. public and nonprofit stations. Recently, various PBS television stations were carrying two British television news programs nightly—Independent Television News and BBC World—thus providing American viewers an opportunity to watch two services that take world news seriously. The domestic CNN, as an around-the-clock, cable news channel, has elicited competition from other U.S. networks. NBC moved ahead aggressively, launching MSNBC—a 24-hour cable news channel owned jointly with Bill Gates's Microsoft—with great fanfare in July 1996. Another NBC cable channel, CNBC, stressed financial and business news here and abroad.

Rupert Murdoch's Fox Network has joined the 24-hour cable news steeplechase with its own Fox News Channel or FNC. With its appeal to more conservative viewers, FNC recently passed CNN in listener ratings. CBS has been trying to get into the 24-hour cable news competition but, so far, has lagged behind the others. Despite this headlong rush, there were serious reservations about whether even two, much less three or four, cable news channels could survive financially when there is no urgent crisis to report.

In any case, this stampede to provide cable news channels probably reflects a sea change in broadcast news. People seem to be getting their electronic news more and more on the run in small snippets from car radios or at home (radio ratings have stayed high), or from cable news flicked on at odd hours and increasingly from the Internet. Less and less are people getting the news from the evening network news shows, which have been steadily losing viewers. During the 9/11 crisis, cable TV channels attracted more viewers than the networks.

Multiple 24-hour cable TV news channels also have important implications for global television. Both Rupert Murdoch and NBC's Robert Wright have had their sights on global television networks similar to CNN International and BBC World. Murdoch is well on his way to achieving that goal with his existing Star TV satellite service based in Hong Kong for Asia and Sky Channel, a satellite TV service in England with a 24-hour news channel drawing on the staffs of his *Times* and *Sunday Times* of London.

NBC has similar global ambitions, and its well-regarded CNBC channel in Europe and the Middle East is widely available overseas. Emphasizing daily business news from New York, it is seen as a precursor for such a global network (Auletta, 1995a).

But again, reservations have been expressed about the economic feasibility for global television news, at least along the lines envisaged by Murdoch and NBC.

Yet as the war on terrorism has shown, global television news services like CNN and BBC World will take center stage again in reporting, explaining, greatly influencing, if not manipulating, the world's response to those events.

3

Freedom of the Press: Theory and Values

The First Amendment reads more like a dream than a law, and no other country, as far as I know, has been crazy enough to include such a dream among its fundamental legal documents. I defend it because it has been so successful for two centuries in preserving our freedom and increasing our vitality, knowing that all arguments in support of it are certain to sound absurd.

—Kurt Vonnegut

Americans have long had lively, irreverent, rambunctious, and scurrilous newspapers, often disrespectful of authority and at times outrageous. People often despise the news media, but they still value their right to freedom of the press.

Thomas Jefferson had strong and ambivalent feelings about the press, as his quoted words indicate: "Newspapers serve to carry off noxious vapors and smoke" (cited in Rafferty, 1975, p. 85), and later, "Nothing can be believed which is seen in a newspaper" (cited in Rafferty, 1975, p. 85). In addition, "The man who never looks into a newspaper is better informed than he who reads them, inasmuch as he who knows nothing is nearer the truth than he whose mind is filled with falsehoods and errors" (cited in Rafferty, 1975, p. 26) And yet, Jefferson, our most intellectual of presidents also wrote these words: "When the press is free and every man able to read, all is safe" (cited in Rafferty, 1975, p. 61), and "No government ought to be without censors; and where the press is free none ever will" (cited in Rafferty, 1975, p. 61); "The press is the best instrument for enlightening the mind of man, and improving him as a rational, moral, and social being" (cited in Rafferty, 1975, p. 61).

Jefferson's ambivalence has been shared by other leaders because newspapers can sometimes be excellent, even indispensable to our political life, and at other times, of course, they can be offensive, dishonest, and hateful. Yet the importance of the concept of a *free press* as essential to a democratic republic has long been recognized, and the American press has been given more protection in our constitutional law than in any other democracy in the world.

The First Amendment to the U.S. Constitution states clearly and unequivocally that Congress Shall Make No Law ... Abridging Freedom of Speech or of the Press.

Freedom of the press in the United States is more than a legal concept—it is almost a religious tenet. The Constitution, as interpreted by the Supreme Court of the United States, is itself virtually a sacred text, and the First Amendment, which also protects religion, rights of assembly and association, and expression in many forms, is a central part of the value system proclaimed by most Americans (Soifer, 1985).

ORIGINS OF FIRST AMENDMENT

America's high regard for the principle of press freedom derives from the Enlightenment and the liberal political tradition reflected in the writings of John Milton, John Locke, Thomas Jefferson, James Madison, John Stuart Mill, and others. A democratic society, it is argued, requires a diversity of views and news sources available—a marketplace of ideas—from which the public can choose what it wishes to read and believe about public affairs. For no one or no authority, spiritual or temporal, has a monopoly on truth. Underlying this diversity of views is the faith that citizens will somehow make the right choices about what to believe if enough voices are heard and government keeps its hands off the press.

In American Constitutional theory, Blasi (1977) saw this libertarian view as based on certain values (and hopes) deemed inherent in a free press: (a) By gathering and publishing public information and scrutinizing government and politicians, the press makes self-government possible; (b) an unfettered press ensures that a diversity of views and news will be read and heard; (c) a system of free expression provides autonomy for individuals to lead free and productive lives; and (d) it enables an independent press to serve as a check on abuses of power by government.

Our press freedom, rooted in English Common Law, evolved slowly during England's long 17th- and 18th-century struggle between the crown, the courts, and Parliament; when none of the three could dominate the others, a free press slowly began to emerge. In the American colonies and the later republic, a press relatively free from arbitrary government controls evolved as printers and editors asserted their freedoms and gradually established a tradition of a free press. The American press today is freer of legal constraints than is the press of other countries.

In American history, however, press freedom has suffered great lapses and defeats, especially at the state and local level. In fact, the key constitutional decisions supporting claims for press freedom have been decided almost entirely since the 1930s, beginning with the great Supreme Court decision on *Near v. Minnesota* (1931), which protected the press from prior restraint or censorship especially when involved with reporting news of government.

How to define it? Our definition of *freedom of the press* means the right of the press to report, to comment on, and to criticize its own government without retaliation or threat of retaliation from that authority. This has been called the right to talk politics. By this demanding test—the right to talk politics—press freedom is comparatively rare in today's world. A free or independent press is usually found in only a dozen or more Western nations that share these characteristics: (a) a system of law that provides meaningful protection to civil liberties and property rights; (b) high average levels of per capita income, education, and literacy; (c) legitimate political oppositions; (d) sufficient capital or private enterprise to support news media; and (e) an established tradition of independent journalism. In any case, freedom of the press really has meaning and can survive only within a framework of law.

Through the decisions of the courts in adjudicating legal disputes involving newspapers, pamphleteers, broadcasters, radical speakers, and others over basic conflicts between written, printed, oral expression and other competing claims, the framework of our system of press freedom has been delineated. In our law, free speech and free press are identical rights; only the form is different. Print and broadcasting are equally protected but radio and television seem less free because they are licensed by the FCC and because broadcasters are not as assertive in demanding their rights as are the print media.

Great Supreme Court justices such as Oliver Wendell Holmes, Louis Brandeis, Charles Evans Hughes, Hugo Black, William Douglas, and William Brennan, in particular, have contributed to our expanding freedom of expression. Legal scholars Zachariah Chafee, Alexander Meiklejohn,

Thomas I. Emerson, Vincent Blasi, and others in their commentaries have filled out the picture.

Some of the press-related issues decided by the courts have involved highly charged loyalty and national security issues: (a) freedom from prior restraint and censorship; (b) freedom to report legal proceedings and to criticize judges; (c) libel immunity when criticizing public officials; (d) freedom of distribution, pretrial publicity, and defendants rights; (e) press rights versus right of privacy; (f) freedom of expression versus obscenity; (g) protection of confidential news sources; and (h) access to information about public records and meetings. In most of these areas, press freedom has expanded significantly in the 20th century.

ESSENTIAL TO DEMOCRACY

That the American press plays a key role in our democratic system, and in fact, is a central requirement for it, is due in part to several factors (Emerson, 1985). First, instead of representing only private or partisan interests (as in the earlier days of the political party press and yellow journalism), the press has moved to representing the public interest. The growing stress on professionalism, the role of investigative reporting as a regular feature of serious newspapers, and even claims made for special treatment such as shield laws (protecting confidential news sources) are all indicators that the press perceives itself as serving the public interest. Certainly not all (or even many) of the news media share these goals (much less achieve them), but the mere existence of the concept is important.

Second, this concept of the *press as serving the public interest* has become the popular as well as legal justification for protecting freedom of the press. Despite widespread criticism of the media, residual support remains for this press tenet among the general public, opinion journals, and legislatures because the serious press does contribute independent and counterbalancing voices to public discourse.

Third, it can be argued that the press, as an institution, constitutes a viable base from which to stand up to government and concentrated corporate power. With the great expansion of state power and the proliferation of giant corporations, the serious press, despite its own links to many large corporations, still provides a significant potential for independence. So, if not constrained by government, the press in a general way remains an important factor in generating political and social ideas and programs.

Finally, the constitutional and legal doctrines that protect the press are stated in general terms and are applicable to all sectors of the press. Free-

dom of the press is an individual right, we all are protected by it; it is misleading to hear, as is often stated, that newspapers are the only business
specifically protected by the Constitution. Corporations are only claiming
a right we all enjoy, including unpopular minorities, such as radicals and
non-conformists. The First Amendment not only protects NBC and
Gannett but also Noam Chomsky or any unpopular dissident or malcontent
handing out inflammatory pamphlets in a mall.

In fact, the First Amendment and the rest of the Bill of Rights can be
seen as primarily concerned with protecting minority or dissident rights.
Thus a free society must tolerate irresponsible, reckless, and tasteless expression in order to protect the rights of all. The majority rarely feels the
need for First Amendment protection, yet the survival of the First Amendment, as both Alexander Hamilton and Alexander Bickel averred, relies
on the support of the people. That is the paradox of the First Amendment
and a reason for its fragility.

VALUES OF THE FIRST AMENDMENT

Several scholars have elaborated on various values they deem central to the
theory of the First Amendment. Emerson (1966) saw four major values, all of
which stressed individual rights. The first was the right of an individual
purely in his own capacity to seek his own self-fulfillment. "In the development of his own personality, every man has the right to form his own beliefs
and opinions. Hence, suppression of belief, opinion and expression is an affront to the dignity of man, an affront to man's essential nature" (Emerson,
1966, p. 5). Second, free speech is the best method of searching for and at-
taining truth. This value is similar to values found in both academic freedom
and the scientific method of inquiry. A journalist seeking important public
information must be free to go wherever the leads take him or her to get the
story, just as a scholar should be free to follow the indications of truth wherever they may lead. Third, free speech makes self-government possible by
encouraging the participation of citizens in social and political decision making. And fourth, by so doing, the system of free expression becomes a safety
valve that helps maintain a balance between stability and change in an open,
dynamic society. If people have access to information and are free to express
their views and address their grievances to authority, they are less likely to
take up arms against their rulers and resort to civil strife.

Diversity is a value directly relevant both to the ownership and performance of a free press. A related concept, the *marketplace of ideas*, which
goes back to Milton, has come into some disrepute because critics say that

truth does not always seem to come to the top and win out in the clash of ideas and programs. Propaganda, public relations, and other persuasive and manipulative communications have made many of us skeptics. Still, even if communication channels are polluted, diversity assures that press freedom is served if people are given a wide choice of information sources, as well as alternative proposals from which to choose rather than having an authoritarian selection imposed on them.

In an antitrust case, *Associated Press v. United States* (1945), Judge Learned Hand expressed well the value of diversity:

> That (newspaper) industry serves one of the most vital of all general interests: the dissemination of news from as many different sources, and with as many different facets as possible.... It presupposes that right conclusions are more likely to be gathered out of a multitude of tongues than through any kind of authoritarian selection. To many this is, and always will be, folly; but we have staked upon it our all. (p. 20)

This view reflects Hand's skeptical view of free speech. The spirit of liberty, he said, is the spirit that is not too sure it is right. Therefore, many views must be available for consideration. Diversity implies the necessity of competition and a variety of differing and even conflicting views. The steady decline of local newspaper competition coupled with the trends of concentration and monopoly of news media have placed this value in some jeopardy.

Another value, also directly linked to press performance, is the checking value, which sees the press as a watchdog on excesses and malfeasance of government. Blasi (1977) revived this neglected value, on which the drafters of the First Amendment had placed great stress, the ability of free expression to guard against breaches of trust by public officials. Influenced by 20th-century wars, Blasi argued that government misconduct is a more serious evil than misconduct by private parties because there is no concentrated force available to check it. The potential impact of government on the lives of individuals is unique because of its capacity to use legitimized violence.

> "No private party—not Lockheed, not United Fruit, not the Mafia—could ever have done what our government did to the Vietnamese people and the Vietnamese land. Private forces could never have exterminated such significant portions of the domestic population as did the Nazi and Soviet governments of the 1930s and 1940s." (Blasi, 1977, p. 527)

The checking value has been rarely invoked by the Supreme Court, but Justice Hugo Black did so in his last written opinion, in the Pentagon Papers case, *New York Times v. United States* (1971), giving it eloquent expression.

In the First Amendment, the Founding Fathers gave the free press the protection it must have to fulfill its essential role in our democracy. The press was to serve the governed, not the governors. The government's power to censor the press was abolished so that the press would remain free to censure the government. The press was protected so that it could bare the secrets of government and inform the people. Only a free and unrestrained press can effectively oppose deception in government. And paramount among the responsibilities of a free press is the duty to prevent any part of the government from deceiving the people and sending them off to distant lands to die of foreign fevers and foreign shot and shell. (*New York Times v. United States,* 1971, p. 717)

KEY CONCEPTS OF FIRST AMENDMENT

The values of press freedom are further buttressed by several key concepts that are well established in constitutional law. One of the oldest—*no prior restraint*—means that government is barred from censoring any printed matter before its publication, a principle that goes back to Blackstone in 18th-century England. The landmark decision, *Near v. Minnesota,* (1931), dealt with prior restraint or prior censorship and struck down a state statute that barred publication of a local smear sheet, *The Saturday Press,* which had been highly critical of Minnesota state officials. The key point about *Near* is that a publication was prohibited from future publication because it had criticized official conduct; the court found this to be an unacceptable restraint on a free press.

Chief Justice Charles Evans Hughes relied on Blackstone's rather narrow view of press freedom:

> The liberty of the press is indeed essential to the nature of a free state; but this consists in laying no previous restraints upon publications, and not in freedom from censure for criminal matter when published. Every freeman has an undoubted right to lay what sentiments he pleases before the public; to forbid this, is to destroy the freedom of the press; but if he publishes what is improper, mischievous or illegal, he must take the consequences. (*Near v. Minnesota,* 1931, p. 702)

And in referring to the sleazy publication barred, Hughes wrote:

> The fact that liberty of the press may be abused by miscreant purveyors of scandal does not make any the less necessary the immunity of the press from previous restraint in dealing with official misconduct. Subsequent punish-

ment for such abuses as may exist is the appropriate remedy, consistent with constitutional privilege. (*Near v. Minnesota,* 1931, p. 705)

As *Near* and other cases demonstrated, press immunity from prior restraint in other situations such as obscenity or wartime security needs was not absolute, but the principle of no prior restraint of press criticism of government conduct (the right to talk politics) took on great and lasting importance from then on.

Another key concept, the *press's right to criticize government,* even wrongly, was spelled out in the celebrated *New York Times v. Sullivan* (1964) decision in the turbulent 1960s. The case involved a civil libel judgment against the *Times* for an advertisement, signed by civil rights supporters, critical of the conduct of public officials during civil rights demonstrations in Montgomery, Alabama. L. B. Sullivan, Montgomery police commissioner, sued for defamation, winning a $500,000 judgment. Upheld by the Alabama Supreme Court, the case went to the U.S. Supreme Court where it was unanimously reversed. The court famously announced a constitutional standard that a public official may not recover libel damages regarding official conduct unless he or she can prove actual malice—that is, knowledge on the part of the critic that the statement was false or "showed reckless disregard of whether it was false or not." Justice William Brennan's decision stressed that Alabama's libel law was unconstitutional because it failed to protect freedom of the press. (Previously, no one ever thought civil libel had anything to do with the First Amendment.) Brennan said that at issue was: "a profound national commitment to the principle that debate on public issues should be uninhibited, robust, and wide-open, and that it may well include vehement, caustic, and sometimes unpleasantly sharp attacks on government and public officials." Brennan rejected the argument that falsity of some statements in the ad destroyed any protection the paper may have had. He said protection did not depend on the "truth, popularity, or social utility" of the ideas and beliefs expressed. He wrote: "A rule compelling the critic of official conduct to guarantee the truth of all his factual assertions—and to do so on paid libel judgements virtually unlimited in amount—leads to a comparable 'self censorship'" (*New York Times v. Sullivan,* 1964, p. 278).

Brennan pointed out a civil libel suit brought by a public official was as dangerous to press freedom as seditious libel. He added that "the court of history" had found that the Sedition Act of 1798 that had authorized punishment for criticism of public officials and government was inconsistent with the First Amendment. Professor Harry Kalven hailed the Times decision as a great constitutional event because the "touch-stone of the First Amendment has become the abolition of seditious libel and what that implies about the function of free speech on public issues in American democracy" (cited in Blasi, 1977, p. 568). Kalven felt that the absence of seditious libel as a crime was the true pragmatic test of a nation's freedom of expression, because politically relevant speech is what press freedom is mostly about.

Another key concept of press freedom is the more general proposition that *expression itself is protected and only actions can be proscribed.* This is related to the view that there are no false ideas, that is, all views and ideas, however heretical or illogical they may seem, enjoy the same protection under the law. Only when the fighting words are closely linked to illegal action can the state step in.

In the long history of national security and sedition cases, the clear and present danger test and similar measures were devised to give as much protection as possible to political speech in the face of sedition laws. Since 1969, the Supreme Court has moved to an even more objective standard. In *Brandenburg v. Ohio,* (1969), the court said a speaker could not be convicted for "mere advocacy" of illegal action; to be constitutional, a statute can only prohibit advocacy where it is "directed to inciting or producing imminent lawless action and is likely to incite or produce such actions" (p. 448). In so doing, the court reached back and adopted a standard used by Judge Learned Hand in the *Masses Publishing Co. v. Patten* (1917) case and greatly expanded freedom of political speech.

Of more direct interest to the news press is the key concept of the *right to know,* which implies that the press not only can publish and comment on the news but also has the right of access to news itself at all levels of government. (One murky question is whether the right belongs to the press or to the public.)

Long ago, the press won the right to be present at open meetings of Parliament and legislatures, including Congress. The Sixth Amendment's guarantee of a fair and public trial has assured the right of a reporter, standing in for the public, to attend and report on public trials. Further, evolution of U.S. contempt-of-court law has given the American press broad powers to criticize judges, report on pretrial news, and criticize the conduct of trials—as the O. J. Simpson trial so well demonstrated.

The right to know about the executive branch with its numerous bureaucracies and vast classified files and records has been a long and contentious problem for serious journalism. Some progress has been made, however, through the Freedom of Information Act and various sunset laws that require the release of classified government records after a specified time lapse. The famous Pentagon Papers case, (*The New York Times v. United States,* 1971) involved overclassification of government records—a secret history of the Vietnam War—and the alleged potential danger to national security posed by *The New York Times'* publication of them. U.S. Judge Murray Gurfein ruling for the *Times*, wrote:

> If there be some embarrassment to the government in security aspects as remote as the general embarrassment that flows from any security breach, we must learn to live with it. The security of the nation is not at the barricades alone. Security also lies in the value of our free institutions. A cantankerous press, an obstinate press, a ubiquitous press must be suffered by those in authority in order to preserve the even greater values of freedom of expression and the right of the public to know. (*New York Times v. United States*, 1971, p. 715)

The Supreme Court upheld the favorable ruling for the *Times*.

Another key concept, *journalistic autonomy*, supports the independence of newspapers from government intrusion into their operations. In *Miami Herald v. Tornillo* (1974), the Supreme Court said a right of reply requirement was unconstitutional when applied to the print media. The Court had ruled just the opposite in a broadcasting case, *Red Lion v. FCC* (1969). In *Tornillo, The Miami Herald* challenged a Florida statute that required newspapers to print free replies to political candidates that the papers had attacked. The Supreme Court ruled unanimously for the *Herald*, supporting editors and publishers. Chief Justice Warren Burger said it was unconstitutional to require a newspaper to print what it otherwise would not. Press responsibility, he said, was a desirable goal, but it was not mandated by the Constitution and like many other virtues could not be legislated. Burger said the law was unconstitutional simply because it intruded into the function of editors. He wrote:

> The choice of material to go into a newspaper, and the decisions made as to limitations on the size and content of the paper, and the treatment of public issues and public officials—whether fair or unfair—constitute the exercise of editorial control and judgment. It has yet to be demonstrated how governmental regulation of this crucial process can be exercised consistent with First Amendment guarantees of a free press. (*Miami Herald v. Tornillo*, 1974, p. 248)

The values of U.S. press freedom may have influenced the professional values of journalists in other nations. One particularly influential concept is that of a *free flow of news*, which captures the spirit of the First Amendment. This concept refers to the need to report foreign news fully, accurately, and quickly across national borders and without interference from foreign governments. Timely and accurate news and other reliable information is deemed essential to the needs of an increasingly interdependent global political economy. This concept collides with the counter view that every nation has a sovereign right to control news and information passing back and forth across its borders. The free flow of news may be often one-sided, erratic, or delayed, and, in some parts of the world, may seem a hopeless ideal. Yet the trend is favorable for more open and free journalism in more and more nations.

CONCLUSION

Most of the basic law protecting freedom of the press is considered settled. For many years, there have no significant challenges to the law protecting freedom of the press. The press has all the legal protection it needs to be free, vigorous, and outspoken.

As this overview of U.S. press law shows, our news media enjoy a wide range of legal rights and privileges enabling them to carry out their essential roles of providing meaningful news and commentary on public affairs. A free, vigorous, and outspoken press is indeed essential to a healthy society. Yet there remains the question of how well the American public understands and supports the First Amendment. A 1997 Roper poll found that few Americans are familiar with the five rights guaranteed by the Constitution's First Amendment. Further, few believe that the right to freedom of the press should be guaranteed at all times. The poll found people see the role of news media as crucial to the functioning of a free society, but the legal processes of press freedom are not well understood. Eighty-five percent could not name press freedom as one of the five First Amendment freedoms. Nearly two thirds said that there are times when the press should not be allowed to publish or broadcast certain things. That, of course, would be prior restraint, clearly illegal under the First Amendment.

One of our greatest judges, Learned Hand, in speaking of the spirit of liberty, sounded a cautionary note:

> I often wonder whether we do not rest our hopes too much upon constitutions, upon laws and upon courts. These are false hopes. Believe me, these are false hopes. Liberty lies in the hearts of men and women. When it dies there, no constitution, no law, no court can even do much to help it. While it

lies there it needs no constitution, no law, no court to save it. (Cited in Gunther, 1994, p. 548)

The greatest threat to press freedom today does not come from the courts. It comes from an American public that has often been disillusioned about the news media and has been bitterly outspoken in its criticism of press performance.

CHAPTER

4

Recent History of the Press

The press as it exists today, is not, as our moralists sometimes seem to assume, the willful product of any little group of living men. On the contrary, it is the outcome of an historical process in which many individuals participated without foreseeing what the ultimate product of their labors was to be.

—Robert Park (1923)

To understand the flaws of the press today, we must first examine several trends in journalism during the 20th century. The dismaying shortcomings as well as the encouraging strengths we see in U.S. news media today have their roots in the past.

The 20th-century history of American journalism has been dealt with in all its complexity and fascination by numerous scholars and writers, some of them journalists. Among other things, our press history is a morality tale with plenty of sinners and bad guys, some high-minded heroes, and even a few saints.

This brief historical overview focuses on several topics related to the main concerns of this book: (a) the rise of the great metropolitan newspapers; (b) trends toward group or chain ownership of daily newspapers; (c) roots of the gossip or scandal-mongering tabloids and their obsession with celebrities; (d) the advent and growing influence of radio and television journalism; (e) new technologies for reporting the world; and (f) criticism of the press.

BIG CITY NEWSPAPERS

By 1900, the press was poised to become big business—the leading papers had attained large circulations, high capitalizations, and profits. High-speed rotary presses that made possible automated printing on both sides of the paper at once, the linotype machine, which speeded typesetting, the typewriter, and the telephone all helped create the big-city dailies. Important, too, was the telegraph, invented in 1844, which enabled newspeople to collect and send news from great distances. These same tools for putting out a newspaper were still utilized well into the 1960s. By then, the new technologies of offset printing, computers (for writing, editing, and storing news), communication satellites, and high-speed data transfers (for instant global news distribution) again revolutionized journalism as well as telecommunications in general.

The great rivals of the 1890s, Joseph Pulitzer and William Randolph Hearst, set the tone for 20th-century journalism, especially for the more lurid and sensational variety. Pulitzer's *New York World* combined a crusading editorial page and thorough news coverage, along with some sensationalism for mass appeal. The *World* had the first sports section and comics, featured brightly illustrated pages, and campaigned against corrupt public officials. By 1892, the *World* had reached a circulation of 374,000. (By 1900, the *Daily Mail* of London was selling 1 million copies per day.) The first mass medium for a mass audience had truly arrived.

Pulitzer's success influenced the young Hearst who did the same things with his father's *San Francisco Examiner.* In 1895, Hearst bought *The New York Journal* and began his famous circulation war with Pulitzer. Hearst hired away some of the *World's* staff, expanded the use of photography, and introduced color printing to newspapers. The circulation competition led to lurid stories about sin and corruption, sensational pictures, and expanded use of the newly popular comics. The intense rivalry produced the shrill debate and jingoistic coverage of the Spanish American War. *Yellow journalism* was the term critics used for the formula of sensationalism that has persisted in varying forms to the present.

Interestingly, intense competition for circulation was a factor in the enduring tradition of objectivity as a standard for reporting. The papers, as well as the budding press associations—AP and later United Press (UP)—wanted all the readers they could possibly attract so it made sense not to turn off some customers with partisan or one-sided stories. Striving to be first to get a "scoop" was another enduring newspaper goal and a reason for extra editions to boost street sales. The UP motto of "get it first, but first get it right" animated journalists even after radio and television provided instantaneous delivery of spot news.

Democratization of news was also a hallmark of Pulitzer and Hearst, both of whom championed the little person and the working class. To maximize circulation meant targeting news to the masses, often recent immigrants, whose tastes and interests affected the newspapers' content. Despite its faults, yellow journalism did much to help the new arrivals off Ellis Island learn about and adjust to a strange, new land. Pulitzer's famous motto, "To comfort the afflicted and to afflict the comfortable," had an underlying commercial motive. Publishers like Hearst, Pulitzer, and E. W. Scripps also acquired readers through the inclusion of some serious social and political content. Bagdikian (1992) wrote, "They secured deep loyalties among readers because their papers crusaded in direct and unmistakable terms for reforms most needed by the powerless majority of the times" (Bagdikian, 1992, p. 126). The young Hearst wrote, "I have only one principle and that is represented by the effort to make it harder for the rich to grow richer and easier for the poor to keep from growing poorer." Pulitzer's editorial position was "Tax luxuries, inheritances, monopolies ... the privileged corporation" (Bagdikian, 1992, p. 127). Such sentiments are rare in today's mainstream press.

The acquisition of *The New York Times* by Adolph S. Ochs more than 100 years ago in 1896 marked the real beginning of modern serious journalism and the acceptance of a responsibility to stress news, rather than trivia and sensation. Ochs stated, "It will be my aim to give the news impartially, without fear or favor" (Johnston, 1979, p. 55). He eschewed yellow journalism and left out comics and other purely entertainment features. Ochs and his editor, Carr Van Anda, stressed persistent and full coverage of significant national and international events. The reporting was objective, the tone somber (some thought it dull) and the contents thorough enough for the *Times* to be considered a "newspaper of record," providing as its front page has long proclaimed, "All the News That's Fit to Print" (Johnston, 1979, p. 55). Following that approach, the *Times* outlived both the *World* and the *Journal* and prospered to become, 100 years later, America's leading newspaper.

After 1900, running a big city paper had become expensive and required revenue, not just from street sales but from advertising, which came from the newly arising department stores, like Macys and Gimbels. In circulation, number of pages per issue, and volume of advertising, the papers grew to sizes never before dreamed of, and the figures representing investments, costs, and revenues reached astonishing totals. Mott (1947) noted that the biggest U.S. paper, *The New York Times* had an annual expenditure of some $2 million and a full-time workforce of 1,300 men and women in the mid-1890s. Combined circulation of its morning and evening editions hit 1 million in March 1897. The *World* was said to be worth $10 million and earning 10% of that sum annually.

Mott (1947) quoted Lincoln Steffens in 1897:

The magnitude of financial operations of the newspaper is turning journalism upside down. "Big business" was doing two things in general to journalism: it was completing the erection of the industrial institution upon what was once a personal organ; and it was buttressing and steadying the structure with financial conservatism. (p. 547)

Prophetic words indeed.

Corporate newspapers marked the end of the personal journalism of earlier America. As Mott (1947) wrote:

The roar of double octuple presses drowned out the voice, often shrill and always insistent, of the old-time editor.... Yet, as was often said in this period, the soundly financed and well-established journal was in a far better position to resist undue interference with proper journalistic functions than the insecure sheet of an earlier day. Ochs of the *Times* could defy even an angry advertiser. And many of the papers of the period were inveterate crusaders against moneyed interests. (p. 548)

GROUP OWNERSHIP OF DAILY NEWSPAPERS

Early in the century, New York City had 14 highly competitive dailies. Many papers lacked the money to compete and were forced to close down, consolidate with a rival, or be bought out. This was the beginning of chain publishing or later, group publishing, whereby several newspapers were owned and operated by one publisher or publishing corporation. (From a peak of 2,460 daily newspapers in 1916, the number of papers declined after World War I and leveled off at mid-century to around 1,750.)

Group ownership, although it made good business sense, was not necessarily good for democracy and the values of diversity and competing viewpoints. In 1900, 10 chains controlled 32 papers, just 1% of all dailies, and about 12% to 15% of total circulation. Chains boomed during the 1920s; the number of chain newspapers doubled between 1923 and 1933. By 1935, 63 groups controlled 328 papers and 41% of total circulation. In 1960, the figures were 109 groups with 560 papers (30%) and 46% of circulation (M. Emery, E. Emery, & Roberts, 1996).

Around 1900, the eccentric E. W. Scripps was the first to establish a major U.S. newspaper chain, 34 papers in 15 states. Scripps broke all of the later rules for acquiring papers; he created new papers (sometimes in competition with existing ones) instead of acquiring established publications. He charged readers as little as he could and took in few ads. He crusaded for socialist reforms and against abuses of working people. Nevertheless, in 20 years, he was a major publisher worth about $50 million.

His success was followed by that of William Randolph Hearst, also a proclaimed socialist and populist early on. By the end of 1922, Hearst owned 20 dailies and 11 Sunday papers in 13 of the largest cities including New York, Chicago, Los Angeles, Baltimore, and San Francisco. By 1931, Hearst had taken control of 42 papers. With the largest chain in 1935, Hearst controlled 13% of daily circulation and 24.2% of Sunday sales.

Hearst was active in politics and used all his papers to push his own ambitions and favorite causes; he was opposed to entering World War I and later waged a long-time national campaign against radicals that was sometimes called "Hearst's red hunt." Mott (1947) noted that Hearst's vast empire, which included numerous major magazines, began to crumble during the 1930s. By 1986, Hearst had 14 dailies which represented only 1.6% of daily circulation.

The press associations or wire services expanded during the rise of newspaper groups. The AP, which was started in 1848 by New York City papers to pool shipping news, expanded greatly in the new century, and although a cooperative, it mainly served morning papers in the larger cities. Scripps founded the UP in 1907 because he feared an AP monopoly of news. Two years later, Hearst started the International News Service (INS) to serve his papers. (In 1958, UP and INS merged to form UPI, which today is nearly moribund.) Few papers could afford to station reporters in Washington or abroad or even to cover news outside their local regions. The wire services filled the gap by cooperative news gathering and distribution by telegraph or leased wires.

Group ownership of daily papers has flourished and expanded. The expertise acquired in handling and merchandising news, boosting circulations, selling advertising space, and the promotion and marketing of their newspapers was, logically enough, carried over to other media—magazines, radio stations, book publishing, television stations, and in some cases, motion pictures. So after World War II, various newspaper chains, including Scripps' and Hearst's and others, were transformed into the media conglomerates of today.

TABLOIDS: SCHOOLS FOR SCANDAL

The Roaring Twenties, following World War I, brought a revival of sensationalism in the form of tabloids patterned after the successful *Daily Mirror* of London. With pages half the size of broadsheet newspapers, which made them easier to read in subways or on buses, tabloids were intended for workers and the foreign-born and stressed crime and sex, ample photographs, and large eye-catching and irreverent headlines. (*Tabloid* refers to both the half-page format and the racy style of journalism.)

The most successful and enduring U.S. tabloid was *The New York Daily News* launched by Joseph Medill Patterson in 1919. Within 6 years, the *News* went to 1 million in circulation, and before World War II had reached 2 million in sales. By 1924, two competitors, Hearst's *Daily Mirror* and Bernarr Macfadden's *Evening Graphic,* which was the most lurid and irresponsible of the three, had joined in. In addition to stressing photos, the tabloids introduced composographs (i.e., faked photos), crime, and lurid stories of show business personalities. The intense circulation war led to what was called the battle of gutter journalism. The *Graphic* folded after 6 years and the *Daily News* gradually moved toward more straight news and less trivia and sensation.

Few tabloids in other big cities were as racy as the New York tabloids, but the quest for sensational news did not end with the 1920s. Today's bawdy and irresponsible tabloids sold in supermarkets, such as *National Enquirer* and *The Star,* continue the questionable practices of the 1920s tabloids but are more directly related to the cynical Fleet Street practices of British journalism.

One tabloid journalist who left an indelible mark (or perhaps blemish) on American journalism was Walter Winchell, who wrote for *The New York Graphic* and then for *The Mirror* in the 1920s and early 1930s. Gabler (1994) wrote that Winchell invented the gossip column, breaking journalistic taboos in the process by chronicling the marital problems, peccadilloes, frailties, finances, and personal information about the prominent and famous, often basing his items on vague rumors or gossip. Winchell successfully kept at it for 40 years, and by one estimate, 50 million Americans either listened to his weekly Sunday radio broadcast or read his daily syndicated column in more than 2,000 newspapers. It was, according to one observer, "the largest continuous audience ever possessed by one man who was neither politician or divine" (Gabler, 1994, p. xi). Winchell's impact on journalism and mass culture was tremendous and deleterious.

Frank Rich (1994) commented,

> The whole oppressive idea of celebrity as we know it today—a fame more often conferred by the press than earned by achievement—also owes its birth to Winchell. The Winchell column may have done more than any other single feature to spread tabloid journalism in its infancy and to speed the rise of the nascent public relations industry. (p. 1)

The way that Winchell and others reported the Hauptmann trial for the kidnapping of the Lindbergh baby in 1935 was a precursor, Rich believes, for the media circus of the O. J. Simpson criminal and civil trials.

In his fine biography, Gabler (1994) wrote (quoting columnist Leonard Lyons): "It was Walter Winchell who rewrote the rules for what was permissible in a major daily newspaper; it was Walter Winchell who first created a demand for juicy tidbits about celebrities and then spent 40 years trying to satisfy it" (p. 552). Gabler went on in his own words:

> If Winchell was responsible for having enlivened journalism, he was also responsible in the eyes of many for having debased it. Once loosed, gossip refused to confine itself to columns. Once loosed, it danced all over the paper, sometimes seizing headlines, sometimes spawning whole publications and television programs, sometimes, and more insidiously, infecting reportage of so-called straight news by emphasizing gossip and personalities at the expense of objectivity and duller facts. Once gossip had been loosed, WE would become jaded. We would always want more and the media would bend to accommodate us.... The legacy remained. We would believe in our entitlement to know everything about our public figures.... Above all, we would believe in a culture of gossip and celebrity where entertainment takes primacy over every other value. (p. 553)

Winchell did not do it all alone. There were others—Broadway and Hollywood gossip columnists (Louella Parsons, Hedda Hopper), *Confidential* magazine, and a panoply of Hollywood fan magazines, as well as press agents and studio publicists, all working overtime to feed the public's appetite for gossip, rumor, and scandal. Winchell, of course, became a celebrity himself, and in part because of him, the circle of celebrities has been widened today to include many prominent journalists and broadcasters.

RISE OF BROADCAST JOURNALISM

In the 1920s, radio provided newspapers with a new form of competition in news. At first, radio's offerings were limited. However, radio had the advantage of involving listeners with events taking places thousands of miles away with a flip of a switch. Also, radio could report news immediately and directly, many hours before newspapers could print and distribute their papers. Radio was the death knell for the extra edition; big city papers soon cut back on the number of editions published daily. (Although radio could get the news out faster, the newspapers still did—and do—gather most of the day's news.)

On November 2, 1920, the Westinghouse Electric Corporation inaugurated the first commercial radio station, KDKA, in Pittsburgh. That day, a crackling KDKA kept a small number of listeners in a restricted area up to date on the tabulations of the presidential election of 1920. At that time, interested voters in remote rural regions of America far from telegraph lines, without telephones, and beyond population centers with daily papers, had to wait 2 weeks before news reached them that Warren K. Harding had defeated James M. Cox for the presidency. (Now, there is not a place in the United States where one cannot follow election night tabulations instantaneously and, indeed, be told the winner's name even before all the polls are closed. Broadcasters have been widely criticized for announcing winners before polls have closed in western states.)

By the end of 1922, some 576 commercial radio stations were operating in America. Local stations started offering news summaries, often in cooperation with local newspapers. Johnston (1979) reported that in 1926, NBC, a subsidiary of David Sarnoff's pioneering Radio Corporation of America, initiated the first network with 24 stations interconnected; in the next year, the first coast-to-coast hookup was achieved with the broadcast of a football game. In 1927, CBS was organized; the Mutual Broadcasting System followed 6 years later.

For years, NBC operated two networks, the Red and the Blue, so dominating radio broadcasting that the FCC later forced the company to give up one. In 1943, NBC sold the Blue network, which became the ABC. Significantly, the three major radio networks, NBC, CBS, and ABC, all moved on in postwar years to dominate the next medium, television, and today each are major parts of giant entertainment conglomerates. (Mutual opted not to go into television.)

Radio's entertainment shows—*Jack Benny, Amos 'n Andy, Burns and Allen,* and others—drew large national audiences and interest in instantaneous, on-the-spot news reports became popular due to the Lindbergh kidnapping trial in 1935, presidential nominating conventions, and FDR's fireside chats. Radio commentators—H. V. Kaltenborn, Gabriel Heatter, and Lowell Thomas—became household names. Radio expanded greatly between 1935 and 1945, when commercial stations reached 900. Daily newscasts were routine and the networks and most major stations had news staffs and reporters in key cities.

Radio played a major role in reporting World War II with direct reports from the fronts and key cities abroad. Edward R. Murrow and his colleagues, William L. Shirer, Eric Sevareid, and Charles Collingwood, reported with distinction for CBS. Murrow became famous for his *This is London* broadcasts.

Radio as a news medium, however, was to be eclipsed a few years later by a new and more immediate broadcasting force. Television came in soon after World War II but it is often forgotten that television was essentially an outgrowth of radio, which provided the norms and the format for early television news as well as entertainment programming. Television took its viewers to the event itself—to show the President speaking, the touchdown being scored, or the sights and sounds of deadly combat. And from the 1950s, television news was in color. The first regularly scheduled network newscasts began in 1948 with Douglas Edwards on CBS-TV and John Cameron Swayze on NBC. As on radio, these were only 15-minute newscasts with the "talking head" reading most of the news. Until the technology improved, live or taped video reports were slow in coming. When the television report finally did present the actual witnessing of an event on a screen, rather than reading a journalist's report, it had considerable impact.

Great social and political impact was felt throughout the nation by televised coverage of the Senate's McCarthy–Army hearings in the 1950s, early space exploration, the Watergate hearings, the Vietnam War, and the tumultuous Democratic convention in Chicago of 1968. Americans felt these traumatic events deeply and viscerally because of what they saw and heard on the little screen.

The nightly newscasts expanded to 30 minutes and drew huge audiences. In the 1970s, an estimated 41 million Americans watched the 7 p.m. news on the three networks. The faces of the newscasters—Walter Cronkite, Chet Huntley, David Brinkley, Howard K. Smith, John Chancellor, and Harry Reasoner—became well-known and trusted. Broadcast journalists were on the way to becoming celebrities. For a time, television news was supplemented by some serious in-depth documentaries. Leading the way were the *See It Now* series and *CBS Reports* of Ed Murrow and Fred Friendly. Although technically much better today, television news no longer enjoys the prestige it had in the 1960s and 1970s. Before they died, Murrow, Sevareid, and Chancellor each expressed disillusionment with trends in television news.

Television news did not replace news on radio or in newspapers and news magazines; it supplemented them. Radio was hardest hit but slowly adapted to television news and has developed its own niche by adopting many new formats. Cronkite once called the evening television news a "headline service," and that is still the case.

Some big afternoon dailies were hard hit by television, but the press generally, especially the serious press, adapted and survived. Numbers of daily newspapers have been generally stable in recent times. However, several journalistic magazines, such as *Colliers, Saturday Evening Post, Look,* and *Life* were electronically executed, not because their circulations declined, but because national advertising moved to television. Magazines, by finding new niche readerships, generally prospered after television; the same can be said for books.

NEW TECHNOLOGY FOR REPORTING THE WORLD

From Gutenburg on, technology has always shaped the way that news is gathered and disseminated. The persistence of certain anachronistic terms attests to the importance of earlier mechanisms. The *foreign correspondent* was the journalist abroad who literally wrote letters transported by ship to his newspaper at home. The *wire editor* handled out-of-town stories that came clattering in over telegraph wires from around the country. The *cable editor* (not cable television) was the foreign news editor sifting through news reports coming from the underseas cable, mainly from London and the British Empire, which long controlled the cables. *Cablese* was a shorthand method used by news services to combine words to save on cable charges, which traditionally cost a British penny a word. As mentioned, in the first half of the 20th century, newspapers depended on the telegraph, the telephone, the typewriter, hot type (i.e., Linotypes), and the rotary press to get out the newspaper. But from about 1960, a wide range of innovations, loosely called the *new technology*, came along and markedly affected journalism and especially news from abroad.

A much-deepened reservoir of information and its rapid dissemination among many more people are the hallmarks of this quiet revolution, which in its broader context, came to be called the *information revolution*. In the print media, high-speed transmission and electronic processing have accelerated and expanded the gathering, storing, and transferring of words for newspapers, magazines, and books. Computerized composition and offset printing techniques have simplified production, leading to desktop publishing. (Today small newspapers exist that are published using a computer, printer, copying machine, and a staff of two or three people.) In broadcasting, minicams, videotape, and remote location transmissions have simplified the delivery of video to the television screen. International journalism has been greatly facilitated by the vast improvement of telephone service, including fax, provided by the INTELSAT system. Foreign correspondents in remote places can be in close telephone or Internet communication with their supervising editors.

Perhaps the major impact of communication satellites on the news industry has been the capability to relay color television reports instantly and globally, often significantly influencing world public opinion and understanding, as during the Iraq War or in Kosovo and Bosnia.

CRITICISM OF THE PRESS

Criticizing the press has long been a popular sport in America, if only because the press has long been so outspoken about our public officials and the establishment. H. L. Mencken once said, "The only way for a newsman to look on a politician is down." He also said: "All successful newspapers are ceaselessly querulous and bellicose. They never defend anyone or anything if they can help it" (Bartlett & Kaplan, 1992, p. 642). If so, they asked for it!

Like the government it supposedly keeps an eye on, the press itself needs watching and throughout the previous century, the press has not lacked critics, including many from its own ranks. One of the earliest critiques was a series of articles titled "The American Newspaper" for *Colliers* written by Will Irwin in January–July 1911. *The Brass Check* by Upton Sinclair in 1919 pictured a false, cowardly press dominated by advertisers and business interests. Walter Lippmann's *Public Opinion* in 1922 raised serious questions about the validity of journalism standards and values. Hearst and other press lords triggered a series of critical books: Oswald Garrison Villard's *Some Newspapers and Newspapermen* in 1923; and in the turbulent 1930s, George Seldes' *Liberty of the Press* and *Lords of the Press*; Harold Ickes' *America's House of Lords* in 1939; and Ferdinand Lundberg's *Imperial Hearst* in 1936. In those depression years, the largely Republican press was much on the defensive. Newspapers still endorsed political candidates and President Franklin Roosevelt claimed that 85% of the press opposed him; he blamed the owners, not the reporters.

Out of the tempestuous 1960s came a spate of journalism reviews, written by journalists themselves and highly critical of press performance. Before 1968, only two reviews existed, *The Montana Journalism Review* and *The Columbia Journalism Review*. *The Chicago Journalism Review*, published from 1968 to 1975, inspired about 40 or so similar publications, but fewer than a dozen survived after 1977, including *More*, a national review; *Accuracy in Media* (AIM) a conservative newsletter; *Media Report to Women, Twin Cities Journalism Review,* and *feed/back.*

Among newsmen who wrote for those reviews, the model of press critics was A. J. Liebling, whose insightful "Wayward Press" pieces in *The New Yorker* entertained readers as he skewered newspaper errors and ethical lapses throughout the 1950s and 1960s. Throughout the considerable literature of press criticism, Johnston (1979) noted that certain themes have persisted: (a) the media are too big and powerful; (b) too tightly controlled by too few people; (c) too standardized in their presentation of news and information; too much "managed" news; and (d) too much attention is paid to gossip, trivia, sex, and violence, and not enough attention to significant social, economic, and political trends. Current press criticism echoes and rephrases some of these themes.

As we see later, criticism of the press is alive and prospering, and there is some evidence that the news media heed their critics.

CHAPTER

5

Bigger, Fewer, and More Like-Minded

Freedom of the Press is guaranteed only to those who own one.

—A. J. Liebling

News has become a big business controlled not by powerful families but by media moguls who place a higher priority on the size of the profits than on the value of their contributions to society.

—Marvin Kalb

A continuing and inexorable trend throughout 20th-century America has been for more and more newspapers, radio and television stations, magazines, book publishers, and other media organizations to become owned and controlled by corporate giants—usually called conglomerates—that have become bigger, fewer, and, in significant ways, more like-minded. The trend continues in the 21st century.

This thrust toward monopoly or concentration of ownership has developed in stages, each of which represent potential threats to diversity of ideas and views as well as to independent and vigorously competing news media. First came the newspaper groups noted in the previous chapter, whereby a number of similar papers are held by one owner. The Gannett Company is currently the largest, with 100 dailies including 17 in England, Knight-Ridder is next largest, with 31 dailies. Similar patterns of group ownership of radio and television stations have characterized broadcasting as well.

Next there were the increasingly common, one-newspaper cities with local media oligopolies whereby the only newspaper in a particular city also owned local radio and television outlets. (The spread of national newspapers plus more suburban papers has allayed this concern somewhat.)

Another stage was cross-media ownerships whereby one company—such as the Tribune Company of Chicago, the Times Mirror Company of Los Angeles, the Washington Post Company, and others—acquired additional newspapers, radio and television stations, book publishers, and magazines scattered around the country. In such companies, media properties come and go as corporate strategies change.

In television broadcasting, groups of stations and networks have been swallowed by bigger fish. In 1986, the ABC network was acquired by the much smaller Capital Cities network for $3.5 billion. General Electric, original owner of RCA, bought it back, including the NBC network, for $ 6.4 billion. In 1990, Rupert Murdoch assembled the Fox network out of the Metromedia television station chain and acquired the film studio, 20th Century Fox. Among the owners of the nation's radio stations, the Clear Channel group was out in front with 1,238 stations.

These various media companies have evolved into the most ominous creature in the media menagerie—the giant conglomerate that owns not only news and entertainment media, but also production and distribution companies as well. These behemoths deal in all of the products of entertainment and popular culture, including in a small corner, journalism.

The world's largest media company was, at recent count, Time Warner, (formerly AOL–Time Warner) but others in the chase, are Disney/ABC, Viacom (CBS), NBC Universal, Bertlesmann (of Germany) and the far-flung empire controlled by Rupert Murdoch operating under the misnomer of News Corporation.

No one has followed the continuing trends of media consolidation more closely than Ben Bagdikian (1992) who has shown that ownership of most of the major media has been consolidated into fewer and fewer corporate hands—from 50 national and multinational corporations in 1983 to just 20 in 1992. In that 9-year period, the companies controlling most of the national daily circulation shrank from 20 to just 11. According to Bagdikian, magazines, a majority of the total annual industry revenues earned by 20 firms in 1983 was amassed by only 2 in 1992; in book publishing, revenues divided among 11 firms accrued to just five in that same 9-year period. This media merger frenzy has continued unabated with no end in sight.

The sheer size of media conglomerates makes them, as publicly held companies, active players in the financial markets, hence they are under pressure to compete for earnings with other highly speculative investments. Bagdikian (1992) commented,

> For the first time in the history of American journalism, news and public information have been integrated formally into the highest levels of financial and nonjournalistic corporate control. Conflicts of interest between the public's need for information and corporate desires for "positive" information have been vastly increased. (p. xxx)

Driven by visions of expanding profits and ever-larger markets as well as the opportunities created by new technologies of telecommunications, the media giants have been acquiring each other at a quickened rate. Grow or perish seems to be the credo; bigger is apparently better. A flurry of mergers of major U.S. media organizations have been occurring since 1995. The continuing trend has broad implications both for the quality of journalism and the nature of the entertainment business here and abroad. These media giants, especially Time Warner, are subject to fluctuations in the economy and during the early years of the 21st century, have taken some severe hits.

DISNEY SWALLOWS ABC

In August 1995, the Walt Disney Company announced the acquisition of Capital Cities/ABC in a deal valued at $19 billion—the second largest media takeover ever. The merged company brought together ABC, then the most profitable network, including its television news organization and its ESPN sports cable service, with an entertainment giant—Disney's Hollywood film and television studios, its theme parks, and its repository of well-known cartoon characters and the merchandise sales they generate. In 1995, the Disney Company sold more than $15 billion worth of Disney merchandise worldwide—a figure more than seven times the global box office for Disney movies (Auletta, 1996).

Both companies announced they would grow faster together. Disney/ABC became the first media company to have a major presence in four distribution systems: filmed entertainment, cable television, broadcasting, and telephone wires through its connections with three regional phone companies. So, ABC's news media operations, including its national news shows, *World News Tonight with Peter Jennings*, and *Nightline,* with Ted Koppel and the admirable ABC television news organization, plus 20 radio stations and eight television stations, publishing operations, *The Kansas City Star, The Fort Worth Star Telegram* (both papers were later sold to Knight-Ridder), Fairchild and Chilton trade publications, and international broadcasting interests were all merged, or better, submerged, into an entertainment giant that generates about $26 billion in revenues yearly. Heretofore, Disney had no involvement with any activity remotely concerned with news or journalism. Now Peter Jennings and Ted Koppel and colleagues were all working for Mickey Mouse. At the time of the merger, no top executive from either Disney or ABC made any statement about how the merger would affect news media and journalists in the new company. (In February 2004, in a bold bid that could have reshaped the entertainment business, Comcast, the nation's largest cable operator, made an unsolicited $54.1 billion takeover offer for the Disney company. Michael Eisner, Disney's chief executive, barely beat off the bid.)

TIME WARNER, TURNER AND AOL

Another merger bombshell came in 1995 when Time Warner Incorporated and Turner Broadcasting System announced they would merge their sprawling operations, reinforcing Time Warner's position as the world's largest communications giant. Time Warner said it would buy the 82% of Turner that it did not already own—at a price tag of $7.5 billion. In this case, both companies had major news-related media. (Time Inc. and Warner Communications had merged in a $14 billion deal in 1989.) Time Warner's major publishing interests included *Time, Life, Money, Fortune, People,* and *Sports Illustrated* as well as Time–Life Books and Warner Books. However, in money terms, these publications were overshadowed by the Warner Brothers. film and television studios, television and cable channels such as HBO, Cinemax, and others, 50 record labels, the world's largest music publisher, film libraries, and other businesses such as Six Flags theme parks. The Turner company had CNN, CNN International, and Headline News cable channels, in addition to its film and television production, other television and cable channels, film libraries, and assorted sports franchises such as the Atlanta Braves baseball team, the Atlanta Hawks basketball team (later sold), and World Championship Wrestling. As with Disney/ABC, the news and journalism operations were in monetary terms a fraction of the corporate pie, and presumably of less importance in the corporate scheme of things.

But all of this was just prelude to the richest media merger to date when in 2000, America Online (AOL), which provided the Internet to many millions, announced that it had agreed to buy Time Warner for $165 billion, providing the best evidence yet that the old and the new media were converging. Time Warner thus admitted that the Internet was central to its music, publishing, and television businesses. AOL with its 22 million paying subscribers, gained access to Time Warner's cable systems. Concerns were expressed that the Internet, with its many thousand sources of information, had itself become prey to corporate consolidations. Some journalists were concerned not that there would be fewer outlets (the opposite was true) but that a few people would have control over them. This biggest of all media mergers was forcing journalists and those who care about journalism to be cognizant of the need to build walls among the multiple compartments of these new information, entertainment, and marketing giants. Some saw the independence and diversity of journalism in peril all across a media world that was being reshaped more rapidly than anyone could have predicted. These concerns proved premature as the new media giant was buffeted badly by the bursting of the dot-com bubble, which wiped out almost $200 billion in shareholder value. This shakeout in the early 2000s showed that AOL's Internet value and importance had been vastly overrated. Balance of power in the company shifted back to the "old media" empire founded by Henry Luce, which promptly dropped "AOL" from its corporate title. Despite its battering, Time Warner is still the biggest revenue earner of the congolomerates.

WESTINGHOUSE, CBS AND VIACOM

Another blockbuster merger came in mid-1995, with Westinghouse Inc.'s takeover of CBS Incorporated, creating the nation's largest broadcast station group, with 39 radio stations and 16 television stations reaching 32% of the nation. This merger brought together two pioneers of broadcasting—CBS started its radio network in 1927 and Westinghouse had launched KDKA Pittsburgh in 1920. There were concerns about how well this merger could run a major network. CBS, once a leader in both ratings and quality of broadcast news, had slipped. The former "Tiffany" network had lost some important affiliates and had no holdings in cable. By the scale of today's mergers, once-mighty CBS was sold for an embarrassingly low price—only $5.4 billion.

Another significant (and related) merger was the marriage of a hot cable television company, Viacom, with a legendary Hollywood studio, Paramount Communications, Inc., for $8.2 billion in 1993. The new company, called Paramount Viacom International, fused Viacom's ubiquitous MTV and Nickelodeon cable channels and Showtime pay television channel with Paramount's film company, Paramount television, and publishing firms—Simon & Schuster, Prentice-Hall, and Pocket Books—and several sports properties, Madison Square Garden, The New York Knicks, and The New York Rangers. (Fabricant, 1996a).

The mega-merger pot kept boiling and in September 1999, Viacom said it would acquire the CBS Corporation for $37.3 billion, creating the world's second largest media company . CBS brought to the merger $1.9 billion in radio properties including 190 radio stations; $4.4 billion in television holdings, including the CBS Network, CBS Entertainment, CBS Sports, 17 television stations, and $546 million in cable properties, including two country music networks, CMT and TNN, and two regional sports networks.

MURDOCH ROLLS ONWARD

Although smaller than several of its U.S. rivals, Rupert Murdoch's News Corporation had expanded into satellite television and programming abroad and had global clout far beyond its size. During these recent mega-mergers, Rupert Murdoch, the most conspicuous big roller among media owners, had not been idle. In 1996, his News Corporation acquired the New World Communications Group, Inc. for $3.4 billion, making him the biggest owner of television stations in this country. The purchase gave Fox network ownership of 35 television stations in 11 of 12 of the nation's largest television markets, extending the company's reach to 40% of American homes. Murdoch's reach was extended even further in 1997 when he agreed to pay $1.9 billion to acquire the cable channel controlled by Pat Robertson, the religious-right purveyor of programs reaching 67 million homes.

Since starting out with a small group of Australian newspapers, Murdoch has been continually reshaping his media empire and juggling his considerable debts. Although long involved in journalism and newspapers, Murdoch has consistently shown a cynical and hypocritical disdain for responsible journalism, apparently considering news just another commodity to be bought and sold. His Fox broadcast network has notably lacked respectable news programming and he has been criticized for using his news operations to further his own political goals and preferences. One critic, Alex Jones, said of him:

> News is a commodity that is of no more importance to Rupert Murdoch than a television sitcom. He crafts news for the audience, but in fact his sense of what the audience wants is skewed to sensation and a lowering, not an elevation, of standards. Murdoch makes no excuses. "Look," he said, "the first thing you have to do in a public company is to survive, and I don't make any apology for a paper or a magazine." (cited in Fabricant, 1996a, p. C6)

His strategy apparently is to own every major form of programming—news, sports, films and children's shows—and beam them via satellites or television stations he owns or controls to homes in America, Europe, Asia, and South America. Murdock commented: "We want to put our programming everywhere and to distribute everybody's product around the world" (cited in Fabricant, 1996b, p. C1).

Murdoch has more than 150 media properties in his constantly shifting empire, based mainly in the United States, United Kingdom, and Australia, and with it, he has carefully put together a vertically integrated global media empire. In the United States, he owns the Fox television network, 20th Century Fox movies and television, *The New York Post, Weekly Standard,* and Harper-Collins Publishers. His 24-hour cable news channel, Fox News Channel, has outperformed CNN and MNBC in attracting cable's news viewers. In Britain, he owns *The Sunday Times, Times* of London, *The Sun, News of the World,* and other media companies. In Australia, he owns Fox Studios Australia for movies; seven television networks; one national newspaper, *The Australian*, and 117 other newspapers, giving him two-thirds of newspaper circulation; two magazines and other media-related companies. Various other holdings include the Sky satellite system in Britain and the Star satellite system in Asia, plus other important TV properties—Star News in India and Phoenix InfoNews in China.

In April 2003, Murdoch agreed to buy control of Hughes Electronics and its DirecTV satellite operation from General Motors for $6.6 billion. The deal gives Murdoch more power in determining what programs are beamed to television sets in the United States and what consumers will pay for them. With the addition of DirectTV, the nation's largest satellite operator with 11 million subscribers, News Corporation becomes, along with Time Warner, one of a few companies that both create and distribute television programs. The FCC approved the deal in December, 2003.

GENERAL ELECTRIC AND NBC UNIVERSAL

The latest major media consolidation took place in October 2003, when the major corporation, General Electric, owner of NBC, television's most profitable network, agreed to buy the entertainment assets of Vivendi Universal, in a deal that would create a new entertainment conglomerate better able to compete with Viacom, Time Warner, the Disney Company, and News Corporation. The new entity, NBC Universal, is owned 80% by General Electric and 20% retained by Vivendi. NBC has added Universal's movie and television studios, theme parks, and three cable channels to its own television and cable networks and TV production, bringing a total value of the new "full service" conglomerate at an estimated $43 billion. NBC Universal hoped to capitalize on technologies beginning to change the television business, such as video-on-demand programs and the multiplication of available channels through the digitalizing of television signals.

The annual revenues of the big five of media conglomerates are Time Warner with $42 billion, Viacom with $25 billion, Disney with $26 billion, General Electric including NBC Universal with $131 billion, and Murdoch's News Corporation with $17 billion.

These mega-mergers positioned the evolving giants—Disney Co., Time Warner, NBC Universal, Viacom, and News Corporation to better penetrate and dominate the growing international markets for television, movies, news, sports, recordings, and other media products. At the time of the merger with ABC, Disney president, Michael Eisner, spoke glowingly of India's middle class of 250 million as a great potential audience for Disney/ABC movies, cartoons, news, and sports programs. NBA and NFL professional games have been gaining large audiences overseas, hence the importance of the ESPN sports networks. The competition between CNN, MSNBC, and Murdoch's Fox network for the top 24-hour cable news channel has strong international potential. Broadcast networks have been looking to international markets as a way of gaining hundreds of millions of new viewers.

OTHER BIG MEDIA PLAYERS

Other conglomerates abroad are also competing for global media markets. Among the bigqger players are Bertelsmann A.G. of Germany, which became a media giant with book and record clubs in Germany, Spain, the United States, Brazil, and 18 other countries. Bertelsmann owns Bantam, Doubleday, and Dell book publishers in America, 37 magazines in five countries, and radio and television properties. In 1998, Bertelsmann surprised the American book industry when it purchased Random House, the dominant general book publisher in the United States, making the German firm by far the most important book publisher in the world. With Random House combined with its other U.S. book properties, Bertelsmann controls a substantial share of the American adult trade-book market.

Possibly the most swashbuckling of the media tycoons has been Silvio Berlusconi of Italy who built a multibillion dollar television and newspaper empire, Fininvest, of unusual power and influence. With 42% of Italy's advertising market and 16% of its daily newspaper circulation, ownership of Italy's three main private television channels, plus other properties, Berlusconi has dominated Italy's media and influenced its politics. Using that power, he won election as prime minister of Italy in 1994. However, he was forced to resign after his media empire was linked to bribes of tax auditors. In 1998, Berlusconi was sentenced to 2 years in jail for illegal political contributions and for bribing tax inspectors. Despite all this—on trial 8 times in eight years—he has become prime minister of Italy, remains the richest man in Italy, and recently has rewritten the law to protect himself from prosecution.

Transnational buying and selling of media are an expected result of the globalization of the economy and the free flow of investment capital across borders. But the United States and other democracies may need to update and revise their own communications policies that were formulated before news, mass culture, entertainment, and other information moved so freely around the world.

CONCERNS FOR JOURNALISM AND PUBLIC INTEREST

A principal concern for public affairs journalism is that the news operations—broadcast news divisions, newspapers, and news magazines—have become just a small part of these giant entertainment companies. The future of independent news gathering appears threatened when news media are submerged into entertainment companies.

Bill Kovach (1996), wrote:

> Though the trend is not new, with the Disney/ABC merger the threat to a form of journalism that serves the interests of a self-governing people crosses a new threshold. Even with the best of intentions, owners and managers are influenced by the fact that they now preside over a corporation that, by the simple act of merger, has drastically reduced the proportionate importance of the news department ... ABC's news division will now have to compete with the enormous energy of Disney's entertainment productions in a company in which ABC's value as an outlet for entertainment is paramount. (p. A17)

The future of journalism as watchdog on government and giant corporations is threatened when big organizations that do business with the U.S. government, like General Electric (NBC), have swallowed major news media. Communications companies in recent years have ingested many news organizations, yet these same companies are involved in lobbying government and seeking government favors. In a recent election campaign, the communications industry was the sixth largest contributor to candidates, giving almost $10 million to political action committees.

A major concern is whether reporters within these entertainment giants will be permitted to objectively and critically report news about their own organizations. Lawrence Grossman, former head of NBC news, reported that when the stock market crashed in 1987, he received a call from Jack Welch, chairman of General Electric, owner of NBC, telling him not to use words in NBC news reports that might adversely affect General Electric stock. Grossman said he did not tell his NBC news staff about the call (Bagdikian, 1992).

"You cannot trust news organizations to cover themselves," said one critic, citing as an example television's meager coverage of the telecommunications debate in Congress that led to major communications legislation in 1996 (cited in Gunther, 1995, p. 36).

Gunther (1995) raised this question regarding mega deals: "Will film critic Joel Siegel of ABC's *Good Morning America* feel free to deliver a withering critique of Disney's next big animated movie?" (p. 37).

Will ABC news be able to report critically about the Chinese government at a time that Disney may be trying to get its movies via satellite into China? We already know what Rupert Murdoch will do; in 1994, in an effort to curry favor with the Deng regime in China, which had criticized the BBC news, Murdoch summarily dropped BBC's World television news from his Star TV satellite service in Hong Kong.

The word "synergy" has become a mantra for CEOs of the recent mergers. When he bought ABC, Disney chief, Michael Eisner, used the term five times in four sentences to illustrate the advantages of merger. When Westinghouse purchased CBS, its CEO said that combining the two companies' broadcasting assets would save hundreds of millions of dollars a year and bring about "tremendous marketing synergies" (cited in Auletta, 1995b).

So far, the jury is out about the advantages of synergy. But what is already apparent is that synergy is no friend of journalism. The business assumptions behind the word—cost savings, a "team culture," the "leverage" of size—can be actively hostile to the business of reporting. (Auletta, 1995b). Rich (1996) defined synergy as the "dedication of an entire, far-flung multimedia empire to selling its products with every means at its disposal." Another critic said, "When you hear the word synergy, you might as well read 'conflict of interest'" (cited in Rich, 1996, p. 15).

Investigative reporters like Brian Ross of ABC News have been learning how far they can go in reporting about their own companies. In October 1998, Ross had what he thought was a solid story involving accounts of pedophilia and lax security at theme park resorts, including Disney World. But his story for *20/20*, ABC's news magazine program, was killed by ABC News executives, who refused to discuss the decision. The Disney Company issued a statement that its executives had nothing to do with the decision. An important question was whether other ABC journalists would feel inhibited from pursuing stories about Disney. When the Warner movie, *Twister*, was released, *Time* magazine just happened to run a cover story on tornadoes, and Time Warner was criticized for committing synergy.

An ominous dispute between media giants occurred on May 2, 2000, when Time Warner Cable removed ABC stations from cable systems it operates in seven cities serving 3.5 million customers including New York, Los Angeles, and Philadelphia. Viewers found themselves without access to *Who Wants To Marry A Millionaire* as well as the *ABC Evening News* and *Nightline*. The dispute involved how much Time Warner should pay Disney (owner of ABC) for carrying its cable channels. But it also touched on larger issues relating to the distribution of entertainment and news programs, including the friction between cable and broadcast industries, the growing competition between cable and satellite firms, and Disney's opposition to the merger between Time Warner and America Online. Time Warner backed off 24 hours later but for critics, the shutting down of a major news outlet, even for a day, was seen as a blow to the public interest and should not be tolerated in a democracy. By the blunt use of its monopoly power, Time Warner suffered an instant public-relations disaster and critics called for a closer scrutiny of its merger with AOL. One critic said the incident took the theoretical danger of media consolidation and control and made it a very real problem.

By comparison, synergy seemed like a modest concern but yet it too has a lot to do with diversity—and marketing. Critic, Edward Rothstein, commented:

> Disney can produce related movies, toys, books, videos, shows and infomercials so that each format feeds the others. A video game turns into a television show, a computer game into a novel. A newspaper reviews its own corporation's products; news shows promote made-for-TV movies with tie-ins. It can seem that much of culture has become a series of products being transported from one technological medium to another, with fewer and fewer hands manipulating the software. (Rothstein, 1996, p. B1)

The media giants' timidity and aversion to controversy was illustrated by recent legal clashes of both ABC and CBS news organizations with major tobacco corporations. In 1994, ABC on its *Day One* magazine show carried a hard-hitting investigative piece called *"Smoke Screen"* about the manipulation of nicotine in cigarettes and the behavior of tobacco companies. As a result, ABC spent 17 months and millions in legal fees fighting a potential $10 billion dollar lawsuit from Philip Morris. Both the producer and on-air correspondent said the story was accurate and ABC lawyers were confident they could win. But soon after the merger with Disney was announced, Capital Cities/ABC management forced the news division to issue a humiliating public apology, which Philip Morris reprinted in newspapers all over the nation. Many journalists were stunned. Why had ABC settled? Most agreed it was not a matter of journalistic ethics ("We were wrong") but more of corporate convenience ("We can't impede the merger"). Auletta called it "the logic of negative synergy" (Auletta, 1995b, p. 9).

A similar ethical embarrassment hit CBS' *60 Minutes* news program soon after and was even more of a *cause celebre*. In November 1995, in an atmosphere of increased tension between the tobacco companies and the press, CBS's lawyers ordered *60 Minutes* not to broadcast a planned on-the-record interview with a former tobacco company executive who was harshly critical of the industry. Many in journalism and the law felt that CBS, facing a multibillion-dollar lawsuit, had backed off from a fight it probably could have won. *60 Minutes* was faulted for not saying that the decision came at a time CBS stockholders were considering a merger with Westinghouse. *The New York Times* editorialized:

> This act of self censorship by the country's most powerful and aggressive television news program sends a chilling message to journalists investigating industry practices everywhere.... But the most troubling part of CBS's decision is that it was made not by news executives but by corporate officers who may have their minds on money rather than public service these days. With a $5.4 billion merger deal with Westinghouse Electric Corp. about to be approved, a multi-billion dollar lawsuit would hardly have been a welcome development. Some of the executives who helped kill the *60 Minutes* interview, including the general counsel, stand to gain millions of dollars themselves in stock options and other payments once the deal is approved.... The network's action shows that media companies in play lose their journalistic aggressiveness when they let lawyers and corporate executives make decisions that ought to be the province of news executives. The same issue was raised when ABC settled its lawsuit with Philip Morris. ("Self-Censorship at CBS," 1995)

Both ABC and CBS took a critical lambasting from the press in general and from academic critics, *Columbia Journalism Review* and *American*

Journalism Review. Many in journalism were asking whether the corporate executives of the big conglomerates will back their own news media in future legal clashes with government or economic power as, for example, *The New York Times* and *The Washington Post* had done in the Pentagon Papers case. The outlook was not promising.

DOMINANCE OF GROUP OWNERSHIP IN DAILIES

The great majority of U.S. daily newspapers have not been swallowed by the huge entertainment conglomerates described earlier. This is important because the daily newspaper is a medium that is mainly involved with marketing news. However, more than 500 of the 1,516 dailies in 1997, including almost all of the largest and most influential, are owned by the 20 largest U.S. newspaper companies, that is, firms mainly concerned with putting out newspapers.

In early 2000, the eight largest newspaper groups, all with total daily circulations of more than 1 million, are in order of total daily circulation: Gannett Company, 96 papers; Knight-Ridder Inc., 31 papers; Times Mirror Company, 7 papers; New York Times Company, 20 papers; Dow Jones & Company, 31 papers; E. W. Scripps, 19 papers, (Chicago) Tribune Company, 4 papers; Washington Post Company, 51 papers.

TRIBUNE COMPANY BUYS THE LOS ANGELES TIMES

This lineup was changed abruptly on March 4, 2000 when the Tribune Company of Chicago announced that it was buying the Times Mirror Company for $6.3 billion, creating the nation's third largest newspaper company. *The Los Angeles Times*, operated for 118 years by the Chandler family, along with *The Baltimore Sun, The Hartford Courant,* and Long Island's *Newsday,* plus 18 magazines, passed over to the Tribune Company, which along with the *Chicago Tribune*, had interests in three other newspapers, regional cable programming, 22 television stations, three radio stations, and the Chicago Cubs. The dailies had a combined 3.9 million circulation and combined 1999 revenues of $6.25 billion. The Tribune Company moved up to second place behind the Gannett Company among the top groups in market value of its assets.

The sale of *The Los Angeles Times* was about more than mergers and financial payouts. The *Times* had played a leading role in the history of southern California and was a dominant influence on the region's political, intellectual, and cultural life. It was a blow to civic pride and to the Angelenos' sense of identity to see their great newspaper pass into the hands of midwesterners. Even the *Times'* many critics hated to see the change.

More importantly, the *Times,* is one of four or five best newspapers in the nation and it faced an uncertain future. Would the Tribune Company do what is necessary to maintain its excellence? Would the *Times'* expensive Washington and foreign news bureaus be maintained? So far, the news was encouraging. In April 2004, the *Times* won five Pulitzer Prizes for its excellence in journalism—a near record for any newspaper.

In the aggregate, 455 individual companies own the nation's dailies. Of these, 129 groups now own 80% of the total. In earlier times, the idea of several daily newspapers competing in one city for news and public support reflected the value of diversity and the competition was considered important for democratic government. New York City once had 14 dailies, and Omaha, for example, had seven. Today, only eight large American cities have more than one daily newspaper under separate ownership and are not involved in joint operating agreements: Boston, Chicago, Denver, Los Angeles, New York City, Trenton, NJ, Tucson, and Washington, DC. However, in most larger communities, the presence of local radio, television, and cable outlets, suburban and weekly papers, and local magazines, plus access to national papers certainly contributes to diversity and the marketplace of ideas.

The steady, inexorable trend toward group ownership seems to go on unabated. The long-standing tradition of the family-owned newspaper may be ending. Media analyst, John Morton (1995) said it cannot last because few family dynasties are left. In 1995, he counted only 77 independently owned, family-controlled newspapers remaining of 30,000 circulation or more; this represented about 5% of the 1,516 or so dailies still in business in the United States. According to industry figures, the total number of independently owned daily papers shrank from 1,650 in 1920 to 850 in 1960, and to just 300 in 1998 and most of these papers had small circulations.

Morton said the unusual thing about the growing concentration of newspaper ownership in the past 25 years, compared with other industries, is that it has come rather late to newspapers. Compared with auto makers, grocers, steel companies, and retailers, the newspaper industry remains diverse in ownership. Moreover, newspaper ownership is much more concentrated in other Western democracies such as Britain, France, Italy, Australia, and Germany.

When Gannett purchased 11 more daily papers in July 1995, Charles Eisendrath commented, "The war is over and the old guys lost" (Glaberson, 1995, Sec. 4, p. 1). The "old guys" were independent newspaper publishers, many of whom had close ties to their communities. Gannett's earlier purchases of respected family-owned papers had raised the issue of whether good journalism and corporate ownership can coexist. Now the question does not seem to come up.

Some major newspapers have been able to withstand the pressures of potential buyers by either adopting a two-tier stock ownership plan, retaining voting power with the founding family, or by distributing ownership of the company to its employees through employee stock ownership plans. Several of the biggest companies in terms of circulation, the New York Times Company, the Tribune Company, Dow Jones, and the Times Mirror Company have had arrangements to ward off potential buyers. (At Times Mirror, it was the contentious Chandler family that initiated the sale of the *Times* to the Tribune Company.)

At *The Milwaukee Journal,* an employee-owned trust was established in 1937 by publisher, Harry Grant, who also acquired an ownership stake that his descendants control today. Grant felt that protecting the company from a buyout would promote superior journalism. But in 2003, because of financial debts relating to the ownership structure, the company's directors decided to turn Journal Communications into a publicly owned company with initial offerings on the New York Stock Exchange. Will the employees lose control of he company? Management thinks not because employees will receive Class B stock worth 10 votes each while Class A public stockholders will get one vote each.

As noted earlier, most of best papers are in groups. The old days of William Randolph Hearst sending out explicit orders from San Simeon regarding his pet campaigns and editorial positions to be carried in all his papers are over. Most group-owned dailies enjoy considerable local autonomy with editors and publishers establishing their own news and editorial policies. Group ownership provides economic stability by efficient business policies that enable papers to survive where they might otherwise fold. The sharing of news through the group and through news services and other cooperative efforts helps papers to survive. In its first years, *USA Today* was greatly assisted by the seconding of staff members from other Gannett papers who remained on the payrolls of their home papers. Nonetheless, papers within a group tend to look alike in format, typography, features, and editorial tone.

PUBLIC OUTRAGE AT MEDIA CONSOLIDATION

From time to time, the public reacts strongly against "media giantism" and the continuing trend toward bigger and fewer media outlets. In June

2003, the FCC narrowly approved, 3 to 2, the most important changes in media ownership in a generation. The FCC relaxed many of the most significant restrictions on broadcast and newspaper conglomerates to expand into new markets and extend their reach in cities where they already have a presence. The ruling would permit a company to own up to three television stations, eight radio stations, a daily newspaper, and a cable operator in the biggest cities. Also, the big television networks would be able to buy more stations. The two FCC dissenters said the rules would lead to more consolidation.

But a firestorm of opposition to the proposed changes erupted from a variety of sources. FCC officials said they received 520,000 public comments, mostly in opposition. Interestingly, the organizational critics were ideologically diverse, including the National Rifle Association, the National Organization of Women, Common Cause, U.S. Chamber of Commerce, U.S. Conference of Catholic Bishops, Writers Guild of America, and the Parents Television Council. The groups said they worried that it would be more difficult to get diverse views on the airwaves.

Congress was besieged with protests from constituents. As a result, the House of Representatives overwhelmingly (400 to 21) passed legislation to block a new FCC rule that would permit the largest TV networks to own more stations.

The Senate approved a resolution to repeal all of the new regulations for media companies to get bigger. The vote of 55 to 40 was not enough to override a possible veto. Then a federal appeals court issued a surprise order blocking the FCC from imposing the new rules a day before they were scheduled to go into effect. It was a sharp setback for both the biggest media companies and for FCC chairman, Michael K. Powell. In November 2003, the White House and Congress settled their long-running dispute over media ownership rules. The FCC had wanted to allow television networks to extend their reach by owning TV stations reaching 45% of the nation's audiences. Congress wanted to roll back the rule to 35%. In the face of a White House veto, congressional negotiators agreed to set the figure at 39%.

Today's media mix presents a paradox. The sources of news and useful information, however wrapped and disguised in gaudy packages of entertainment and persuasive communication—marketing, advertising, propaganda and PR-driven messages—are greater than ever. This vast, expanding landscape also includes cable channels, magazines, and books (just visit a Border's or Barnes & Noble bookstore), the Internet, CD-ROM and other electronic outlets, and even mail order.

On the other hand, another reality is that the economic units—the media companies and organizations that produce, market, and distribute the news that enlightens us and the entertainment that diverts and beguiles us—are rapidly becoming gigantic in size, fewer in number, more remote, and more like-minded. That is certainly cause for concern.

6

News on the Air:
A Sense of Decline

Radio, if it is to serve and survive, must hold a mirror behind the nation and the world. If the reflection shows radical intolerance, economic inequality, bigotry, unemployment or anything else—let the people see it, and rather hear it. The mirror must have no curves and must be held with a steady hand.

—Edward R. Murrow

For more than 50 years, television has been a powerful information force, focusing a nation's attention on great events—a presidential election, a disastrous war in Vietnam, a historic struggle for civil rights, and more recently, the fall of Communism and prime time wars in the Persian Gulf and Yugoslavia.

In 1963, the three networks began their 30-minute evening newscasts (originally 15 minutes as on radio) which became the "front page" from which most Americans increasingly received their news. But in recent years, things have changed. There has been a pervading atmosphere of unease about television news, a sense that broadcast journalism has lost its way and is in decline.

In addressing the shortcomings of today's journalism, it should be understood that some criticisms are peculiar to television news (either broadcast or cable), others to news on radio, and still others to newspapers and magazines. Yet, many broad-brush indictments of poor journalistic performance blame all news media equally; that is patently unfair. Some criticisms such as mixing entertainment with news may seem to cut across several media but not in the same ways. The problem of journalists as celebrities is mainly in television. Many media differences persist, exacerbated by the rise of cable and the Internet.

The media are not a monolith, but a complex and heterogeneous collection of diverse organizations and individuals often with quite different motivations and goals. Journalists, whether at *The Daily Chronicle,* or ABC news or station WGN are members of a news organization and their performance is shaped by and is a reflection of where they work. Some journalists do their jobs well, others not so well at times. So bear in mind that the criticisms that follow usually apply to only part of the news media. For clarity, television, radio, and the print media are analyzed separately as much as possible.

In its transition from radio to television, broadcast news was for many years a loss leader, a public service intended to attract serious viewers. Profits, if any, from newscasts were incidental. The best-known broadcasters—Edward R. Murrow, Eric Sevareid, Walter Cronkite, Chet Huntley and David Brinkley, Howard K. Smith, and John Chancellor—enjoyed a stature and credibility with the public rarely found among today's anchors. As the pioneering broadcast giants, William Paley at CBS and David Sarnoff at NBC, faded away, conventional corporate interests took control—General Electric at NBC, real estate magnate, Lawrence Tisch (and later Westinghouse and then Viacom) at CBS, and Capital Cities (and later Disney Company) at ABC. News programs were increasingly expected to attract large audiences and bring in revenue, and that required higher ratings and mass audiences.

The short television life of the early high-quality but low-rated documentaries soon ended, and the evening news broadcasts began to stress more crime, scandal, and celebrities, all of which tended to crowd out foreign and public affairs news.

After the ratings success of CBS' *60 Minutes* in the 1980s, the networks found money was to be made from the so-called news magazine shows. Imitators, such as *20/20, Prime Time Live, Turning Point, 48 Hours, Dateline NBC, Eye to Eye With Connie Chung,* and *Day One,* soon clogged the airways. The quality varied widely from the newsworthy to such trivia as Connie Chung seriously interviewing Tonya Harding, an Olympic skating hopeful who caused injury to a rival, and Heidi Fleiss, a Hollywood madam in trouble with the law. These news magazines had a semblance of journalism, but were increasingly emulating the popular pseudojournalistic television shows such as *Hard Copy, A Current Affair,* and the talk shows of Oprah Winfrey and Phil Donahue.

Don Hewitt, a 50-year veteran of CBS News, doesn't like the recent trends in television news. "For the old news giants, the motto was 'news is news and entertainment is entertainment and never the twain shall meet.'

Well, the twain have met. And it's not good," he said. He didn't just mean that television news has gone soft or is excessively trying to entertain a fickle audience. He has a broader worry: that television news programs are being used as filler for prime-time slots in which entertainment shows have faltered. (Mifflin, 1998, p. C5) During the summer of 1999, *Dateline NBC* was on 5 hours a week; at ABC, *20/20* was on 4 hours a week; and at CBS, *60 Minutes* was on 2 hours a week, and *48 Hours* was on 4 hours a week. Such programs were cheaper to produce than entertainment shows and yet attracted good audiences. Yet critics considered the journalistic quality of most such shows to be diluted and trivialized.

Veteran television anchors expressed their concerns. Walter Cronkite, who anchored the CBS evening news for 17 years, wrote that in the face of rising competition from cable, VCRs, and more aggressive local newscasts and tabloid shows, the big three newscasts, "frequently go soft. Their features aren't interpretive to the day's events, and the time could be better spent" (cited in Rottenberg, 1994, p. 34). Cronkite blamed two developments. First, the networks have cut news budgets "so practically an amputation has taken place. The reduction of the foreign bureaus is a crime. It is simply not possible for anybody to intelligently and adequately cover a distant foreign beat without living there" (cited in Rottenberg, 1994, p. 35). Second, Cronkite saw television news evolving away from the networks into something in the pattern of daily newspapers. That is, he said, "the local television station really does all the news—some international, some national, and some local. And many local journalists—smaller markets, smaller money—are not as good as those on the network" (cited in Rottenberg, 1994, pp. 34–35). John Chancellor, long-time NBC anchor and commentator, berated television for neglecting its coverage of politics:

> The networks are spending far less than they ever did on covering politics. I sense in the networks an unwillingness to go into much detail as far as politics is concerned. The people who run the news divisions feel that unless it's an unusual election, the public isn't all that interested. (cited in Glass, 1992, p. 1C)

Chancellor was the last news commentator on an evening network show. Daniel Schorr, NPR commentator, said, "Television deals badly with talking heads, especially when they are also thinking heads" (cited in Glass, 1992, p. 1C).

The dramatic decline in the quality and quantity of network news, especially foreign coverage, has been called the single most significant development in journalism in recent years. The closing of expensive foreign news bureaus by the networks has been mentioned. ABC has only six bureaus today compared with 13 in the peak 1980s. Similarly, NBC has six bureaus compared with 13 in the 1980s and CBS news has six bureaus compared with seven in the 1980s.

The decline of public affairs news on television was further signaled by the decimation of network news staffs in Washington, DC, the major source for news of government and politics. In a 2-year study of 75 Washington correspondents and producers at ABC, CBS, and NBC, Kimball (1994) found not just a slump in coverage but "the end of an era in broadcast history" (p. 5). Overall, he found that the CBS and NBC Washington bureaus, which once had 30 correspondents each, were down to about 13 each; ABC had just eliminated seven reporters. The White House, Congress, and the Supreme Court, and federal agencies all received diminished attention. Beats such as the environment and individual agencies were eliminated. Kimball found the networks relying more and more on shared pool coverage and voice-overs, or tape shot by a freelancer or syndicate and narrated by a home-based correspondent who had not been to the scene of the story. (Similar practices became prevalent in foreign news coverage.)

In this regard, the print media did not do much better. A survey of 19 key government agencies in Washington, DC, found that newspapers are also jettisoning their traditional beat coverage. For example, the important Department of the Interior, which controls the use of 500 million acres of public land, including the National Park Service, and agencies like Indian Affairs, Fish and Wildlife, logging, mining, and so forth, had no newspaper reporters assigned full time. (Herbers & McCartney, 1999)

With the decline of television network news, there has been a dramatic rise in alternative news outlets such as prime-time news magazines, radio talk shows, cable news and talks show, and Internet outlets, which do little news gathering.

The soft "infotainment" news that has largely replaced public affairs news on network newscasts has been called "your news," "news lite," or "news you can use." A newspaper ad touted NBC's hottest story, "Marriage 'Boot Camp': Could It Save Your Relationship?" On any given evening, one third or more of the 21-minute news hole is given to features such as "Sleepless in America" (the growing problem of insomnia), "Starting Over" (on keeping New Year's resolutions), "The Plane Truth" (airline safety), or "Going Home" (NBC journalists return to their roots). A consistent leader in ratings, NBC also puts soft news into regular segments like "In Their Own Words," "In Depth," "The Family,"

"The American Dream," and "Norman Schwarzkopf's America." ABC and CBS have similar non-news segments regularly on their evening network shows.

IMPACT OF 24-HOUR CABLE NEWS

The growing influence of CNN, MSNBC, and Fox News Channel have directly affected the ways the networks report the news. Increasingly important breaking news stories are often first reported on cable. Networks may interrupt their program for a major news story but then will often return to scheduled programming while CNN, Fox, and MSNBC will usually stay on the air with the developing story, especially if it has high audience appeal. Further, the precarious economics of broadcasting (billions are now spent on sports coverage) have forced the networks to cut news budgets. Satellite and computer technology have enabled networks to report news faster and easier and to rely on footage from two giant video news agencies: Reuters Television and Associated Press Television News (APTN). So the networks have retreated from original or direct news coverage and become retailers of other journalists' reporting.

The evening news shows identified with Jennings, Brokaw, and Rather can often be technically and visually quite impressive, especially for special events such as those marking the new millennium. But during the lively political primaries leading up to the presidential election of 2004, to get the latest breaking news and in-depth analysis, viewers had to turn such cable news channels as CNN and MSNBC. In the more leisurely past, Americans would usually wait for the evening news shows of Dan, Peter, and Tom to learn the day's news. Now with important breaking news available all day long on cable, radio, the Internet, and on the early evening local TV stations, the networks have been scooped—again and again.

Although their audiences are much smaller than the networks, (except during a major breaking story) the three cable news channels are profoundly influencing news over the air. Competition between CNN, FNC (Fox) and MSNBC (NBC) has been intense and at times personal. (CBS and ABC do not have cable news channels but not for lack of trying.)

During April 2003, as the Iraq war was winding down, television news executives noted an unexpected trend: Viewers were increasingly tuning out the broadcast networks' evening news shows. In the first 16 days of the war with Iraq, the networks not only saw the gains of the first days vanish, they also suffered a drop off from the average viewership during the preceding weeks of the television season. CBS and ABC lost nearly 2 million viewers or a combined 10% during the period. Only NBC, which unlike the other two, has a cable news operation, showed a slight increase.

The overall decline in the evening news programs ratings came at the same time that the three cable news networks showed gains of over 300%. This perhaps could be a watershed moment on how Americans get their news on television.

And to the surprise of many, the Fox News Channel has risen to the top of cable news ratings. The Iraq war was expected to be CNN's war, but FNC, owned by Murdoch's News Corporation, emerged as the most watched source of cable news by far—with anchors and commentators that skewered the mainstream media, disparaged the French and attacked anyone who disagreed with President Bush's war effort. Fox showed there were huge ratings in stressing opinionated news with an America-first flair. Fox has successfully applied a new approach to television news by casting aside traditional notions of objectivity, showing contempt for dissent, and eschewing the skepticism of government that was long at the core of mainstream television. Fox's newfound success may be because, in part, that it attracts millions of conservatives who perceive the evening network news shows as too liberal and too anti-Bush.

MSNBC has responded to this "Fox effect" by adding two outspokenly conservative commentators, Joe Scarborough and Michael Savage, to their lineup of commentators. The battle for dominance in cable news has had the effect of dragging down the standards of broadcast news. When the war on terrorism and debates over Iraq are not hot topics, the cable news channel compete for tidbits of news and rumor about the latest crime or celebrity scandals (snipers, Kobe Bryant, Winona Ryder, JonBenet Ramsey, or Laci Peterson.) Howard Kurtz of *The Washington Post*, reported that the Laci Peterson murder case has been examined 79 times on Fox by Greta Van Susteren; 40 times by Dan Abrams, and 20 times on Chris Mathews' *Hardball*, both on MSNBC; 38 times by Hannity and Colmes and the O'Reilly Factor, both on Fox; and 34 times on Larry King on CNN.

Ironically, the 24-hour cable news channels were originally intended to provide a constant stream of breaking news around the clock. CNN has tried to do this, gathering news from 28 overseas news bureaus but has learned that the audience is not that interested unless it involves American lives at peril abroad. FNC has led the cable field with only minimal efforts at gathering original or "exclusive" news (let the AP and big dailies do that). Fox has shown that the public will instead watch outspoken and opinionated commentors "haranguing" the audience and appealing to their prejudices and predispositions. And for now, MSNBC and CNN seem to be following the Fox formula.

DECLINING VIEWERSHIP OF TELEVISION NEWS

The changes and decline in quality of television news seems related to its continuing loss of viewers; as audiences splinter or evaporate, network producers seem to use more soft features, as well as sensational and entertainment-oriented news to attract a greater audience. A study by the Pew Research Center for the People and the Press (1996) reported that television news was in trouble with the American public and especially with younger viewers; fewer adults watch it regularly.

Viewership of evening network news was particularly hard-hit. In 1996, less than half the public (42%) regularly watched one of the three nightly network broadcasts, down from 48% in 1995, and 60% in 1993. Among viewers in 1996 under the age of 30, only 22% watch nightly network news, down from 36% in 1995; that is a drop of one third in just 12 months.

Local television news broadcasts attracted more viewers overall in 1996, but their audience declines were also steep. Among all adults, 65% said they regularly watch local TV news; it was 72% the previous year in 1995. But among those under age 30, 51% said in 1996 they watched local news, down from 64% 1 year before in 1995. Survey Director, Andrew Kohut, said, "The networks are facing a serious problem, with increased competition within their industry (from cable, VCRs, pay TV, Internet, etc.) and with a decreased appetite for news, especially among young people" (cited in Mifflin, 1996b, p. C5.) Network officials said the falloff is due to the fact that news is following the trend of cable—drawing viewers away from networks. As viewers grow older, they will watch more news just as today's older viewers watch more news than younger viewers do. Kohut partly agrees but is convinced they will be far fewer in number. "They will grow up and watch less news than the previous younger generation that is now middle-aged. I really think it's not a life-cyclical pattern, it's generational" (cited in Mifflin, 1996b, p. C5).

How does television news viewing compare with newspaper reading? Newspaper reading is a bit more stable. Half of those polled (50%) said they read a newspaper "yesterday," (compared to 52% a year earlier). In contrast, the percentage saying they watched TV news "yesterday" slipped to 59%; the percentage had been as high as 74% in 1994. Regular CNN-watching in 1996 was also less (26%) than in 1995 (30%) and 1994 (33%). Interestingly, the 1996 Pew study found that listening to radio was largely unchanged in 1996, as it has been for more than 5 years.

As mentioned before, it appears that many people are getting their news on the run—from car radios, television and cable news snippets at all hours, newspaper headlines, or the Internet but the disquieting trend is that young people do not include reading or listening to news in their life-style. Apparently a growing number of young people—tomorrow's lead-ers—are not interested in news.

IMPACT OF TELEVISION ON NEWS
AND ON JOURNALISTS

Newspapers and television both report the day's news, but, increasingly, television news is becoming packaged entertainment with less hard news. According to James Fallows (1996), there are two significant differences in methods. In television, news becomes a kind of spectacle, designed to fully engage the viewers for a moment or longer but then moves on to other dis-crete and separate spectacles. This contrasts with the press's view that news is a process and that events have a history that should be explained. Televi-sion's natural emphasis is on the now. Fallows (1996) said, "Part of the press's job is to keep things in proportion. TV's natural tendency is to see things in shards. It shows us one event with an air of utmost drama, then for-gets about it and shows us the next" (p. 53).

Television's second impact concerns its effect on the concept of being a reporter. Television has shown that the most successful way to be a journal-ist is to give up most of what is involved in being a reporter. Fallows (1996) argued "behind the term 'reporter' is the sense that the event matters most of all. Your role as a reporter is to go out, look, learn—and then report on what you have learned" (pp. 53–54). Although television journalists still call themselves "reporters," it is their personality (i.e., celebrity status) that of-ten is the real story they report. When Dan Rather travels to Afghanistan, the subject of the broadcast is not Afghanistan, it is "Rather in Afghani-stan." When Diane Sawyer conducts a high-profile interview, the real story is the interaction between two celebrities. One of them is a politician, movie star, or athlete, but the other is a particular sort of television "journal-ist." Diane Sawyer, Barbara Walters, Mike Wallace, and Katie Couric (among others) are not paid multimillion dollar salaries because they are reporters in the traditional sense.

CREEPING TABLOIDIZATION

The changing perceptions of journalists and other factors have made television news most vulnerable to charges of *tabloidization*. The term refers to the featuring of stories of crime, violence, or scandal in a sensa-tional or lurid fashion, preferably about celebrities, as was the practice of some New York tabloid papers such as *The Daily Mirror* and *Daily News* of the 1920s, or the supermarket tabloids of today such as *The Star* and *The National Enquirer.*

Of course, sensationalism and triviality have long been found in American journalism. But in recent years, television, both broadcast and cable, have seemed to erupt with stories of sensation, bad taste, and lurid scandal, usually involving celebrities or notorious persons, appearing on the scheduled news programs.

David Shaw (1994), press critic of *The Los Angeles Times*, sounded the alarm.

Twenty years ago, there were essentially seven gatekeepers in the American news business—executive editors of the *New York Times* and *Washington Post*, executive producers or anchors of the CBS, NBC, and ABC evening news shows, and editors of *Time* and *Newsweek*. Occasionally, someone else—*60 Minutes, Wall Street Journal. Los Angeles Times,* or *The New Yorker*—would break a big story that would force everyone to take notice. If a story didn't make it past one of these gatekeepes, it didn't fly and often the *New York Times* editor was the key one. Now, all of that has changed. Well, almost all. Now the *New York Times* and the other six no longer decide. There are dozens of gatekeepers or none at all. (p. 4)

The "fire walls" that formerly separated the serious media from the trivial and sordid have disappeared. Another perceptive media critic, Howard Kurtz (1996) of *The Washington Post*, said

We have become a talk-show nation, pulsating with opinions that are channeled though hosts and reverberate through the vast echo chamber of the airwaves. The Old Media—the big newspapers, magazines and network newscasts—still cling to some vestige of objectivity, the traditional notion that information must be checked and verified and balanced with opposing views before it can be disseminated to the public. (p. 3)

But talk shows, Kurtz (1996) said, revel in their one-sided pugnacity, spreading wild theories, delicious gossip, and angry denunciations with gleeful abandon. "Anyone can say anything at any time with little fear of contradiction…. The gatekeepers of the elite media have been cast aside and the floodgates thrown open" (p. 3). (Such "talk shows" have increasingly become a staple of cable news shows.)

Important news events are now discussed, analyzed, and snap judgments made as they are happening. Did George W. Bush win or lose in tonight's televised debate?

Kurtz (1996) believed the talk culture has been further vulgarized by the popularity of tabloid television, which has increasingly set the agenda for mainstream media.

Diane Sawyer was roundly criticized for her sympathetic and uncritical interview of just-married Michael Jackson and his wife on *Prime Time Live*. The show promoted Jackson's latest Sony album and attracted an audience of more than 60 million for the network. Television critic Walter Goodman (1995) wrote:

> It was an expertly modulated hour of synthetic collision and wholehearted collusion. Sony could be sure ABC's star would not put Sony's star in harm's way. Mr. Jackson did a little dance as the credits rolled. Why not? This hour meant millions for him. And then a voice announced, "This has been a presentation of ABC News." (p. B1)

Earlier news commentators at the time of columnists Walter Lippmann or James Reston tried to influence informed readers on serious public issues, whereas the electronic talkers of today play to the audience. News of public issues is either pushed aside or trivialized in the new media mix of scandal, sensation, gossip and commercial promotion carried on television, cable, and radio talk shows.

The O. J. Simpson criminal trial—the "trial of the century"—was a major cultural phenomenon that for a year and a half transfixed millions of viewers and raised continuing controversies. When the first verdict was announced at midday, about 107.7 million people, or 57% of the nation's adult population watched on live television. Another 62.4 million watched the recap later in the day. The drawn-out trial strained many aspects of American life—race relations, violence against women, the criminal justice system, and the integrity of the news media.

The continuing story had to be reported, of course, but did it have to dominate the news for so long? CNN covered the entire trial live from gavel to gavel for months and drew large audiences. Night after night, the network news shows on ABC, NBC, and CBS, as well as local television news, led off with the day's developments and often devoted large chunks of their daily 21 minutes of news time to the trial.

When he retired from public television, Robert MacNeil had harsh words for the trend in television news toward ever more sensational stories. Singling out CBS and NBC coverage of the O. J. Simpson trial, MacNeil said:

> Here were these prestigious news organizations saying in effect night after night last year, "Mr. and Mrs. America, this is the most important thing that

happened today." The journalists knew perfectly well that O. J. Simpson was not the most important thing that happened that day. But they were scared to death—at least at CBS and NBC—that all the bottom feeders, as I call them, were going to steal more and more of their audience. (cited in Kolbert, 1995, p. H39)

GROWING INFLUENCE OF LOCAL TELEVISION NEWS

As network television news has declined in both audiences and journalistic quality, local television news programs have gained in influence, especially in the metropolitan areas where local news shows are on the air 1 hour or more before the evening network shows begin. Because of cable news, the networks are no longer first with breaking national and foreign stories.

According to Tom Rosenstiel (1994), CNN has significantly, if unintentionally, affected broadcast journalism's control over its own professional standards. In the mid-1980s, CNN, in order to generate more revenue, began selling its vast footage to hundreds of local news stations. Before that, the three networks had jealously protected their own footage, well-aware that exclusive coverage of the day's biggest story was one of their competitive advantages. CNN did not have that concern. In turn, CNN could make deals to acquire local footage from these subscribing stations, thus expanding its own coverage reach, even if CNN news crews had not produced the pictures.

Next, the networks' local affiliates began pressuring the networks for more network footage so that they could compete in the local markets. Soon the networks' control over national and foreign footage had ended. In 1986, the three networks fed affiliates about 30 minutes of footage a day. By 1990, they averaged about 8 hours a day. This greatly changed the business, and the networks became subservient to local stations. The network shows began doing more "you news" features and less hard-news reporting, as well as often sending Tom Brokaw, Dan Rather, and Peter Jennings off to cover floods, fires, and presidential trips live, thus hyping some stories beyond their intrisinic importance.

Local television news, although often highly competitive, is usually less professional, less responsible, and more sensational then network news. The Rocky Mountain Media Watch in Denver analyzed the tapes of 100 programs in 58 cities on a single night, and found a disheartening sameness. The typical 30-minute program offered about 12 minutes of news, more than 40% of it depicting violent crimes or disasters. Commercials averaged more than 9 minutes and sports and weather nearly 7 minutes, leaving 2 minutes for promotions. Of the 100 programs, 37 led off with crime, 15 with disasters. On 70 stations, the favorite disaster that night was a mild California earthquake, one of 200 that month, which caused no injuries and little damage. Commenting on the study, Max Frankel (1995) wrote: "Virtually, no station offers thoughtful coverage of important local issues, including crime. Few ever try to analyze the local economy or the school, transportation and welfare systems" (p. 46). About the late-evening local news, Frankel (1995) wrote:

> Their newscasts are distinguishable only by the speed and skill with which they drive the audience from rage and fear to fluff and banter, leading the way to long commercials that exploit aroused emotions. Sports results, too, are delivered at a manic pace, spiced with scenes of violence or pathetic pratfalls, and even the weather reports are used to drive our moods up and down, from alarm to calm and back again. (p. 47)

Production costs are the usual explanations for this kind of journalism. A television crew takes 1 to 2 hours to visit the scene of a murder or a fire; it may take days or weeks to report on the causes of crime or the poor state of housing. Murders, fires, or accidents—the grist of today's local television news mill—are relatively simple stories to cover. It's not that local newsrooms have a built-in predilection for violence. It's just that it's there—easy to get—and it can be enhanced by production techniques. How many times have you seen on the 11 p.m. news on a New York City channel a reporter standing in front of a precinct house, reporting "live" on a murder that might have happened 15 hours earlier? It happens on Chicago television practically every night. (Frankel, 1995)

In some cities, news on public television stations deviates from this pattern but still is criticized for not covering local news more thoroughly.

RADIO NEWS: STABILITY OR DECLINE?

Although viewers for both network and local television news seem to be disappearing, many people are listening to the news on radio. In a poll cited earlier by Pew Research Center for the People and the Press (1996), the percentage of people who listen to radio news was largely unchanged in 1996, as it has been for the previous 5 years. Four in 10 people (44%) said they listened to news on radio "yesterday" in the current survey, compared to 42% in 1995. The survey found 13% of respondents reporting they were regular (NPR) listeners, which was not significantly different than the 15% recorded in the 1995 study.

Yet radio news has been undergoing changes just as radio itself has. De-velopments in radio news have been both good and bad. First, the positive. Lou Prato (1996) reported that an official at ABC News Radio said in 1996 that radio news overall was stronger than it had been in 15 to 20 years. "Ra-dio is still the medium in which most Americans first hear a breaking news story. It's fast, ubiquitous, and a growing industry," according to Bernard Gershon (cited in Prato, 1996, p. 52).

At the same time, consolidation of station ownerships has been proceed-ing at a rapid rate.

After the Telecommunications Act of 1996 removed many restric-tions on media, Clear Channel Communications in San Antonio became the nation's largest owner of radio stations. In March 1996, Clear Chan-nel owned 62 stations; in 2003, it owned 1,238 This created the world's largest radio company in both revenues and numbers of stations, which reach a weekly audience of about 100 million. In 1996, there were 10,257 stations with 5,133 owners; in 2003, there were 10,807 stations with 3,408 owners.

Not so encouraging is the trend of more and more radio stations to get out of the local news business altogether. In 1994, the percentage of commer-cial stations with no employees devoted to gathering local news increased to 16.9%. The survey also found that television news staffing had continued to grow modestly since 1987, even as radio news staffs declined at the steepest rate in more than 10 years. Since 1981, station owners no longer have been required to broadcast news and public interest programming in order to maintain operating licenses.

Grossman (1998) had some disturbing words to add to this:

Improbable as it seems, television's unglamorous 75-year-old sibling, radio, now reigns as the most profitable of all media. Radio's recent tidal wave of corporate consolidations, its cheap production costs, and its high cash flow have transformed it into the darling of Wall Street. One troubling result of ra-dio's remarkable financial turn-around: the elimination of serious news re-porting. It is fast disappearing from stations across the nation, replaced by talkers, "shock jocks," syndicated headline services, or no news at all. Ex-cept at public radio and a few all-news stations, radio reporters have become a vanishing breed. (p. 61)

The radio industry increasingly has relied on syndicated material—news, music, and talk shows—transmitted by satellite and offered by networks on a barter basis in exchange for commercial time. The decline in local news pro-gramming was also related to radio's move to specialized music formats ranging from bluegrass to polka; station owners have turned to narrow formats as a way to attract a specific audience desired by advertisers.

Neal J. Conan, of NPR, a noncommercial service that does report the news well, commented that the decline in local radio news does not mean that listeners are less well-informed. "I'm not sure a three-minute newscast was vastly informative. It's not a tremendous loss" (cited in Adelson, 1994, p. C8).

A different litany of complaints and concerns from the public relate to the printed press. These are discussed in chapter 7.

The Fading
American Newspaper?

*The newspapers! Sir, they are the most villainous—licentious—abomina-
ble—infernal—not that I ever read them—I make it a rule never to look into a
newspaper.*

—Richard Brinsley Sheridan (1779)

At this time of rapid change in public communication, newspapers as well
as news magazines have been undergoing modifications similar to those
of broadcast journalism. Publishers and editors of group-owned papers
are increasingly under pressure to expand their profits and their attractive-
ness to Wall Street investors. And they are worried about the Internet. As
in other industries, many newspapers have been downsizing to increase
their profitability. In addition, many editors, in pursuit of greater circulation, are stressing more entertainment-oriented, celebrity-soaked
infotainment, as well as soft features that relate to the personal concerns
of readers. Newspapers are not adverse to pick up on the current
sensationalistic stories carried on television.

SLIPPING MORALE

There are indications that the morale of reporters and editors on many newspapers is low—a sense that working for a newspaper is no longer an exciting
and respected calling. One former newsman, C. S. Stepp (1995) wrote:

> For all the trials of poor pay, lousy hours, and grinding pace, the payoff (in
> earlier times) was high: deference, entitlement, the buzz of recognition, the

glory of it all. Readers grumbled but they paid attention.... These are different days. The newspaper person (today) is just one more harried molecule in
the maligned Media Horde. Newspapers are old news, byte-sized cogs in giant information conglomerates.... The criticisms were bearable, honorable
scars from the ramparts. But irrelevance truly singes, the gnawing feeling
that the spotlight has moved on forever.... The result: angst and anxiety are
pandemic across American newsrooms, as newspaper people collectively
sense the end of an era. (p. 15)

Similar feelings were found in a 1995 survey ("Nieman Poll Finds,"
1995) of 304 former Nieman Fellows—working journalists who had studied 1 year at Harvard University. General findings were that:

- Overall quality of the media is declining and the basic principles of
  the journalism profession are being eroded.
- The distinction between news and entertainment is increasingly
  obscure.
- Television and radio are gaining in influence but declining in journalistic quality, whereas newspapers struggle to maintain quality
  and are losing ground.
- Media proprietors are more concerned with profits than product
  quality.
- The public is losing confidence in the media.

The Nieman survey was largely validated by a much broader national survey in 1999 of the news media, including newsroom staff, managers, and executives on journalistic values and principles. Sponsored by the Committee
of Concerned Journalists and the Pew Research Center on The People and
the Press, the survey was headed by Bill Kovach and Tom Rosenstiel, who
summarized the findings on the Internet (see www.cpj.com). In brief, the survey found that not only is the public increasingly disaffected from the press
but journalists now agree that something is wrong with their profession.
News professionals see two overriding trends that worry them: They believe
the news media have blurred the lines between news and entertainment and
that the cult of argument is overwhelming the cult of reporting. A broad majority feel that way, about 70%, including top executives. These journalists
also see problems of reporting the news fairly and factually and avoiding sensationalism. And things are getting worse. Concerns about punditry overwhelming reporting, for instance, have swelled in only 4 years. In short, the
report said, a large majority of news professionals sense a degradation of the
culture of news—from one that was steeped in verification and a steadfast re-

spect for the facts, toward one that favors argument, opinion-mongering, haste, and infotainment.

Although a good many newspapers, when viewed objectively, do a better job than ever of reporting the day's news and serving their communities, many publications no longer enjoy the prestige in their communities that they formerly had. Once great regional newspapers such as *The Minneapolis Star and Tribune* (now the *Star-Tribune*), *The St. Louis Post-Dispatch, The Milwaukee Journal* (now the *Journal Sentinel*), *The Louisville Courier Journal, The Atlanta Constitution,* and *The Denver Post* are perceived as having diminished in influence and stature even though they are still excellent newspapers.

Yet, daily newspapers remain going concerns and are more prosperous than most corporations. But what concerns many in the newsrooms is that public service and thorough news coverage are being neglected in the scramble for profits.

"Job satisfaction in newspapering appears to be in significant decline," wrote David Weaver and Cleve Wilhoit in their survey of working journalists. "Only 25% say they are very satisfied with their job, about half the satisfaction rate of 20 years ago.... More than 20% ... said they plan to leave the field within five years, double the figure of 1982–1983" (cited in Stepp, 1995, p. 17).

Yet a similar study from Indiana University in 2002 found that job satisfaction had been building slightly after a 20 year decline. More than 33% of journalists said they were "very satisfied" with their jobs. That's 6% higher than in 1992. All but 11% had college degrees, and of these, 36.2% were journalism majors ("A Changing Profession," 2003, p. 9)

This crisis of confidence may be caused by a number of factors: (a) the declining number of independently owned papers; (b) the slow but steady drop for some papers in readership and advertising revenue; (c) less interest by the public in serious news; and (d) competition from the "new media"—cable, VCRs, and the Internet. In university schools and departments of journalism, newspaper careers have been losing their appeal; the best students more often opt for careers in advertising, public relations, and online journalism.

The same 2002 study, sponsored by the Knight Foundation, found that the median age of those in the news business (daily and weekly papers, radio, TV, news magazines, and wire services) was 41 years, compared with 36 in 1992. One third of the country's journalists were women, most of them on news magazines. Although there were more journalists of color than ever before, the 9.5% was significantly lower than the percentage of minorities in the population—30.9% in the 2000 Census. All those with white collars had an average salary of $43,600, up 6% from 1992.

But for some time, newspaper journalists have come to think of themselves as trapped in a sunset industry, and many are more concerned about protecting their financial interests and meager salaries than about serving the public interest. The long-term shift from family-owned to group-owned chains is probably the most demoralizing factor in the newspaper business today. Family-owned papers had their faults and would often play favorites and beat up on their enemies, yet much of the success of numerous great newspapers was due to their strong-willed and high-minded family owners. One thinks of the Sulzbergers of *The New York Times,* the Grahams and Meyers of *The Washington Post,* the Niemans and Harry Grant of *The Milwaukee Journal*, the Bingham family of *The Louisville Courier- Journal*, John Cowles of *The Minneapolis Star and Tribune,* and the Pulitzers at *The St. Louis Post-Dispatch.*

Group ownership brings the problem of a counting-house mentality determined to downsize the newsroom and cut expenses to satisfy demands for quarterly earnings. The Gannett chain, with its 117 daily newspapers and 22 television stations, has been very profitable and is considered a pacesetter in this trend.

Today, four widely admired dailies—*The New York Times, The Washington Post, The Los Angeles Times, and the Wall Street Journal*—have all been protected in some way from the imperatives of quarterly reports—family members control enough stock to affect the newspaper's policies and prevent hostile takeovers.

The *Los Angeles Times*, however, after a loosening of family control, suffered a rude shock and much unfavorable national criticism in October 1999, after an inexperienced new publisher made a major ethical mistake. Publisher Kathryn Downing apologized to an assembled newsroom and asked for the staff's forgiveness for having negotiated a profit-sharing deal with the new Staples Center, a major new sports arena in downtown Los Angeles. The two companies had shared $2 million in advertising revenues from the October 10, 1999 *Times* Sunday magazine, which was devoted to publicizing the Center. The deal, reached without the knowledge of the editorial staff and without informing *Times* readers, was a serious journalistic blunder because news media are not supposed to have financial relationships with organizations about which they report. The *Times'* news staff was incensed and then came a scathing open letter from Otis Chandler, former publisher and scion of the Chandler family that had controlled the paper since 1882. Chandler, retired but a major stockholder, criticized what he called management's "unbelievably stupid and unprofessional handling of the special edition." He said, "I am sad to see what I think may be a serious decline of the *Times* as one of the great newspapers in the country." (cited in Waxman, 1999) The paper's staff was demoralized by the unfavorable publicity about this breaching of the "wall" between the editorial and advertising departments. Critics blamed the *faux pas* on the paper's CEO, Mark Willes, and Publisher, Browning, neither of whom had prior newspaper experience. These events were followed in January 2000 by the abrupt sale of the Times Mirror Company to the Tribune Company of Chicago. The sale was precipitated, some said, by disagreements among Chandler family heirs over how the paper should be managed.

The Wall Street Journal is considered protected by its niche market for financial and industry readers and advertisers. The Bancroft family has owned the paper for over 100 years and has fended off numerous efforts to buy out the paper. That may happen because the paper has been under some pressures from family stockholders to increase profits, as was the case at the *Los Angeles Times*.

The most biting criticism of newspapers today often comes from journalists themselves. *New Yorker* editor, David Remnick (1995) wrote:

> With one eye on Wall Street and the other shut tight, newspaper owners everywhere except for a few … are following the path to deadening mediocrity. Everything that cannot be made blandly profitable is killed outright. Spoiled by the profits of the 1980s, the owners rarely have patience for a more modest future…. In a growing number of cities and regions newspaper owners have abused their franchise, slashing staff, cutting the "news hole," dropping aggressive reporting and leaving little behind but wire-service copy, sports, and soft local stories designed to make readers feel all warm and fuzzy and inclined to place a classified ad. (p. 82).

FINDING A PRINT NICHE IN A CHANGING ENVIRONMENT

At a time when news and entertainment seem inextricably mixed, newspapers have been constantly seeking a niche in the changing news picture. The decline of downtown department stores, and other changes in marketing from mail-order catalogues to WalMart have led to cutbacks of retail advertising in metropolitan dailies.

After radio and television usurped the first reporting of breaking news, newspapers began offering more interpretive and analytical pieces, thus introducing more opinion into news stories. Professional standards have often suffered because often the first news reports, as on cable or radio, may be fragmentary, lacking details and occasionally may be distorted or incorrect. Then, instead of waiting for fuller and more-rounded reporting, both broadcast and print reporters immediately start interpreting the meaning of it all and offering opinions on the event's future impact.

Time, *Newsweek,* and other news magazines also have been struggling to find a role for themselves in an age of instant and saturated news coverage and more in-depth and opinionated daily press stories. Talk radio, personified by Rush Limbaugh, Gordon Liddy, Don Imus, and others, plus the television news magazines, have also skimmed off more and more news readers.

When television first appeared, newspapers tried to ignore it by fully reporting stories television news did not cover and, in some cases, not even carrying program listings. Now the printed press tends to report fully on television's big stories plus much news about television itself, including its celebrities. A Super Bowl game seen by many millions on television will be fully reported and analyzed by newspapers, following the sound assumption that people like to read about events they already know about, whether it is a movie seen, a televised event, or sports competition. Further, comings and goings of television's personalities, programs, gossip, and trends are reported as well. The British popular press carries this trend even further and has become, in effect, a mere adjunct of British television.

The print media have responded to television and radio talk shows' approach to the news by offering readers more and more of the news through the proliferation of signed columns or bylined interpretive pieces. In earlier times, few bylines appeared in newspapers on hard news stories; the story itself was the important thing and the name of the reporter was incidental. In general, bylines were given out sparingly for unusually well-written features or soft news stories. Stories in *Time* and *Newsweek* rarely carried bylines.

Today, *Newsweek,* for example, presents its major news stories through the often lively, irreverent, breezy words of its stable of star writers—Howard Fineman, Jonathan Alter, Evan Thomas, Alan Sloan, Ellis Cose, and others—who not only tell you their version of what happened last week and what it means for you, but what you should think about it. Often, the slant or spin on the story is more important than the content. *Newsweek* assumes most readers already know the basic facts but would still like to read something insightful or at least clever or funny about the story.

The New York Times has certainly joined the trend from mostly straight news to news liberally mixed with opinion. Diamond (1993) noted that until about 1960, there were never more than four or five columnists in the

Times, one or two on the editorial page, a "Sports of the Times" columnist, and on the local page, Meyer Berger's "About New York" column. By the 1990s, the *Times* had about 48 columnists scattered through the paper, who reported and/or commented on a much wider and softer variety of subjects than the traditional no-nonsense hard-news fit to print. In addition to signed editorials in "Editorial Notebook" and the op-ed page's regular columnists and guest writers, the proliferating columnists reflected a wide variety of reader interests: "The Practical Traveler"; four or more sports columns plus one of commentary on sports on television; "Peripherals" for computer users; "Personal Health"; "Pop View"; "Keeping Fit"; "Parent and Child"; "Runways" for fashion; "Patterns" for the garment industry; "Books of the Times"; "Media," and so on. Other newspapers, of course, have been following the trend; some like *The New York Daily News* and *The New York Post* have long been collections of signed columns. Small dailies rely heavily on syndicated columnists.

Proliferation of signed columns reflects a much more broadened approach to what is meant by "news." This translates as less public affairs news (government, politics, and foreign affairs) and more news and useful information that, as on television news, readers can relate to personally such as personal health, medical advances, and sundry advice for coping with life's daily trends and challenges. More interpretation and explanation is not a bad thing if done carefully and does not sink to just opinion and speculation.

Daily newspapers have been greatly influenced in recent years by Gannett's *USA Today*. This innovative paper was launched in 1982 as a national daily available almost everywhere through satellite production and aimed at travelers. Taking its cue from television, the paper used lots of color, imaginative graphics—graphs, maps, photos, and large, detailed national weather maps. At first, *USA Today* reported the news in the print equivalent of sound bites—short takes on complicated matters as well as on lighter themes and without jumps to inside pages. Sports are covered in great statistical detail, but at first the paper maintained no foreign correspondents. Although criticized for reducing news to spoon-sized pellets, and called "McPaper" or "USA OK," many smaller dailies imitated its compacted news presentation and especially its color graphics.

Without a doubt, *USA Today* sells papers: Peterson, (1996c) reported the Friday edition, sold throughout the weekend, passed 2-million average circulation in 1996, while the Monday–Thursday editions have reached 1.6 million, making it second only to *The Wall Street Journal*. But 55% of sales came from newsstands and 25% was purchased in bulk for free distribution by hotels and airlines. Millions read the paper but not the same readers every week; hence, there is little reader loyalty, and as a result, advertising has been sparse. The paper finally began to turn a profit in 1993 after more than $250 million in losses since 1982. In 1996, the paper was under pressure to improve its scant profitability and began changing its news approach. Instead of its light, feel-good news, the paper began stressing more hard news in longer explanatory stories, including some important investigative stories. Said one newspaper editor: "Having ruined half of the rest of the newspaper industry with three-inch briefs, they're finally going the other way" (Peterson, 1996c, p. C8). Clearly, *USA Today* was moving back toward the mainstream and by 2003 was the nation's largest paper with a circulation of 2,162,454.

LOSING READERS AND PROFITS

Newspapers are not as profitable was they once were, even though newspaper profits have been at about 12% or twice the Fortune 500 average. The industry has cut about 6,000 newsroom and production jobs and many others have gone unfilled. Some critics think newspapers should be spending more, not less, on news gathering and publishing.

Aside from the largest and best-quality papers, losses of circulation overshadowed gains for most in 1995. John Morton (1995) reported that in papers under 500,000 circulation, 60% lost or showed no gain in readers. For papers under 25,000 circulation, about 65% showed losses. However, for the total circulation for newspapers, there was still a decline but a smaller one than in the past—.1%. So circulation seemed to be getting worse at a slower rate (Morton, 1995, p. 68). During the first Iraq war and 9/11 terrorist attacks, newspaper circulation soared for a brief time but then settled back to earlier patterns. (Morton, 2003)

With the proliferating electronic news and cable media, online journalism, and other Internet services, the place of daily newspapers in the new market place of ideas, would to be diminished. Freedom of expression is much less dependent on the printing press than in the past and that is a reason for concern because printed journalism has always been the great champion of freedom of the press.

Some newspapers are seeking more personal connections with their readers in order to reverse trends faced by newspapers—an aging readership, declining circulations, and weaker ties between readers and their papers (Peterson, 1997). *The San Jose Mercury News* turns most of a weekly features section, called "Celebrations," over to articles written by readers; it is one of the paper's most popular features. Typical of the more popular articles were "Quotable Kids," "How I Met My True Love," and "The Seven-Second Philosopher." (p. C1).

The *Washington Post* is certainly one of the most successful papers in the United States, reaching a greater percentage of households in its market than any other major daily. And yet readers are steadily abandoning the *Post*—in the last 10 years about 100,000 paying customers stopped getting the Sunday Post, reducing its circulation to 1.5 million. Daily circulation has fallen off by 70,000 to 757,000. These losses have occurred at a time the region had added 700,000 people. The *Post*'s circulation losses, especially among the age 18 to 34 demographic, are not unusual as circulation continues to seep from most U.S. dailies. But this happened to a great newspaper in the most affluent and well-educated market.

In July 2003, the *Post* moved to reclaim its lost readers by announcing a 125,000-circulation, 20-page tabloid called the *Express*, to be published Monday through Friday. The Post Company plans to distribute the paper by hand at Metro stops. This plan follows similar moves in Chicago by the Tribune and Sun-Times, which launched *Red Eye* and *Red Streak*, respectively, in late 2002. These papers carry a $.25 cover price but are often delivered free. All three papers are aimed at the same market—teens to early thirties. Other newspapers are following these experiments with interest (see Shafer, 2003)

GETTING IN BED WITH SUPERMARKET TABLOIDS

The relationship of mainstream newspapers with the so-called supermarket tabloids has been uncomfortable and a reason for concern. Headlines for these lurid weeklies can be read at the checkout counters of 29,800 supermarkets in America—"Six Signs That PROVE the World is Coming to an End," "Liz's Hubby's Drug Bust," and "How to Tell if Your Dog Worships Satan." Most stories are not news by any definition.

Until a few years ago, most newspapers did not pay much attention. But nowadays, some of the stories that publications like *The Star* or *The National Enquirer* dig up on political and entertainment celebrities find their way to front pages of the better newspapers and on network evening news. These are stories that reputable journalists would not ferret out themselves, but once they are published, many editors and broadcasters believe they must go with the story or be left behind.

The National Enquirer's stories and pictures of Senator Gary Hart's escapade with Donna Rice ended Hart's political career. The *Star's* stories on Gennifer Flowers threatened Clinton's political fortunes in the 1992 campaign. And in the O. J. Simpson criminal trial, the tabloids put out a string of scoops the mainstream media felt they had to follow. *The New York Times'* publishing information first reported by the *Enquirer* about the Simpson case provoked journalistic criticism of the *Times*. But the *Times'* reporter, David Margolick (1994) said of the *Enquirer*, "Mainstream reporters may grumble about its checkbook journalism, laugh at its hyperbole, talk vaguely about its inaccuracies. But always, they look at it" (p. 6).

The 1996 political campaign was roiled briefly by *The Star's* revelations that President Clinton's closest political adviser, Dick Morris, had a year-long relationship with a prostitute. The *Star* paid the $200-a-night call girl well for the expose. The story had short but intense coverage: CNN, ABC, and NBC gave it excited play the first day, and both *Time* and *Newsweek* put Morris on their covers. However, much press reporting was more restrained in part because Morris was so quickly fired and the political impact was minimal.

But as Howard Kurtz noted, "The established media is increasingly covering the same sorts of things as the tabloids and finding that the supermarket papers are often better at the game" (cited in Zane, 1996, Sec. 4, p. 2). The paradox is that even as the mainstream media are inexorably moving toward the tabloid style of journalism, the tabloids are gaining relevance and credibility by operating a bit more like their respectable brethren. The tabloids are becoming more conventional in how they gather news and are entering into the political arena more often. Kurtz said that the cross-pollination may be sowing the seeds of a new hybrid form of news. Peterson (1996b) said that the tabloids are facing more competition from mainstream media. One response to increased competition has been for the major supermarket tabloids to merge. In November 1999, American Media, which owns *The National Enquirer, The Star,* and *The Weekly World News,* announced that it was buying *The Globe* and its sister tabloids, the *Sun* and *National Examiner.* Despite the consolidation, the papers have not improved much in quality.

BAD ATTITUDE: CYNICISM, ELITISM, AND OTHER COMPLAINTS

Fibich (1995) said that tabloid journalism contributes to one of the press' major problems today—a feeling by the public, and many thoughtful journalists as well, that the press has become too cynical and negative. "Journalism is too negative, too negative, too negative," said Andrew Kohut, director of the Pew Research Center. "There's criticism of the way the press conducts its business, particularly its watchdog role. And the attitude is more fundamentally negative than in years" (cited in Fibich, 1995, p. 17). Gallup surveys show that from 1981 to 1993, the share of Americans who felt that journalists had high ethical standards slid from 30% to 22%. One survey by Kohut found that the public had a favorable attitude toward the press but objected to some of its practices. The press was judged as too intrusive, too negative, driving controversies rather than just reporting them. (as cited in Fibich, 1995, p. 18)

A 1997 Roper poll, commissioned by the Freedom Forum, found the public quite critical of journalists. People trust most or all of what ministers, priests, rabbis, and doctors say, but only 53% place similar trust in their local television anchors. Even fewer trust what network anchors say and just under one third trust newspaper reporters.

Ethically, the public sees journalists not as equals of teachers and doctors, but as being among those with agendas to advance—politicians, lawyers, and corporate officials. The public also believes, according to the poll, that special interests are pulling strings in newsrooms. The public believes that profit motives, politicians, big business, and advertisers, as well as media owners, influence the way the news is reported and presented. Also, a majority of those polled (64%) said a major problem with news is that it is too sensational.

Sometimes the negative comments are entertaining and selectively true yet they show cynicism for the political scene. Maureen Dowd's now famous lead in *The New York Times* on Clinton's visit to Oxford in June 1994 illustrates the point: "President Clinton returned today for a sentimental journey to the university where he didn't inhale, didn't get drafted, and didn't get a degree" (cited in Walsh, 1996, p. 286). Clever indeed, but did it belong on page 1?

It should be noted, said Fibich (1995), that the press owns up to a lot of its criticisms. Kohut's study found that a majority of the news people surveyed thought that public anger with the press was justified, either totally or in part. A majority of journalists agreed about the validity of the charge that "the personal values of people in the news media often make it difficult for them to understand and cover such topics as religion and family values" (p. 19).

Joann Byrd said that during her 3 years as ombudsman for *The Washington Post,* she received 45,000 telephone calls and she concluded that "people don't see journalism as public service anymore." Instead, they believe "that journalists are engaged in self service—getting ratings, selling newspapers, or making their careers ... that our ideas about detachment are so much hog wash.... They feel cheated, I think, that the rules changed and nobody told them" (cited in Fibich, 1995, p. 18).

Public annoyance at reporters and the bad news they bring is not new; this annoyance has a long history. However, there is the feeling that a healthy skepticism has crossed the line to a virulent cynicism that assumes all in public life are guilty until proven otherwise. Cynicism and negativism, some feel, has become a virus that has contributed to a decline in faith in democratic institutions.

A media reporter for *The New York Times,* Iver Peterson (1996a) wrote: "Nobody would dispute the importance of a skeptical mind and tough questioning, and few want reporters to be cheerleaders. What the critics are arguing is that newsroom cynicism has crossed the boundary between being tough and being mean" (p. C7).

The solution is to strive for balance, according to Sig Gissler, a former editorial page editor of *The Milwaukee Journal* and now a journalism professor. He wrote: "We're great at raising people's anxieties but we don't leave them with much sense of hope or remedy. So I always thought it was a good idea to at least shade in some potential solutions to all those problems we see" (cited in Peterson, 1996a, p. C4).

Elitism and a sense of being out of touch with the rest of the nation is another problem for journalists who work for the national news media. (Elitism is not considered a problem apparently on smaller newspapers and local broadcast outlets.) Journalist Richard Harwood (1995) noted that the elitist label is being pinned on journalists and journalism in unflattering ways:

> Journalism's ills are a symptom of a poison infecting all professional elites. Increasingly removed from the realities of manual labor, community ties, or ordinary life in general, professionals have disdain for those they see as inferiors and for any genuine achievement or heroism. Nothing is properly understood until it is exposed as corrupt, duplicitous, or hypocritical. (p. 27)

Journalists in New York City , Washington, DC, and other major cities tend to identify with the affluent professional classes and follow their lifestyles. A 1995 survey found significant differences in attitudes between the mainstream media and the public. For example, more than 50% of the public said that homosexuality should be discouraged, whereas eight out of ten national journalists said it should be accepted. Two out of five Americans said they attended a church or synagogue regularly, compared with only one out of five national journalists.

Thirty-nine percent of Americans said they were politically conservative, compared with only 5% of national journalists. (Nearly 66% of national journalists identified themselves as moderates, and 22% said they were liberals.) More than 50% agreed that the press was too cynical and negative in covering Congress, whereas eight out of ten national journalists disagreed (Walsh, 1996).

LOSS OF CREDIBILITY:
JOE KLEIN'S "PRIMARY COLORS"

Many of the ethical problems faced by journalists today, including cynicism and elitism, relate to matters of credibility—the quality or power of inspiring belief, essential for public acceptance of serious journalism. Some say that credibility is the journalists' and the news media's most precious asset. Often, loss of press credibility is self-inflicted as two recent examples—one at *Newsweek* and the other at *The New York Times*—illustrate.

The first involved a best-selling novel, *Primary Colors*—a tale of political intrigue and deceit, whose author was identified only as anonymous. The book was a commercial success and after months of emphatic denials, Joe Klein, a political columnist for *Newsweek* and commentator on CBS, admitted publicly that he was indeed the author. Klein offered no apologies for lying to friends and colleagues and said he guarded his secret the way journalists protect their news sources. *Newsweek's* editor, Maynard Parker, was privy to the secret and not only kept it out of his magazine but misdirected one of his own reporters who wrote a piece about the mystery in the magazine.

The response from the press was mixed. Stephen Hess, a media expert at the Brookings Institution, was amused. "Look, people lie to reporters every day. What annoys journalists was that this was a member of their own community, a friend of theirs" (Peterson, 1996b, p. C5). Most were much tougher on Klein. Rem Rieder (1996), editor of the *American Journalism Review*, wrote:

> Lying is lying. For a journalist, it is poison. Credibility is crucial. Why should *Newsweek's* readers believe what Klein writes when they know they can't believe what he says? And we're not talking little white lies here. No coy deceptions for Joe Klein. "For God's sakes, I didn't write it," he told *The New York Times*. (p. 6)

Editorially, *The New York Times* was critical of Klein, reflecting the views of many in the working press. The *Times* said:

> Their behavior (Klein and Parker) violates the fundamental contract between journalists, serious publications and their readers. If journalists lie or

publications knowingly publish deceptively incomplete stories, then readers who become aware of the deception will ever after ask the most damaging of all questions: How do I know you are telling me the whole truth as best
you can determine it at this time? ... Mr. Klein wants his colleagues to view
his actions as a diverting and highly profitable whimsy. But he has held a
prominent role in his generation of political journalists. For that reason, people interested in preserving the core values of serious journalism have to
view his actions and words as corrupt and—if they become an example to
others—corrupting. ("Colors of Mendacity," 1996, p. A14)

THE NEW YORK TIMES AND JASON BLAIR

Ironically, the same issues of credibility and trust just cited also framed a
major crisis for *The New York Times* in 2003 after a reporter, Jayson Blair,
27, was found to have committed frequent acts of journalistic fraud while
covering major stories for the *Times*. In an unprecedented four-page detailed "accounting" of plagiarism and fabrication in some 36 news articles,
the *Times* said the misdeeds "represented a profound betrayal of trust and a
low point in the 152-year history of the newspaper." Blair's misdeeds were
multiple and varied: His dispatches purportedly from Texas, Maryland, and
other states were actually written from New York; he made up quotes and
comments; he concocted scenes; he stole material from other papers and
wire services, and he selected details from photographs to create the impression that he had been in places and saw people that he had not.

People inside and outside the *Times* wondered how such fraudulent reporting could have gone on so long without detection. Howell Raines, the
Times executive editor, before a large meeting of 500 staff members accepted blame for the breakdown of communication and oversight that allowed such frequent acts of journalistic fraud to happen. But Raines also
spent most of the 2-hour meeting responding to angry complaints and questions about his managing style and acknowledged that many reporters
viewed him as "inaccessible" and "arrogant."

Two weeks later, the *Times* newsroom again erupted in anger over star reporter, Rick Bragg, and his aggressive defense of relying heavily on stringers and interns, with many reporters denouncing the practice and insisting
that was not the way they worked. Bragg, a Pulitzer Prize winner, had relied
almost entirely on the reporting of a freelance journalist to compose a feature about oyster fishermen in Apalachicola, Florida. Bragg later resigned.

The *Times'* woes elicited a good deal of criticism from other journalists.
David Broder, columnist of *The Washington Post*, said it was far more than
a black eye for the *Times* and called it a serious blow to the credibility of the

press, and at a time when public trust was fragile. Some critics said that racial preferences were involved and that Blair, an African American, had received favored treatment from Raines. Blair had joined the paper with scant experience and, critics said, was raised to a national reporter much too quickly. Such preference programs, it was charged, implied that lower quality work would be tolerated. Yet with Blair and Bragg both long gone, unhappiness on the *Times* staff continued until *Times* Publisher, Arthur O. Sulzberger, Jr., was forced to accept the resignations of both Howell and Managing Editor, Gerald Boyd. Raines was the first editor to leave in disgrace since the Ochs/Sulzberger family purchased the paper more than a century ago. More significant perhaps, the *Times* scandal was the first institutional crisis of its kind to unwind in real time. Reports of events inside *The New York Times* were transmitted via the Internet, media news sites, online magazines, and newspaper editions, blogs, and e-mail. Each turn in the scandal and every memo issued by Sulzberger, Raines, or Boyd were immediately posted on the Internet. Then, one after another, unhappy *Times* reporters began sending their blistering comments to the popular news media Web site of Jim Romenesko at the Poynter Institute. Within hours, a sort of rhetorical "free for all" among *Times* staffers was on display for the whole wired world. Raines and Boyd were forced to issue a memo defending themselves. Pressure began to build on the Sulzberger family to act—and they did. Raines and Boyd were forced to step down and retired top editor, Joe Lelyveld, was brought as acting executive editor. And it was the new world of Web sites, blogs, online editions, and e-mails that set the pace for Raines' exit. (Rutten, 2003)

A month later, Bill Keller, 54, was named executive editor—a popular choice with the huge staff. An important result of the scandal was that the *Times* appointed two new watchdogs, a public editor to critique the paper and a standards editor to serve as an internal ethics czar. The *Times* had belatedly joined about 30 U.S. newspapers who have such internal critics or ombudsman to respond to the public complaints about the paper's practices. One of the dismaying aspects of the Jason Blair affair was that almost none of the many people who were inaccurately or fraudulently "interviewed" by Blair bothered to complain to the *Times*. Allan Siegal was named the standards editor; he will be a sounding board for staff members who have complaints or doubts about the paper's content. Daniel Okrent, a longtime magazine editor and author, was named the first public editor. Operating outside the management structure, the public editor or ombudsman, will address reader's complaints, raise questions of his own, and write about them in commentaries that will be carried in the paper.

Although the scandal enthralled the journalists and media watchers, the public in general was not much concerned. A Pew Research Center survey for June 19–July 2, 2003, found that problems with false stories and plagiarism at the *Times* had surprising little impact on overall public attitudes toward the news media. Americans are highly critical of the press on a number of issues, faulting it for inaccuracy, arrogance, and political bias, but no more than in recent years. (Pew Research Center for the People and the Press, July 13, 2003).

However, plagiarism problems for the press did not end with the Blair case. By March 2004, at least 10 other daily papers had confirmed instances of plagiarism, or fabrication. Most notable was the continuing investigation of Jack Kelley, former foreign correspondent for *USA Today*. Kelley was found to have fabricated portions of at least eight major stories and lifted two dozen quotes and other material from competing publications.

DUBIOUS PRACTICE OF BUYING NEWS AND PHOTOS

The British press has a long and dishonorable tradition of paying, and paying well, for scoops, exposes, and photos about the rich and famous, especially prominent politicians and the royal family. Fleet Street tabloids will pay $200,000 to $300,000 for a story that has lasting interest. Provocative pictures of Princess Diana commanded prices up to $6 million. This practice undermines the credibility of news because of the suspicion that sources will exaggerate to make a better and more profitable story or photo. Unfortunately, although resisted by mainstream news media, paying for news has become more commonplace in U.S. journalism and its disreputable tabloid fringe. After the second Rodney King trial, *The Los Angeles Times* reporters found themselves excluded from post-trial interviews with certain jurors because reporters not willing to pay them. Today, tabloid television shows routinely pay for interviews, whereas mainstream magazines like *Sports Illustrated* and *Redbook* have paid for news exclusives.

The practice is not new; in the 1970s, *60 Minutes* paid Nixon-aide, H. R. Haldeman, $25,000 and Watergate burglar, G. Gordon Liddy, $15,000 for interviews. But the practice (and the prices) have escalated lately, even more bad news for journalism's slipping credibility with the public. The high (or better, low) episode of checkbook journalism came when President Clinton faced impeachment over the Monica Lewinsky affair. Larry Flynt, publisher of *Hustler* magazine, placed an advertisement in *The Washington Post* in October 1998 offering up to $1 million to anyone who could prove that a member of Congress or a high-ranking public official had carried on an adulterous affair. Before the year ended, information turned up by the ad ended the career of House Speaker-designate, Bob Livingston. Flynt told a well-attended press conference that all news organizations are going to be paying for stories. That has not happened—yet. But the serious press often faces a dilemma of whether or not to pick and up use a paid-for news story.

The violent death of Diana, Princess of Wales, in a high-speed car crash while being pursued by paparazzi photographers in Paris had ominous lessons not just for tabloid journalism but for the mainstream press as well. The immediate public reaction was revulsion aimed at the press, even though much of the public are eager consumers of scandal and gossip about the celebrities they have come to know well from tabloids and television.

Tabloids have little interest in serious news but will pay much more for intrusive and revealing photos of the rich and famous and hence have triggered intensive competition among the paparazzi, who use hidden vans, planes and motorboats to stalk and harass celebrities, often invading their privacy. The problem for mainstream journalism is that such lurid and distorted photos and the companion gossip and scandal find their way into the more respectable publications and TV news. *Time* and *Newsweek* are regular users of tabloid by-products. *People* magazine ran 43 covers featuring Princess Diana. U.S. news media carry little serious news about England but most Americans are very well informed about the scandals and peccadilloes of the royal family. The unprecedented public grief and mourning in Britain at the Princess's funeral was stark evidence of the power of celebrity-driven gossip and scandal to affect the lives of many millions. It's also an indictment of mainline media when they give excessive and sustained coverage to such celebrity-driven stories.

Journalism's credibility problems have been exacerbated as well by the antics of certain celebrity journalists whose names and faces, as well as incomes, are almost as well-known to the public as are rock stars or movie personalities. These are discussed in chapter 8 along with the related questions of bias and trust.

CHAPTER

8

Why the Public
Mistrusts the Media

*I should make my bias clear: I have been a journalist for 60 years, in print,
on radio, on television. I have been appalled to watch "the press" metamor-
phose into "the news media" and, ultimately, into "the media," occupying a
small corner of a vaster entertainment stage.*

——Daniel Schorr

*When it comes to arrogance, power, and lack of accountability, journalists
are probably the only people on the planet who make lawyers look good.*

—Steven Brill

No question about it, many of the most prominent personalities in journalism today have become unpopular with segments of the American public.
This is shown in public opinion surveys as well as in caustic comments
from a wide range of commentators including from within the press itself.
In general, many people feel that journalists, along with politicians, are not
dealing with the real concerns of the people.

Public affairs news, the heart of serious journalism, is the focus of this
criticism, striking most deeply at a press perceived as estranged from its
readers and viewers. Journalist Jonathan Schell (1996) wrote:

> On one side is the America of those who are political professionals. It com-
> prises politicians, their advisers and employees, and the news media. Politi-
> cians waste little love on the newspeople who cover them, and the news-
> people display a surly skepticism towards politicians as a badge of honor.
> Yet if the voters I met on the campaign trail are any indication (and poll data
> suggest they are), much of the public has lumped newspeople and politicians

into a single class, which, increasingly, it despises. Respect for the government and respect for the news media have declined in tandem. More and
more the two appear to the public to be an undifferentiated establishment—a
new Leviathan—composed of rich, famous, powerful people who are di-
vorced from the lives of ordinary people and indifferent to their concerns.
On the other side of the division is the America of political amateurs: ordinary voters. (p. 70)

Schell believes that the activity of politics has become an interaction
between the media and people running campaigns. Everyone else is an
onlooker. Walsh (1996) believed good reasons exist for concern about the
cultural chasm between the public and the Washington press corps. A
1996 survey for *U.S. News and World Report* found that 50% of Americans thought that the media were strongly or somewhat in conflict with
the goals of ordinary citizens, whereas only 40% thought the media were
strongly or somewhat friendly to their goals. This was the worst approval
rating of any group measured—lower than prime-time television entertainment providers, welfare recipients, even lower than elected public officials, whose goals were judged to be in conflict with those of ordinary
citizens by only 36%. Even lawyers did better, with 45% of Americans
saying attorneys' goals conflicted with the public's. Clearly, the media
were seen as part of a strongly disliked governing elite. When asked about
"the people running the government," 52% of those surveyed said they
had little or nothing in common with them.

Further evidence of the public's low regard for journalists came in a
1998 survey during the Clinton–Lewinsky scandal and based on 3,000
telephone interviews. The public said the credibility of all news media
has suffered in what was perceived to be a ceaseless chase after the
saucy, sexy story. Responding to the statement, "Journalists chase sensational stories because they think it will sell newspapers, not because
they think it's important news," 53% agreed and 27% strongly agreed.
Among the more intriguing findings: 76% of respondents said journalists can be manipulated by people in powerful positions; 75% said journalists do not demonstrate consistent respect for their readers and
communities; and the people who say that journalists do not slant their
reporting to suit their political beliefs are more likely to be Democrats.
One encouraging finding for print media: only 23% of respondents see
print reporters as the worst perpetrators of bias, while another 42% see
another more pervasive purveyor of bias: television (American Society
of Newspaper Editors Poll, 1998).

DEBASING PUBLIC AFFAIRS JOURNALISM?

Instead of reporting the news as carefully and fully as possible, many political journalists today are seen as too arrogant, opinionated, and biased in their comments on major issues, particularly when appearing on television. Rather than just telling the news straight, reporters often go beyond the news report itself and predict the future impact of the news. Needless to say, such predictions, so widely strewn on television talk shows, often prove wrong.

Newspaper reporters covering a presidential campaign were accused of letting opinion replace straight news. Because editors know that by morning most people learn from radio and television what the candidate had said the day before, the usual hard news story was often replaced by an analytical or opinion piece. One critic said that one third to one half of every campaign story reflected some level of analysis. (But interpretive pieces, if carefully done, can be free of opinion or bias; it is a fine line.)

Critical of the cozy relationship between journalists and Washington insiders, columnist, David Broder, calls this a "blurring of the line" when journalists become pseudo experts on television talk shows. He told one audience, "On television, the 'punditocracy' has begun to look like the last scene from Orwell's *Animal Farm*. You can't tell the journalists from the politicians, the watch dog from the running dog. It's not just that they're in bed with each other. It's that they have become one and the same" (cited in Fibison, 1996, p. 1).

Matters are not helped when some journalists move back and forth between journalism and high political positions. David Gergen, for example, worked in the White House for both Presidents Reagan and Bush before joining *U.S. News and World Report* and the MacNeil/Lehrer News Hour. Then he joined the Clinton White House for a time and later returned to journalism. Pat Buchanan, once a Nixon White House aide, has used talk shows, especially CNN's *Crossfire* and his newspaper column, as springboards to his presidential campaigns of 1992, 1996, and 2000. After 4 years of advising President Clinton, George Stephanopoulos resigned and became a political analyst for ABC News.

ABC apparently believed that any conflict of interest of their new star analyst was more than balanced by his celebrity status and good looks.

BIAS OR PERCEPTION OF BIAS?

Many Americans mistrust the media because they believe or perceive that the media are biased. What does that mean? Earlier, bias was a synonym for partiality or partisanship, was opposed to the idea of "objectivity," and often implied a deliberate effort to distort facts.

More recently, bias has meant an "unconscious slant" and, according to conservatives, introduced by the "prevailing liberal tendencies of the media." Journalists, it is said, make subjective decisions every minute of the way. So some media critics argue that the best interests of balance are better served by openly partisan commentary than by the traditional "objective" reporting . But interestingly, charges of bias seem to be applied only to those who will not own up to having an ax to grind. Rush Limbaugh or Michael Moore, for example, are clearly expressing their opinions but ABC, NBC, or CBS journalists, for example, may imagine they are getting the facts right and not just fitting facts to fit their ideology, or so their critics charge (Nurnberg, 2003).

The recent success of the clearly conservative Fox network and Fox cable channel in gaining audience share in television news may be due in part because many conservative viewers perceive that news reports of Peter, Tom, and Dan are biased whereas the news on Fox channels is "fair and balanced," as the network claims.

Of course, most working journalists honestly believe they are not biased and are reporting the news as fairly and objectively as possible. Objectivity and fairness may be difficult to achieve, it's said, but it is important to always try to be balanced and fair. Bias, it could be said, is in the eye of the beholder. If you agree with the slant, it's news; if you don't, then it's bias or even "lies."

Bernard Goldberg's book, *Bias: A CBS Insider Exposes How the Media Distorts the News,* became a best seller during 2002–2003 and popular with conservatives but was firmly rejected by Dan Rather and his colleagues at CBS News who believed their former colleague got it all wrong. The book was not widely reviewed by the national press.

Some observers think we are coming to the end of the era of "objectivity" that dominated journalism for many years. A new ethic is needed that lends legitimacy to opinion, honestly disclosed and disciplined by some sense of propriety. It's argued that in the new torrent of instant radio, cable television, and now the Internet, with its countless bloggers, supplying all the bulletin board news but also strong and varied opinions as well, that it's necessary that the press—the printed word—must not just report events but explain them. And explanations can become a matter of opinion.

The problem of "media bias" (it's almost one word) is exacerbated by the ideological, political, and social divisions within American society, sometimes referred to as the "culture war." Deep and emotional differences exist on such issues as abortion, gay marriage, family planning, capital punishment, school prayer, religion in public life, legalization of drugs, as well as regional, economic, and generational issues, and so forth. For example, a religious, wealthy Republican from a small town, in say, Alabama, would see the world and the news quite differently than a 30-year-old Democratic school teacher in Manhattan. A further complication is that national journalists, by and large, tend to be affluent, liberal Democrats, who probably inject a good deal more opinion into their news stories than earlier and this opens the press to accusations of bias and distortions. As Geoffrey Nunberg (2003) wrote:

> If objectivity is an illusion, we are free to disbelieve any report we find inconvenient and uncongenial on the grounds that it is colored by a "hidden agenda"—another expression used by unhappy readers. Partisan polarization always leads to the creation of parallel universes. (p. 4)

Yet an effective democratic society requires agreement on the broad facts of reality. Today more than in the past, readers and viewers tend to reject news and opinion at odds with their personal worldview.

Within the media itself, in the mud-slinging over who is and who is not biased, neither side seems to be willing to give ground. And because that is the case, many conservatives will continue to see *The New York Times, Newsweek,* and *ABC News* as clearly, if unconsciously, biased and partisan, whereas liberals will feel the same about the Fox network, *The Wall Street Journal*, and *U.S. News and World Report*.

My personal view is that the bias controversy, real or perceived, will never reach a resolution within such a robust, free-wheeling, perverse, and hyperactive news media as we have in America. Our best hope, I believe, is for a press and media system that is as diverse as possible—expressing a wide range of both news and views. As Judge Learned Hand (1945) wrote in an antitrust action against the Associated Press:

> The (newspaper) industry serves one of the most vital of all general interests: the dissemination of news from as many different sources, and with as many different facets as possible.... It presupposes that right conclusions are more likely to be gathered out of a multitude of tongues and through any authoritarian selection. To many this is and will always be folly, but we have staked upon it, our all. (p. 372)

CELEBRITY JOURNALISTS AND BIG BUCKS.

Critics have long advocated that political journalism should get away from the insider game and move closer to the audience. That, however, is not where the rewards are these days for national journalists. A root cause of this animosity toward the press stems from the fact that due to exposure on television, many journalists have become well-known celebrities themselves and highly paid ones at that. Many among the public can instantly identify Barbara Walters, Tim Russert, Jane Pauley, Paula Zahn, Katie Couric, Sam Donaldson, or Mike Wallace, but they have no idea what the editors of *The Washington Post* or *Time* magazine look like, nor do they know their names.

As previously explained, news on television is becoming packaged entertainment. The role of celebrity journalists in such circumstances is not just to report the news, but to embellish and "spin" the news with lively and entertaining commentary, much of it opinionated and speculative. Newspaper and magazine journalists in Washington, DC and New York City have learned that the way to become prominent and affluent in journalism is to appear on the television talk shows such as *The Capital Gang, Washington Week in Review, Meet the Press, McLaughlin Group, Reliable Sources, Crossfire, Inside Politics, Hardball,* and others that have proliferated in the nation's capital since 1980. Some talk shows are carried nationally, but all are seen in Washington. Compared to prime-time network television or even the daytime talk shows, these political confabs attract scant audiences but are inexpensive to produce because participants receive little pay. But plenty of journalists want to be on them for the visibility and opportunities that can result from their appearances.

Some talk shows have became known as "food fights" because the format requires guests to be opinionated, loud, witty, and, of course, to disagree with other panelists. One participant said the less she knew about a topic, the better she was able to argue about it. These shows provide little time for measured and thoughtful comments on the news and public affairs. (Some journalists see these shows as pure entertainment but others considered them an embarrassment and a disservice to serious journalism.)

But the talk shows provide visibility, and for many, they have been the path to affluence. Rem Rieder, the editor of the *American Journalism Review* commented: "It is a package. You say outrageous things to get attention on the shows so that you can become a regular, and once you become a regular you can get the speaking fees" (cited in Fallows, 1996, p. 96).

For example, *Newsweek* reporter, Howard Fineman, a regular on various talk shows, was hired to speak to a group of lawyers on a 12-day cruise from Holland to Russia. Margaret Carlson, the *Time* columnist, said her speaking fees doubled to approximately $10,000 after she became a regular member on *The Capital Gang.*

Kurtz (1996) said a partial sampling of journalists' speech making income from 1994 shows that Sam Donaldson got $30,000 a speech, Pat Buchanan received $10,000, and William Safire, frequent *Meet the Press* panelist, pulled in $20,000 a talk. ABC's Cokie Roberts got at least $20,000 per lecture and was said to have earned $300,000 one year. Mike Wallace of CBS earned $25,000 an outing and CNN's Larry King received $50,000 for each appearance and was said to earn $1 million per year.

Because these hefty lecture fees usually come from a variety of for-profit organizations and interest groups, it is legitimate to ask whether ethical problems or conflicts of interest are involved here Many in the national press have been unhappy at the spectacle of this "buckraking" by so many of their colleagues. Fallows (1996) wrote:

> The bluntest way to criticize journalists on the lecture trail is to say, simply, that they are corrupt. Some day, in some form, they may have to write about the groups they are addressing. If they have taken big money from these groups, they can't give the reader an honest—or as honest-sounding—assessment as if they had kept their distance. (p. 103)

Similarly, Alan Murray, then of *The Wall Street Journal,* said:

> You tell me what is the difference between somebody who works full-time for the National Association of Realtors and somebody who takes $40,000 a year in speaking fees from realtor groups. It's not clear to me there's a big distinction. (p. 103)

Prominent television journalists who do not accept money for speeches include Peter Jennings, Tom Brokaw, Dan Rather, and Brian Lamb of C-SPAN. They make speeches but not for money (Fallows, 1996). Jim Lehrer of the PBS news show no longer accepts speaking engagements.

The drumbeat of intramedia criticism of journalists speaking for lucrative fees has had an effect and in recent years, networks have restricted such activities by their journalists.

Kurtz (1996) summarized the ethical dilemma nicely:

> The essence of journalism, even for the fiercest opinion-mongers, is professional detachment. The public has a right to expect that those who pontificate for a living are not in financial cahoots with the industries and lobbies they analyze on the air. Too many reporters and pundits simply have a blind spot on this issue. They have been seduced by the affluence and adulation that comes with television success. They are engaging in drive-by journalism, rushing from television studio to lecture hall with their palms out-

stretched. Perhaps when they mouth off on television, a caption should appear under their names: PAID $20,000 BY GROUP HEALTH ASSOCIA-TION OF AMERICA, TOOK $15,000 CHECK FROM AMERICAN MEDICAL ASSOCIATION. The talk show culture has made them rich, but, in a very real sense, left them bankrupt. (p. 227)

This problem is not as serious as it was a few years ago but it does point out the hubris of some national journalists. Another reason the public resents some journalists relates to the money they earn. Even more than large lecture fees, the huge salaries earned by prominent media figures are fairly accurate indicators of their celebrity status and the extent that some of them are really more entertainers than they are serious journalists.

According to the 1999 salary report of *Brill's Content*, the big names at ABC news seem to do best: Barbara Walters was paid $10 million; Peter Jennings got $8.5 to $9 million; Ted Koppel, $8 million; Diane Sawyer, $7 million; and Sam Donaldson, $3 to $3.5 million. Over at CBS, Dan Rather was paid $7 million; Mike Wallace, $3 million; and Lesley Stahl, $1.75 million. At NBC, Tom Brokaw earned $7 million; Katie Couric also got $7 million; and Matt Lauer, $2.5 million.

In the print media, even the most highly placed journalists received considerably less annual remuneration. Walter Isaacson, when he was editor of *Time,* earned $975,000 to $1.05 million; Joe Lelyveld, former executive editor of *The New York Times,* was paid $450,000 to $600,000; a senior writer for the *Wall Street Journal* gets $130,000; a senior reporter for the *New York Times* gets $80,000 to $100,000. And at the lower end of salaries: Ed Agre, the news director, anchor, and reporter at tiny KXGN at Glendive, Montana, was paid $22,000 and a starting salary for a reporter with 2 years experience at the *New Haven Register* was $26,000 to $28,000 ("Who Gets Paid What," 1999)

SELF-CRITICISM OF THE PRESS

The continuing squabble over money earned on television talk shows and the speaking circuit reminds us of the importance of self-criticism by the press. The news business does have recognized professional standards, and most journalists are sensitive and often responsive to the criticisms of press performance that come from such regular or occasional media critics as Howard Kurtz, David Shaw, James Fallows, Ken Auletta, Tom Rosenstiel, Bill Kovach, Richard Reeves, Jonathan Alter, Tom Shales, and Jon Katz, as well as from the *American Journalism Review, Columbia*

Journalism Review, and *Nieman Reports.* The Internet has provided further venues for media criticism including online "magazines" *Slate* and *Salon,* which regularly take on the media as well as the numerous bloggers who can overwhelm the Internet with heated comments (and invective) when a hot press issue surfaces.

A built-in problem for many of these critics—some who critique the media only part-time and do other kinds of editing or reporting—is that they have jobs with various news organizations. Hence, they never seem to zero in on the foibles or errant behavior of their own paper, newspaper group, magazine, or broadcast station, much less the conglomerates of which they are a small part. Further, sometimes critics themselves can get caught crosswise on ethical concerns.

Incisive intramedia criticism is an important way the press improves itself at times. The talk show and lecture fee brouhaha struck a raw nerve with both management and individual journalists. Washington journalists are showing more sensitivity and have drawn back from some of the "food fight" shows and questionable lecture stints.

MORE PROFOUND CONCERNS ABOUT JOURNALISM

The concerns already mentioned about the press' cynicism, negativism, trivialization of news, and decline of serious public affairs journalism have led to some somber assessments of today's journalism, originating from academics, both left and right, and from respected journalists.

Cynicism is at the heart of the new critique. According to Glaberson (1994), journalists are bringing a self-canceling message: Everything—from the O. J. Simpson case to the health care debate and on to journalism itself—is a game about nothing more than winning and losing. Thomas Mann of the Brookings Institution said, "We're now at a point of believing it's all a scam, everyone is looking out for his own narrow interests and the job of the reporter is to reveal the scam" (Glaberson, 1994, Sec. 4, p. 1). The longtime concern about liberal bias in the press has been partly replaced by a concern that a politically neutral bias now shapes news coverage by declaring that all public figures, indeed, all people in the news, are suspect.

This journalism, it is felt, is undermining its own credibility. Professor Kathleen Jamieson said:

> Journalists are now creating the coverage that is going to lead to their own destruction. If you cover the world cynically and assume that everyone is Machiavellian and motivated by their own self-interest, you invite your

readers and viewers to reject journalism as a mode of communication because it must be cynical, too. (Glaberson, 1994, Sec. 4, p. 1)

Studies, backed by statistics, strongly suggest that the press nearly always magnifies the bad and underplays the good. Since the 1960s, reporters have served America a steady diet of trends and events of such a fundamentally negative nature that we have undermined the country's faith in itself. Walsh (1996) wrote:

Of course, the press has to report such stories but they have taken their toll. The media are no longer seen as society's truth-sayers. By embellishing the bad and filtering out the good, a negative picture emerges. It is understandable that Americans have come to associate the press with everything that has gone wrong. (p. 281)

Fallows (1996) thought that the ascendancy of star-oriented, highly paid media personalities involves a terrible bargain:

The more prominent today's star journalists become, the more they are forced to give up the essence of real journalism, which is the search for information of use to the public.... The best-known and best-paid people in journalism now set an example that erodes the quality of the news we receive and threaten journalism's claim on public respect. (p. 7)

Further, Fallows (1996) sees an even more ominous future:

The harm actually goes much further than that, to threaten the long-term health of our political system. Step by step, mainstream journalism has fallen into the habit of portraying American public life as a race to the bottom, in which one group of conniving, insincere, politicians ceaselessly tries to outmaneuver another. The great problem for American democracy is that people barely trust elected leaders or the entire legislative system to accomplish anything of value. (p. 7)

Other forces are involved, but Fallows believes the media's attitudes have played a surprisingly important and destructive role in public affairs.

Unless the press changes its ways, some feel that legal protections of the press will be rolled back within 10 years. The public does not care anymore about protecting the press, it is argued, because most Americans no longer think the press informs them well. Libel laws may be weakened and access laws tightened to make it more difficult for the press to cover news and investigate abuses in government and the private sector. Recently, jury awards for libel soared as the public's trust in the press declined.

One solution to all these criticisms is that journalists should place more stress on reporting the news and leave the task of assessing its impact to others. Criticism of investigative stories, such as Whitewater, White House fund-raising, or alleged Chinese espionage, some journalists say, suggests a naive belief that without the press, the news would somehow be better. Richard Wald of ABC thinks the current criticism is based on nostalgia for a past that never really existed. He thinks there is a broad societal skepticism today that erodes the influence of all institutions, including the press.

What may be significant, however, is that growing numbers of working journalists talk more and more about de-emphasizing coverage that focuses on conflict and scandal, and others say they are rethinking their aversions to positive news stories. These ideas are related to a significant but controversial trend in newspaper journalism today called public or civic journalism. This approach is an attempt to help the public participate in public affairs without the press taking stands on issues. Instead of covering elections as contests or horse races that reduce citizens to mere bystanders, public journalism attempts to ground its coverage in a citizen's agenda or a list of problems and issues that citizens want discussed by the candidates. The press is divided over public journalism but the controversy is a welcome sign of a state of unrest in the news business.

Geneva Overholser, former editor of *The Des Moines Register*, said:

> The public is right to question whether newspapers are acting in the public interest. I think what readers are asking is "Are you really giving us a reflection of what is happening or are you just discouraging us?" We're so good at reporting all the negatives and all the infighting that we give people a sense it is all hopeless. (cited in Glaberson, 1994, Sec. 4, p. 1)

These concerns seemed to come together and reach a new level of public disapproval of news media performance during the prolonged scandal involving President Clinton and a White House intern in 1998–1999. This scandal is covered in chapter 9.

CHAPTER

9

The Clinton Scandal and "Mixed Media"

There is an old piece of advice I think every young reporter in a good news-room gets: Do your own work. And I think the lesson of this whole thing for reporters comes down to some pretty simple standards like that one.

—Michael Oreskes

Major scandals that dominate the news, such as the prolonged Presidential crisis over President Clinton's involvement with Monica Lewinsky, seem to bring out a bit of the best (the serious press *did* get the basic facts right) but mostly the worst in the news media.

In part because this cautionary tale was a prolonged *political* scandal (as well as a constitutional crisis), with charges and allegations flying back and forth, everyone connected with it was, to some extent, besmirched and dis-credited—not only President Clinton but also the presidency, many in Con-gress, Kenneth Starr and his investigation, the impeachment trial, and especially the so-called *mixed media*.

Mixed media is a recent term, popular with media critics, and intended to describe the recent trends, some technological and others organizational and financial, that have altered the news media in mostly deleterious ways.

Critic Steven Brill (1999) wrote that the Monica Lewinsky affair put all the dynamics of that mixed media culture on display:

- The speed of today's never-pausing news cycle that demands instant reactions from the players.
- The way 24-hour cable news channels love to fill the air with two screaming sides of every argument, as if the two sides are always

equal and as if there is always credible disagreement about whatever the issue at hand happens to be.

- The brutal competition across a vast array of profit-hungry news providers that are typically subsidiaries of giant corporations.
- The carnivorous appetite for any shred of news that has even the slimmest claim to being "new."
- Sinking standards for sourcing.
- Shrinking attention spans, and the ability of the story *du jour* to drown out other news. (p. 84)

Mixed media in hot pursuit of a scandal seemed to bring out the worst of American journalism. Many journalists were highly critical of their colleagues' performance during the scandal. David Halberstam spoke for many when he wrote:

> The past year [1998] has been, I think, the worst year for American journalism since I entered the profession 44 years ago.... What is disturbing about the profession today is that, I think, many of the critics are right, and the people who have been performing as journalists in the past year have in fact seriously trivialized the profession, doing what is fashionable instead of what is right.... In some ways, this particular crisis, so much of it driven by technological change, has been coming for more than a decade, as the power of cable television and the effect of it on mainstream media have gradually changed the nature of what constitutes television broadcasting, giving us an ever-escalating diet of sensationalized tabloid reporting, and an endless, unquestioning search for access to celebrities on their own terms. (cited in Kovach & Rosenstiel, 1999, p. ix)

The most thoughtful and penetrating analysis of media performance during the Clinton scandal was done by Bill Kovach and Tom Rosenstiel (1999) in their book, *Warp Speed: America in the Age of Mixed Media*. Their study was conducted within the framework of the mixed media culture (and similar to Brill's [1999] views), which they said has five main characteristics:

- *A Never-Ending News Cycle Makes Journalism Less Complete:* In the 24-hour news cycle, the press is increasingly reporting allegations, rather than digging out the truth. Stories begin as bits of evidence or speculation, to be filled in and sorted out in public as the news cycle continues. And then journalists vamp and speculate until a response is issued. So stories come out less complete and reporting takes on a chaotic and unsettled quality. This makes it difficult to separate fact from spin, argument, or innuendo.

- *Sources Are Gaining Power Over Journalists:* The move toward allegation over verification is compounded by a shift in the power relationship toward the sources of information and away from the news organizations who cover them. Sources increasingly dictate the terms of the interaction and the conditions and time frame in which the information is used, whether it is a celebrity promoting a new movie or a leaker negotiating which paper or prime-time television show to give the interview to. With more news outlets, it reflects a rising demand for the news "product" and a limited supply of newsmakers. Media manipulators as well are growing more sophisticated.

- *There Are No More Gatekeepers:* The press is now marked by a much wider range of standards of what is publishable and what is not. With so many more outlets, the authority of any one outlet (such as a *New York Times* editor) to play a gatekeeper role over the information is diminished. Journalism may be becoming more innovative and democratic, but there has been an abandonment of professional standards and ethics. In fact, the lowest standards drive out the higher standards, creating a kind of Gresham's Law of journalism. The news medium with high standards is often faced with the dilemma over using a story of high interest already "out there" but poorly sourced and of doubtful news value.

- *Argument Is Overwhelming Reporting:* The "reporting culture" (which rewards gathering and verifying information) is being overrun by the "argument culture," which devalues the practices of verification. Due to the information revolution, many new media outlets now merely comment on information rather than gather it. The rise of 24-hour cable news stations and Internet news and information sites place demands on the media to "have something" to fill the time. Further, the economics of new media demand the product be produced as cheaply as possible. Comment, chat, speculation, opinion, and punditry cost far less than assembling a team of reporters, producers, fact-checkers and editors to cover the world. Whole new news organizations such as MSNBC are being built around such chatter, creating a new medium of "talk radio TV."

- *The "Blockbuster Mentality":* As the television audiences fragment, television tries to reassemble the mass audience with a big running story. These blockbusters tend to be formulaic stories that involve celebrity, scandal, sex, and downfall, be it O. J., Princess Diana, or Monicagate. Part of the appeal to news organizations is that it is cheaper and easier to reassemble the audience with the big story rather than by covering the globe and presenting a diversified menu of news. (Kovach & Rosenstiel, 1999, pp. 6–8)

Kovach and Rosenstiel believe these aspects of mixed media are creating a new journalism of assertion, which is less interested in substantiating whether something is true and is more interested in getting it into the public discussion. The trend contributes to the press being a conduit of politics as cultural civil war. Their concern is whether the journalism of verification will soon be overwhelmed by the journalism of assertion. The authors seem to imply that television's lower standards now trample the once dominant standards valued by the best of the print media.

WHAT HAPPENED AND HOW MEDIA REACTED

Most of the turmoil of the scandal occurred during 1998—the so-called "Year of Monica." As most will recall, Linda Tripp's recordings of her phone conversations with Monica Lewinsky, a former White House intern, contained lurid comments about her sexual relationship with President Bill Clinton, and launched the story, which for many months Clinton vehemently denied. Michael Isikoff, a *Newsweek* reporter, had been following events and was readying a scoop when *Newsweek* hesitated and decided to wait a week after Kenneth Starr promised a complete accounting for the following week. The delayed scoop somehow was leaked to Matt Drudge, one-man Internet gossip and news agency. He decided the public had a right to know the story even if the facts could not be verified. So the biggest political scandal in years broke first in cyberspace—a new player in mixed media.

Needless to say, the story spread like wildfire and in the first hectic days, there was a feeding frenzy as media pursued the relatively few tidbits of information—mostly leaks from lawyers and investigators—but various restraints kept the public from knowing with certainty the sources of key elements of the saga. The most important finding of the Kovach & Rosenstiel (1999) study of the scandal was the extraordinary degree to which reporting and opinion and speculation were intermingled in mainstream journalism. A snapshot of network news, newspaper reporting, and cable news that typified what an American might see and hear showed that 41% of all the reportage in the first 6 days of the story was not factual reporting at all ("here is what happened") but instead were journalists offering their own analysis, opinion, speculation, or judgments—essentially commentary and punditry. Another 12% of content was reporting attributed to other news media but unverified by those reporting it. Taken together, it meant that more than half of the reportage of the first week (53%) was either passing along other people's reporting or commenting on the news (Kovach & Rosenstiel, 1999).

Veteran journalist, Jules Witcover, commented:

> Into the vacuum created by a scarcity of clear and creditable attribution raced all manner of rumor, gossip, and especially hollow sourcing, making the reports of some mainstream outlets scarcely distinguishable from supermarket tabloids. The rush to be first or to be more sensational created a picture of irresponsibility seldom seen in the reporting of presidential affairs. (Witcover, 1998, p. 19)

Not until the story settled somewhat did the serious media begin to report in a manner expected of them. Many news media did act with considerable responsibility considering the early demand for news. And the Clinton White House, in full damage-control mode, seized on the leaks and weakly attributed stories to cast the news media as either a willing or unwilling collaborator of sorts with Starr's probe (Witcover, 1998).

Dire predictions of a premature end of the Clinton presidency were heard almost at once. "Is he finished?" asked a coverline on *U.S. News and World Report* and *The Economist* of London commanded, "If It's True, Go." ABC's Sam Donaldson speculated on January 25 that Clinton could resign before the next week was out, "If he's not telling the truth" (cited in Witcover, 1998, p. 19).

After the initial story, there was much piling-on by broadcast and print media and this did not sit well with the public. A *Washington Post* poll taken 10 days after the story broke found that 56% of those surveyed believed the news media were treating Clinton unfairly, and 74% said they were giving the story too much attention.

The public's sense of overkill was exacerbated by the 24-hour cable channels, and Internet sites, which assured the story of nonstop reportage and rumor, augmented by late night rehashes and TV talk shows. Despite the public's criticisms, viewing and listening audiences swelled as did circulations of print media.

Journalists' methods came in for sharp criticism—far more rumor mongering instead of fact checking, and the unattributed appropriation of the work and speculations of others. The old yardstick applied by *The Washington Post* in the Watergate story—that every revelation had to be confirmed by two sources before publication—was quickly abandoned by many news outlets. Often reports were published or broadcast without a single source named or mentioned in an attribution so vague as to be useless. The public was told repeatedly that this or that information came from "sources," a word that only conveyed the notion that the story was not pure fiction. Seldom in a story of such major importance was the public left to guess where the allegations came from and why. Leakers were violating the rules while the public was left to guess about their identity and about the truth passed on through the news media, often without the customary tests of validity (Witcover, 1998).

Yet the fact remains that in all the major aspects of the story, the press was essentially accurate. Kovach and Rosenstiel (1999) wrote that contrary to White House claims, "the press usually relied on legitimate sources and often was careful about the facts in the first account." (p. 90) This turned out to be the case with ABC News and its story of the stained blue dress which indeed proved to be accurate and indisputably relevant; and later became the pivotal evidence against the President. But the key words were "first account" because "others then used the reporting from elsewhere to engage in sometimes reckless speculation and propaganda" (Stewart, 1999, p. 8).

TELEVISION'S ARGUMENT CULTURE

Another dimension of the Clinton scandal coverage was the proliferation of television talk shows in which pundits, in and out of the news media, would face off in loud, argumentative debates either attacking or defending the President. At various stages of the long-running story—the posting of the Starr report on the Internet, release of taped phone conversations between Linda Tripp and Monica Lewinsky, Clinton's grand jury appearance, and the impeachment proceedings in Congress—viewers were besieged with charge and countercharge but little news or rational discussion and analysis in these programs.

These political "shout shows" were mainly a cable television phenomenon on MSNBC, CNBC, CNN, and the Fox News Channel. CNBC's *Rivera Live* with Geraldo Rivera and CNBC's *Hardball* with Chris Matthews were probably the noisiest and the most polarized in their political sentiments. But these cable food fights were soon spilling over into the networks and onto the news magazine formats and onto such respected shows as *Meet the Press*. Unwritten rules seem to require that one person or side must defend the President, the other attack him. Critics felt such shows tend to turn off viewers about the political process by trivializing the news and turning a difference of opinion into a shouting match.

Former TV newsman, Marvin Kalb, of Harvard said, "One of the dangers of programs of this sort is that they convey an impression about politics as being a negative, argumentative forum. And politics is a lot more than that. And a lot more serious than that." Moreover, he added that these pundit shows are for those who enjoy "the veneer of news and the essence of gossip." (Shepard, 1999, p. 22)

The cumulative effect of such shouting matches was a public left hopelessly confused about what is true. "The biggest damage being done is not just losing viewers but to our democracy, because viewers just aren't being informed," wrote Deborah Tannen in her book, *The Argument Culture.* "If you reduce everything to two sides fighting, you are not exploring anything. People are not getting the information they need. It also promotes a real cynicism about the political process." (cited in Shepard, 1999, p. 24)

Such talk shows were, of course, one more manifestation of the "culture of assertion" overwhelming the "culture of verification" in public affairs news and, as such, contributed to public disdain of the media.

WHAT CAN THE PRESS DO?

The Clinton–Lewinsky saga with its nonstop coverage highlighted many of the journalistic shortcomings of the mixed media age. Journalists no longer had the luxury of taking either hours or days while pondering a news decision or arguing over a story. Today, battered by technology, competition, the rise of pseudo news and the decline of audiences, serious journalists are faced with the task of how to separate honest, serious journalism from the all-encompassing culture of entertainment that has pervaded modern life.

In their thoughtful study of the paradox, Kovach and Rosenstiel (1999) concluded that newspapers, magazines, Web sites, and television stations will have to distinguish themselves—and establish their brands—by what they choose to report on and the values they bring to their journalism. Some will publish only what they know is true. Others will publish rumor and innuendo to have the most startling and comprehensive account. Some will separate information carefully from opinion. Some will separate fact from fiction. Others will blend them into a kind of infotainment. (p. 91)

To accomplish this, the authors proposed three steps for news media to follow:

- *Step One:* Each news organization should do a great deal more to decide what its news values and policies are. News media must make these decisions in advance and not wait until a blockbuster story is breaking.
- *Step Two:* The news organization must make it clear to those who work there that these are the values in place. Reporters, they said, are

motivated by the values of the institution and by a sense of mission. They need to know what that mission is to thrive.

- *Step Three:* Once a newsroom has defined its standards and values and genuinely made them clear to its reporters and editors, it must then make these values clear to the audience. In effect, they said, a newsroom must make a covenant with the public about what it stands for. The covenant is crucial since it is the only way for the audience to fairly judge what it thinks of a news organization. (pp. 91–93)

Some may doubt the efficacy of such standards and covenants when the next big blockbuster of a story—replete with scandal, sex, celebrity, and malfeasance—hits the new mixed media. But these are certainly three steps in the right direction.

CHAPTER

10

Foreign News Revived?

In an age of real-time, multimedia, interactive forms of communication, there is a tendency to declare obsolete (or at least dispensable) the diplomat and the foreign correspondent in the field. We will do so at our peril. The myriad forms of instantaneous communication threaten to substitute immediacy for insight, reaction for reflection, sentiment for judgment, hyperbole for reality, and deniability for integrity.

—Peter Krogh

You know, being a foreign correspondent is like being a maitre d' *in a fine restaurant. You meet so many distinguished people under such humiliating circumstances.*

—Quoted by Stephen Hess

International news gathered by foreign correspondents—that far-flung and glamorous specialty of American journalism—has been undergoing some traumatic changes in recent times. Because of new technologies and financial concerns, less news from abroad is reported especially by the broadcast services, and in very different ways. The correspondents are becoming a different breed of journalist than in the bad (yet, journalistically, good) old days of the Cold War.

The aforementioned paragraph describes foreign affairs journalism *before* the momentous events of September 11, 2001. For weeks and even months after the terrorist attacks on New York and Washington, DC, foreign news dominated the media and the public at first could not seem to get enough of it. Yet editors and broadcast executives asked themselves how long would that interest last?

During the superb coverage of the terrorist events and the war on Afghanistan, and later in Iraq, the U.S. media threw all its resources into comprehensive and very expensive journalism. Even its severest critics praised the magnificent coverage by the media.

Television broadcasters lost nearly $100 million a day in local and national advertising because their broadcasts ran mostly without commercial breaks. Opening new bureaus abroad, staffing them, and using the latest technologies cost news organizations about $25 million in the first weeks as reporters flocked to Pakistan, Afghanistan, and other Middle Eastern venues. Set-up costs for satellite communications equipment to send words and images can be about $70,000 for each uplink and about that much a week to maintain it.

As the crisis seemed to ease, audience ratings for broadcast war news began to drop and television soon cut back on its overseas news and reverted to regular programming. Yet most print media, especially the great national dailies, felt obligated the follow the story of the asymmetrical war on terrorism wherever it led.

One significant shift: During and right after 9/11, most Americans were turning to cable news for breaking stories. A Pew Center survey found that fully 54% of respondents cited cable as their primary source for news on the crisis, versus 17% for network television and 18% for local television. The number relying mostly on newspapers for war news had increased from 11% to 34%. Some 66% of respondents said they were more interested in foreign news now than before September 11, but few journalists expected this newfound interest to continue except for the occasional "big story," such as beginning of the war in Iraq and the later capture of Saddam Hussein.

During the decade before 2001, news media (and their customers) were mostly indifferent to foreign news at a time when ethnic conflicts killed millions and globalization trends touched most American communities. A Harvard study found that during the 1970s, networks television devoted 45% of its total coverage to international news. By 1995, foreign news represented only 13.5% of international coverage. During that time period, broadcast budgets and staff had been trimmed cut, bureaus closed, and broadcast programming had shifted to entertainment/trivia and economic concerns.

Yet serious journalists have long held that foreign news is important and should be reported well and thoroughly. Much that happens overseas has a direct impact on American lives, as the rise of Hitler and Stalin, World War II, and the Korean and Vietnam Wars amply demonstrated. In a democratic society, an interested public, it is argued, must know what is happening in the greater world in order to judge how well its own government responds to threats and challenges from abroad. Further, foreign news is considered necessary to inform our leaders and decision makers about foreign dangers and opportunities. In his *mea culpa* on disasters in foreign affairs, Robert McNamara interestingly blamed the press for not better informing State Department officials about Vietnam.

Despite globalization of our economy, for many Americans, foreign news does not seem important. Who is to blame? The national press? The "media"—broadly speaking, with its pervasive cultural and social influences? Perhaps the public itself?

Without a crisis story intruding on the public's attention—China threatening Taiwan, famine in Ethiopia, civil strife in Kosovo, or terrorism in Israel or Ulster—the typical daily newspaper does not print much news from overseas—usually about six or more short items about 8 inches or less—unless American soldiers or hostages are involved. Anyone regularly watching network television is aware that foreign news has been typically reduced to several brief items ("And now the news from abroad"), unless some video with violent footage is available. (Fifty percent of television's foreign news does portray violence.) At the networks, foreign news has been pushed aside in favor of more personalized, self-help, and advice stories—so-called "you news" and the occasional celebrity scandal story, for instance, O. J. Simpson or Michael Jackson.

Who cares? Apparently, not the public. The Pew Research Center for the People and the Press (1996) survey of the American public found that among the regular users of the news media, the topics of most interest were crime, local news about people and events, and health news. International news ranked ninth, well behind sports, local government, science, religion, and political news.

One cross-national study found that 78% of Germans read a newspaper yesterday, whereas only 49% of Americans did so. When asked to identify the current secretary general of the United Nations, 58% of Germans came up with his name, compared with only 13% of Americans. (Kofi Annan was the current secretary general.)

This declining audience interest means that as a culture, we are missing the connective tissue that binds us to the rest of the world. The British have been long involved with far-off places, a legacy of their receding empire. For many Europeans, the consequences of two world wars are still keenly felt. For Americans, the experience of World War II, when everyone knew someone who was in it, and the aftermath of the rising Third World with its involvement with Soviet hegemony and the Cold War, deeply affected two generations of citizens concerned about the outside world.

Now the consensus in the news business appears to be that you can rely on international news to turn a profit only when it is actually domestic news. The most certain way to become domestic news is through a U.S. military intervention—when it is "our boys" who are "over there." The 9/11 terrorism story was certainly a domestic story as well as an international one.

Others blame the news media for skimping on world news. "A great shroud has been drawn across the mind of America to make it forget that there is a world beyond its borders," complained Max Frankel (1994), former editor of *The New York Times:*

> The three main television networks obsessively focus their cameras on domestic tales and dramas as if the end of the cold war rendered the rest of the planet irrelevant. Their news staffs occasionally visit some massacre, famine, or shipwreck and their anchors may parachute into Haiti or Kuwait for a photo op, but these spasms of interest only emphasize the networks' apparent belief that on most evenings the five billion folks out there don't matter one whit. (p. 42)

One indicator of this trend: In its heyday, CBS maintained 24 foreign bureaus; by 1995, it had reporters in only four capitals: London, Moscow, Tel Aviv, and Tokyo (*ABC News* and *NBC News* made similar cutbacks). Dan Rather has not hesitated to speak out. "Don't kid yourself;" he told Harvard students,

> The trend line in American journalism is away from, not toward, increased foreign coverage. Foreign coverage is the most expensive. It requires the most space and the most time because you're dealing with complicated situations which you have to explain a lot. And then there's always somebody around you who says people don't really give a damn about this stuff anyway.... "if you have to do something foreign, Dan, for heaven's sake, keep it short." (cited in Hess, 1996, p. 61)

FEWER COVER STORIES

The covers of the three major news magazines, each of which has long emphasized foreign news gathered by their numerous overseas correspondents, reflects the declining interest in international news. By late September 1996, *Time* had run five covers that year on international topics, versus 11 in 1995. *Newsweek* featured four international covers by September, compared to 11 in 1995. *U.S. News* published no international covers as of late 1996 but ran six in 1995. Why the difference? The decline in interest surely was greatly accelerated by the major historic event of the late

20th century—the ending of the Cold War. In the still dangerous and confusing post-Cold War period, (and before 9/11), foreign correspondents and news organizations had been going through an identity crisis over what is news and what is not news. The Cold War provided reporters with a coherent global road map, in terms of what to cover and how to cover it. Don Oberdorfer of *The Washington Post* added, "Since the fall of the Berlin Wall and the end of the Cold War news filter, the task of making sense of global events has become less manageable for the media." The press is not used to reacting to a world full of conflicts and violent encounters that, as George Kennan put it, offer no "great and absorbing focal points for American policy" (cited in Hachten, 1999, p. 127). The American public has been confused as well and has turned inward. A major effect of the "war on terrorism" is that it has focused the attention of Americans on the dangers that lurk abroad and security and safety within our borders.

Another view holds that only a very small portion of the American public is seriously interested and concerned about the outside world. These are mainly teachers and scholars, some business executives and travelers, and some public officials and journalists, especially those who have worked abroad. One editor said that at any given time, only about 2 million people in America are really interested in foreign affairs. The great majority of Americans are concerned about matters closer to home ("all news is local") just as people in other countries are.

Hess (1996) said "audiences with more cosmopolitan interests can find detailed information in the prestige press or outside the mainstream media" (p. 88). Maybe so, but that prestige press or national press is covering less and less foreign news. With the three television networks and the big news magazines continuing to slough off serious foreign news coverage, the major journalistic outlets seem to have narrowed to a handful of "national" papers—*The New York Times, The Washington Post, The Wall Street Journal, The Los Angeles Times,* and a few others, which have long maintained significant numbers of reporters stationed overseas. Other important daily papers and the number of bureaus abroad in 2003 included: *Baltimore Sun,* 5: *Boston Globe,* 5; *Chicago Tribune,* 10; *Christian Science Monitor,* 7; Cox Newspapers, 9; *Dallas Morning News,* 5; Knight Ridder papers, 14; *Newsday,* 5; *Philadelphia Inquirer,* 4; and *USA Today,* 4.

Hence, knowledge and concern about global events has become one more of the separators between our two media systems. Foreign news may be a main dish for the elite media but is only an appetizer for the popular press. The one exception to this trend, as noted in chapter 2, is the rapid increase in business and financial news from overseas—a direct result of the globalization of the world's economy. For example, *The Wall Street Journal* employs 109 corespondents and that includes reporters for its Asian and European editions as well as its main domestic edition. Many of these reporters report only news of business and industry.

HOW THE WORLD IS COVERED BY THE PRESS

For many years, the prevailing pattern of international news has been an east–west–east flow across the northern hemisphere. Three cities—New York, London, and Tokyo—comprise the key centers of the axis. From those metropolises, news is relayed and returned from the southern regions: Latin American news to New York; European, Middle Eastern, and African news to London; and Asian news to Tokyo.

Needless to say, the news that Americans receive about most of 190 nations from Afghanistan to Zimbabwe is sporadic and uneven. In a sense, most news comes from where journalists are stationed, and the U.S. television networks keep their crews in residence in England, Japan, Germany, Russia, and Israel covering happenings in those areas. But because U.S. television crews are there, a certain amount of soft news comes out of these capitals as well; for example, one more story, picked up from Fleet Street tabloids about Britain's royal family. From London, Tokyo, or Tel Aviv, reporters and cameras can be quickly dispatched elsewhere to a breaking story in the world's crisis areas. With modern air travel, broadcast journalists can quickly get to the scene and, standing before mobs of homeless Africans, can report back "live" from, say, Goma, Congo.

In his 7-year survey of network news, Hess (1996) found that among 190 countries, six were "constant (news) countries" (i.e., Russia, Germany, England, Israel, Japan, and France); 22 were "crisis countries," and 77 "others" rarely reported. His study looked at 2,300 stories from outside the United States. Most countries are rarely covered, particularly on television, and then only because they host an important event, have well-known tourists, or are the locale for the odd human interest story.

Confirming what other studies have shown, Hess (1996) found that 21 countries accounted for 79% of foreign dateline stories on network television from 1988 to 1992. Crisis journalism dominated the evening screens. For 16 nations, the news was wholly or mostly about serious unrest in their regions. A major effect of television news was the reinforcing of stereotypes: Stories from Colombia were often about drugs; in Germany, about neo-Nazis; in Italy, the Mafia. Stories from England ignored business, focusing instead on something offbeat or the royal family.

A more disturbing but not surprising conclusion of Hess' survey was television's concern with violence. When combining the categories of combat (32.8%), human rights violations (13.7%), accident/disaster (2.3%), and crime (2.5%), the total showed that more than 50% of the television network news stories were concerned with some aspect of violence. Further, a correlation was found between violence and the distance of the story from New York City: The farther away from home, the more likely the cameras have been lured there by something violent.

In her recent book, *Compassion Fatigue,* Susan Moeller (1999) argued that the volume and character of disaster coverage can lull audiences into a "compassion-fatigue stupor" and damage the prospects for remedy and recovery. Comparing such stories as famine in Sudan, war in Iraq, and Ebola fever in Congo, she argues that news coverage is usually formulaic and sensationalized. Such foreign news stories, she says, all sound alike with causes and solutions often oversimplified. As one crisis bleeds into the next one, she says, it takes more and more dramatic coverage to elicit the same level of sympathy as the last catastrophe (Moeller, 1999).

In mid-2003, there was evidence that America's television audience was burned out on serious news. At a busy news time—American soldiers dying daily in Iraq, Marines poised off the Liberian coast, California's governorship up for grabs, and pro basketball star Kobe Bryant accused of sexual assault—television viewers were tuning out. The total evening news audience on the broadcast networks had been lower in summer 2003 than in the summer of 2001, when the pressing stories of the day were shark attacks and the disappearance of Chandra Levy. CBS News was particularly hard hit; in June 2003 it had one of its least-watched weeks for Rather's evening news show in at least 10 years. The audience of *ABC News* was down 600,000 from the year before.

TECHNOLOGY PRODUCES
A NEW KIND OF CORRESPONDENT

For most of the last century, the foreign correspondent was a journalist who was "posted" to a distant, foreign capital—Paris, Moscow, Cairo, Buenos Aires—often staying for several years, learning the language, making contacts, and closely following politics and various facets of the particular society. Some stayed a long time: Henry Shapiro of UPI covered Moscow for 40 years, but most reporters were rotated after 4 or 5 years. Because of poor communications, these reporters were pretty much on their own, and they liked it that way. They decided what to report and usually sent back their stories by cable or sometimes by erratic radio telephone, telex, and even by mail. Dispatches were often crafted in a more leisurely fashion, with much thought and reflection. Editors back home tended to go along with what their correspondent reported. Foreign news enjoyed high credibility. A *New York Times* story from Moscow with Harrison Salisbury's byline really meant something as did a CBS television story from Berlin by Daniel Schorr.

Things have changed due to the revolutionary developments in telecommunications, particularly communication satellites, which make it possible to send a news story or video report instantly from one place to many others. The volume and speed of international news has been greatly accelerated. With the great improvement in telephone communication, thanks to INTELSAT, that lone foreign correspondent out there is no longer cut off from an editor, who now may be on the phone several times a day with advice and instructions, often when the reporter is on deadline.

With the availability of impressive gadgets—satellite telephones, lightweight versatile computers, the Internet, reliable phone connections, faxes, and uplinks to send video reports via satellite—foreign reporting, when combined with air travel, is made much easier and has become a lot different.

These technological advances have not always been for the better. Mifflin (1996a) quoted Dan Rather on how the traditional foreign correspondent's mobility has changed.

> Jet travel and technology—with smaller and better cameras, satellites, and cellular phones—have made it easier to send correspondents in and out of places swiftly. That means bureaus have been closed and correspondents, as well as anchors, make quick visits instead.... In 1996, I can literally go any place on the planet, hit the satellite and get up [on the air for a live transmission] instantaneously. (p. C5)

But what about thorough news gathering and reflection by a resident correspondent who knows the country?

Now broadcast news is being collected in other, less costly ways. Just a few years ago, if you saw a foreign news story on the *NBC Evening News*, chances are that it was reported by an NBC reporter at the scene and the film was shot by an NBC crew. Now, however, the networks are relying more on less expensive, and often less experienced, freelancers and independent contractors as well as video news agencies; their products are rarely identified on the air, leaving the impression the story was covered by network staffers. This practice gives rise to a growing concern about quality control. "By the time, the tape gets on the air, nobody has the foggiest idea who made it or whether the pictures were staged," contended Tom Wolzien, a former *NBC News* executive (cited in Hess, 1996, p. 99). More loss of quality or authenticity results when U.S. network correspondents based in London add voice-overs to stories they did not cover.

Bert Quint, former CBS correspondent, said, "There's no reason to believe the person [doing the voice-over] because odds are he or she was not within 3,000 miles of where the story occurred" (cited in Hess, 1996, p. 99). Martha Teichner of CBS's London bureau, recalled, "I was asked to do Somalia for the weekend news and I've never been to Somalia and I think, oh my God, what am I gonna do? I get every bit of research I can find, but even if I'm correct and accurate, I'm superficial. And I don't want to be superficial" (cited in Hess, 1996, p. 100).

When a big story breaks, such as the plight of 500,000 Rwandan refugees in eastern Congo, literally hundreds of journalists and camera crews, few of them knowledgeable about the area, quickly arrive, do their stories, and video the reporters standing among the hungry mobs, and then just as quickly get out. Satellites and jet travel have made such "parachute journalism" not only feasible, but cost effective, often at the expense of serious news coverage.

The global war on terrorism has spawned another innovation in foreign reporting. General assignment reporters are sent out to cover a specific story—such as a terrorist attack in a remote region—then report back by cell phone and return home.

Lack of follow-up and failure to provide context are two frequently heard criticisms of today's foreign coverage, according to Hickey (1996). The brilliant spotlight of powerful color television pictures of the 1989 Tiananmen Square uprising by student demonstrators played to millions around the world. During those dramatic days, CBS, NBC, and ABC aired 357 stories on China—more than they had done in the entire decade from 1972 (when China opened up to the West) through 1981. Afterwards, China reportage plummeted from 14.6% of foreign news dateline stories in 1989 to 1.4% in 1990.

Foreign correspondents are changing in various ways. Fewer of the U.S. media's correspondents abroad are American citizens. Foreign journalists are not only less expensive but often have a grasp of local languages and knowledge of their countries that American journalists cannot match. The AP uses many "locals"—nationals of the countries they cover in their many foreign bureaus. Journalist Scott Schuster (1988) saw the trend as due to a global acceptance of English as a media language and the global influence of American journalistic methods. Schuster said, "American influence is most profound among broadcasters and foreign broadcast journalists need only turn on their TV sets [to CNN] to receive lessons on how to do the news American style" (p. 45).

Increasingly, print has joined the broadcast media in relying more on stringers or freelancers to deal with rising costs and tighter budgets. Another survey by Hess (1994) found that 26% of 404 foreign correspondents working for U.S. news media were freelancers. Moreover, many of these were underemployed with 40% saying they do other work as well. All suffer the usual fate of freelancers: low pay, no benefits, and a precarious relationship with their employers. Hess found six types of stringers: (a) "spouses" of other correspondents; (b) "experts" who know languages and the area; (c) "adventurers" like Oriana Fallaci, the Italian writer; (d) "flingers," a person on a fling who may be starting a serious career; (e) "ideologues" or "sympathizers" who are often British; and (f) the "residents" who are often long-time residents and write occasional stories. Although stringers and freelancers remain marginal, many famous foreign correspondents started that way including Stanley Karnow, Elie Abel, Robert Kaiser, Elizabeth Pond, Caryle Murphy, and Daniel Schorr.

One of the significant changes has been the increased number of women among foreign correspondents, especially as war reporters. Before 1970, their numbers were small, although there had been a few outstanding reporters: Dorothy Thompson, Martha Gellhorn, Marguerite Higgins, and Gloria Emerson. Hess (1996) found that by the 1970s, about 16% of new foreign reporters were women; this doubled during the 1980s to about 33%. The total leveled off in the early 1990s. This ratio of two men for every woman was also found in Washington media as well as in U.S. journalism generally. In the war in Iraq, another generation of women reporters distinguished themselves. A number of women correspondents have established outstanding reputations. Among them are Caryle Murphy of *The Washington Post,* Robin Wright of *The Los Angeles Times,* and now *The Washington Posts'* syndicated columnist Georgie Ann Geyer, and Elaine Sciolino and Barbara Crossette of *The New York Times.*

Christiane Amanpour, who reported with distinction for CNN, has become something of a celebrity because of her aggressive and frankly committed reporting style. She listed the Gulf War, famine in Africa, and civil war in the former Yugoslavia as her most memorable stories. Other networks bid for her services. She agreed to do some foreign stories for CBS' *60 Minutes* but decided to stay with CNN, for whom she reported in Iraq. A large number of reporters covering the Iraq war have been women.

PHYSICAL DANGERS FOR CORRESPONDENTS

Because much of foreign reporting deals with war, civil unrest, and other forms of violence, the work is dangerous, perhaps the most hazardous in journalism. Among the world's many troubled and unstable nations, journalists, both foreign and domestic, are frequently singled out as targets for arrest, beatings, or all too often, assassination. Sometimes they are just in the wrong place at the wrong time.

The Committee to Protect Journalists (CJP) keeps track of such violence worldwide and reported in March 2003 that during the year 2002, there were 500 cases of media repression in 120 countries, including assassination, assault, imprisonment, censorship, and legal harassment. A total of 20 journalists were killed worldwide as a direct result of their work in 2002; in 2003, 36 journalists were killed worldwide with 13 of them killed in Iraq. For the second year in a row, the number of journalists in prison rose sharply. There were 136 journalists in jail at the end of 2002, a 15% increase from 2001, and a shocking increase of 68% since the end of 2000, when only 81 were in jail. China, the world's leading jailer of journalists for the fourth year in a row, arrested five more, ending the year with 39 journalists behind bars.

In the Afghanistan war, eight journalists and cameramen were slain in about a week's time, one of the highest tolls in the shortest time span for journalists. In February 2002, Daniel Pearl of the Wall Street Journal became the tenth journalist and the first American to die covering September 11 and its aftermath. While investigating a terrorist in Pakistan, Pearl was kidnapped by terrorists, held hostage for several weeks, and then executed.

In conclusion, as international news and foreign correspondents continue to evolve due to the imperatives of instantaneous communication and financial pressures, there is real danger that our foreign news coverage may be losing something important. Dean Peter Krogh of the Georgetown School of Foreign Service, commented:

> Over the past 25 years, the numbers of foreign bureaus and foreign correspondents have declined. Deeply informed individual insight from the field is fast disappearing. News and media services compound the problem by making the news more homogeneous. The media are reduced to establishing a fleeting physical presence only after CNN announces there is a crisis abroad.... Yet CNN itself is, by its very nature, flawed. It provides unevaluated and sometimes exaggerated reports of developments abroad which drive a domestic rush to judgment and a correlated reaction. (cited in Geyer, 1996, p. 10)

Krogh added, "As the world gets bigger, the foreign policy agenda simultaneously grows longer. Replacing the set agenda of the Cold War is a veritable avalanche of pressing international issues. Our diplomats and journalists need to inhabit these issues where they reside in a far-flung world" (cited in Geyer, 1996, p. 10). There still are a number of the traditional foreign correspondents sending in thorough and thoughtful news reports from distant capitals but their influence may well be diminishing.

The American public may not show much interest in distant and exotic places, but the media and the public do become very concerned when American soldiers, sailors, and airmen are sent off to those very places. How the press covers our wars is discussed in chapter 11.

CHAPTER

11

Covering Wars
in an Era of Terrorism

The first casualty when war comes is truth.

—Senator Hiram Johnson

War is God's way of teaching Americans geography.

—Ambrose Bierce

Recent wars from the 1991 Persian Gulf War to fighting in Afghanistan and Iraq have dramatically altered the ways that armed conflicts are reported to the American people. Although long-standing frictions and suspicions still persist between war reporters and military officials, the use of new communications technology has altered journalism for the great throng of journalists competing for the story.

In the 42-day Persian Gulf War, or the first Iraq war, television, especially CNN, turned much of the world into a global community witnessing a televised real-time war as the brief struggle evolved from armed confrontation to spectacular aerial bombardment and finally to lightning ground action. That war became the biggest global news story in years, and the telling of it utilized the full resources of the U.S. news media and much of the international news system. More than 1,600 print and broadcast journalists and technicians were on hand to report it.

The NATO bombing campaign against Serbia as its ground forces were mauling Kosovo was a new kind of war: an effort, dominated by U.S. air power, to bomb a nation into submission without deploying ground troops, taking minimal casualties. As in the Gulf war, the U.S. press accused the military of withholding information and of "spinning" its combat reports for political and strategic reasons. The 78 days of NATO bombing in mid-1999 at last succeeded in forcing Serbian dictator, Slobodan Milosevic, to yield and permit 16,100 NATO soldiers to chase the fleeing Serbian forces out of Kosovo and to bring relief to the battered ethnic Albanians. In that last war of a bloody century, news coverage was greatly facilitated by satellite communications, particularly the satellite telephone, 24-hour cable news reporting, and for the first time, the Internet.

The first Gulf war produced great television. But news coverage provoked a bitter controversy among the U.S. press, the White House, and the Pentagon over how the war, any war, was to be reported. In the air war over Yugoslavia, press/military relations were less abrasive because NATO controlled much of the war news and the press corps was more multinational.

The vague and amorphous war on terrorism opened in September 2001 and the Bush Administration made it clear that the news media would receive less access to news of the new asymmetrical conflict. Yet news media here and abroad have poured out a torrent of news, speculation, commentary and pictures since the 9/11 attacks. In Afghanistan, unlike earlier wars, reporters could now deliver news from war zones in real time. In this "videophone war," the closest views of the fighting were provided by reporters using videophones, which are literally cameras plugged into satellites. Because of the remote nature of the conflict, fewer reporters were in Afghanistan.

The legions of reporters from here and abroad followed the U.S. and British forces into the short and violent war in Iraq that toppled the regime and Saddam Hussein in spring 2003. The now refined new technologies of the video or satellite phone (satphones), cell phones, e-mail, Internet, and global television greatly facilitated the flow of 24/7 war news. Despite previous restrictions on battlefield access, the Pentagon did an about-face and permitted some 770 reporters to be "embedded" with combat units during the rapid invasion from Kuwait to Baghdad. The news media approved the new access, which led to some brilliant and moving accounts of the war. After the fall of Baghdad, the war did wind down as expected but has turned into a drawn-out guerrilla war that is straining the occupying troops and troubling the American public. News media have continued their role of reporting, explaining, and criticizing that phase of the war, but because of the embedding policy, there were fewer clashes over Pentagon news policies.

BACKGROUND OF PRESS RESTRICTIONS

War correspondents long have been a kind of specialized foreign correspondent—they work abroad under difficult and often highly dangerous conditions, and are often subject to restraint or censorship, usually from their own government's military, and their adversaries as well. Whatever the conflict, the U.S. press strongly believed that it had the right to report a war involving American citizens without being unduly barred by military censorship.

The acerbic and suspicious relations between American journalists and the military developed over time. In World War I, some 500 American correspondents for various periods covered the conflict for newspapers, magazines, and press associations in France; unlike British and French reporters, they were free to go to the front lines without military escorts. Still, everything that well-known reporters like Richard Harding Davis, Will Irwin, or Floyd Gibbons wrote was passed through the censorship of the press section of the Military Intelligence Service. Details about specific battles, numbers of casualties, and names of units could be released only after being mentioned in official communiqués.

Military censorship followed the same general pattern in World War II, with the added feature of controlling radio broadcasts. The Office of Censorship was headed by Byron Price, an AP editor, who handled with distinction the most difficult part of his job—the direction of voluntary press censorship—that applied to newspapers, magazines, and other printed materials outside the combat zones. In far-flung combat areas, reporters were generally free to move about and join military units, but were always subject to possible censorship. The U.S. Navy long withheld details of the Pearl Harbor disaster and of the sinking of ships in the Pacific, but in most theaters, the news was broadcast promptly. About 500 full-time American reporters were abroad at any one time and provided war coverage that many considered the best and fullest ever seen.

With mobile units and tape recordings, radio coverage greatly increased. Many broadcasts were memorable: Cecil Brown of CBS describing the fall of Singapore; Edward R. Murrow flying over Berlin in a hazardous 1943 bombing raid; George Hicks of ABC broadcasting under German fire from a landing craft on D-Day in Normandy. The best-known U.S. reporter of World War II was Ernie Pyle, a columnist for Scripps-Howard, who attached himself to U.S. combat troops and followed GIs through North Africa, Italy, France, and the Pacific, where he died in battle. Relations between the military and correspondents were mutually trusting and supportive. Despite occasional conflicts over withheld information, everyone seemed to be on the same team. During the Korean War, press–government relations were pretty much the same.

The change began in the Vietnam War, when relations between the American journalists and the U.S. military soured and reached their lowest ebb. Reporters and camera crews, working within military guidelines, were given free access without field censorship to roam Vietnam. Some called it the best reported war in history. Yet many in the U.S. military believed critical press reporting contributed to the later U.S. defeat by overstressing negative aspects, including graphic pictures of dead and wounded, highlighting scandals such as the My Lai massacre, and misinterpreting key events such as the Tet offensive, which the military pronounced a defeat for North Vietnam, not a victory as the press reported. Such reports, the military argued, aided the antiwar movement at home and turned the American public against the war. The press felt that the U.S. military had misled and lied to them in Vietnam and that officials consistently painted a much rosier picture of the war than the facts justified. Given the record of deception, the press, it was argued, was correct in being skeptical of the military. A view prevailed within the military that the free rein given journalists in Vietnam led to reporting that seriously damaged morale and turned American public opinion against its own troops. If news or information is a weapon, then, the generals argued, it should be controlled as a part of the war effort.

The war news issue surfaced again on October 25, 1983 when U.S. forces invaded the tiny island of Grenada. The Defense Department barred all reporters from covering the initial invasion. After 2 days of vigorous protests by the press, a pool of 12 reporters was flown in with a military escort. By the end of 1 week with the fighting winding down, 150 reporters were ferried to the island and allowed to stay overnight. The press, however, was not mollified. Walter Cronkite said the Reagan administration had seriously erred, arguing, "This is our foreign policy and we have a right to know what is happening, and there can be no excuse in denying the people that right" (cited in Hachten, 1999, p. 157). But, as in the later Gulf War, public opinion polls showed the American people generally supported the ban on press coverage. Max Frankel of *The New York Times* wrote, "The most astounding thing about the Grenada situation was the quick, facile assumption by some of the public that the press wanted to get in, not to witness the invasion on behalf of the people, but to sabotage it" (cited in Hachten, 1999, p. 157).

As a result of the furor, the Defense Department appointed a commission that recommended a select pool of reporters be allowed to cover the early stages of any surprise operation and share its information with other news organizations. This seemed a fair compromise between the military's need for surprise and the public's need for information.

The new guidelines were first tested in December 1989 when U.S. forces invaded Panama. The press arrangements failed miserably. The Pentagon did not get the 16-reporter pool into Panama until 4 hours after fighting began, and reporters were not allowed to file stories until 6 hours later. Most critics blamed the White House for the mix-up and for not insisting that the military facilitate press coverage.

THE FIRST WAR WITH SADDAM HUSSEIN

Global television came into its own as CNN and other broadcasters stationed in Iraq reported a war as it was happening, or as it appeared to be happening. After hostilities began early on January 17, 1991, reporters described antiaircraft tracers in the night sky of Baghdad and flashes of bomb explosions on the horizon. On succeeding nights, viewers were provided with live video reports from Tel Aviv and Riyadh of Scud missiles, some intercepted by Patriot missiles, exploding against the night sky and television reporters donning gas masks on camera.

The press talked of the "CNN effect"—millions anchored to their television sets hour after hour lest they miss the latest dramatic developments. Restaurants, movies, hotels, and gaming establishments all suffered business losses. Ratings for CNN soared five to ten times their prewar levels.

The Gulf War was a worldwide media event of astonishing proportions. Global television never had a larger or more interested audience for such a sustained period of time. Television became the first principal source of news for most people as well as a major source of military and political intelligence for both sides. CNN telecasts, including military briefings, were viewed in Baghdad as they were being received in Riyadh or Washington, DC, as well as in other non-Western countries.

Western journalists chafed at the restraints on news coverage of the war itself. Most coalition news came from military briefings and from carefully controlled and escorted pools of reporters. Some official news released at the briefings was actually "disinformation" intended to mislead the enemy, not inform the public. For example, viewers were led to believe that Patriot missiles were invariably successful in neutralizing Scud missiles; such was not the case.

Public opinion polls showed that the overwhelming majority of Americans supported both the war and the military's efforts to control the news; further, some favored more controls on press reporting. A *Los Angeles Times* Mirror poll found that 50% of the respondents considered themselves obsessed with war news, and nearly 80% felt the military was "telling as much as it can." About the same proportion thought that military censorship of press reporting may be "a good idea."

But after the war, many in the American press felt that the traditional right of U.S. reporters to accompany their combat forces and report news of war had been severely circumscribed. Michael Getler of *The Washington Post* wrote: "The Pentagon and U.S. Army Central Command conducted what is probably the most thorough and consistent wartime control of American reporters in modern times—a set of restrictions that in its totality and mindset seems to go beyond World War II, Korea and Vietnam" (Getler, 1991, p. 24).

President George Bush and the Pentagon followed a deliberate policy of keeping negative and unflattering news from the U.S. public lest it weaken support for the war. American casualties were reported, but there were few pictures of dead and wounded. Details of tactical failures and mishaps in the bombing campaign were not released, nor was the information that at least 24 female soldiers had been raped or sexually assaulted by American servicemen.

The shooting war itself started just as the evening news programs were beginning on January 17 at 6:30 p.m. Eastern Standard Time. The networks and CNN interrupted their prepared news shows to report that aerial bombing had begun in Baghdad. Then followed one of most memorable nights in television history: the opening phases of a major conflict reported in real time—as it actually happened—by reporters in Iraq, Saudi Arabia, and Washington.

During this early bombing phase of the war, the Pentagon placed restrictions on interviews with troops and returning pilots. Reporters could go into the field only in designated pools. (One reporter likened a press pool to group of senior citizens on a conducted tour.) All interviews with soldiers were subject to censorship before they could be released. Most information came from the daily briefings held by military spokesmen in both Riyadh and at the Pentagon but much of this information was rather general, vague, and deliberately incomplete. The military had coherent arguments for its restrictive policies. Destroying Iraq's military command and communications capability was a high priority of the bombing strategy, and it was important to withhold useful information, via the media, that would reveal troop movements and intentions of coalition forces. Keeping Iraq's forces off-balance and without reliable information was a key part of U.S. strategy.

However, some news executives and critics claimed the press restrictions went well beyond security concerns and were aimed at both preventing politically damaging disclosures by soldiers and shielding the American public from seeing the brutal aspects of war. If the war had been unsuccessful, the press would have had difficulty reporting the negative aspects. With more than 1,600 reporters in the theater, only about 100 could be accommodated by the pools to report news about the 500,000 American forces. As the ground war began, the large press corps became increasingly restive and frustrated at this lack of access.

The response of some reporters was to "freelance"—to avoid the pools and go off on their own. Malcolm Browne (1991) reported,

> Some reporters were hiding out in American Marine or Army field units, given G.I. uniforms and gear to look inconspicuous, enjoying the affection (and protection of the units) they're trying to cover—concealed by the officers and troops from the handful of press-hating commanders who strive to keep the battlefield free of wandering journalists. (p. 45)

Had the ground war been longer, more heavily contested, and taken a higher toll in U.S. casualties, relations between the military and the freelancing journalists probably would have turned quite acrimonious. But these journalists felt they were doing what they were supposed to do in time of foreign war—maintain the flow of information that Americans need to know when 500,000 of their countrymen are at risk.

The Gulf War certainly conditioned viewers everywhere to keep their television sets tuned to CNN (or its future imitators) during times of high crisis. Perhaps the news today places too much emphasis on immediate and fast-breaking news "as it happens." Video shots of F15s roaring off runways, of smart bombs scoring direct hits, of Tomahawk missiles flying through Baghdad, and tank formations rolling through the desert made memorable viewing. Yet after the fog of war cleared, the press and the public found that the Gulf War had not been quite what they thought it had been. In the Gulf War, hundreds of journalists were in the war theater, but were allowed little freedom to cover the actual fighting. On the Iraqi side, the few foreign reporters in Baghdad were severely restricted. From all indications, both the U.S. military and the Bush Administration were pleased with the results of their media policy and would do the same thing again. But among the press, the general conclusion was that the press had been unduly and even illegally denied access to information about the war. (In the Iraq war in 2003, things would be quite different.)

LESSER CONFLICTS

The incursion of U.S. Marines into Somalia in December 1992 was intended to provide military protection to the relief organizations trying to feed starving Somalis caught in the crossfire of warring clans. Under these conditions, the Pentagon decided not to place any restraints on the media. Kurtz (1993) called what happened the most embarrassing moment ever in media–military relations:

> The infamous night in December 1992 when Navy SEALS hitting the beach in Somalia were surrounded by a small army of reporters and photographers who blinded them with television lights, clamored for interviews, and generally acted like obnoxious adolescents. That sorry performance, turning a humanitarian mission to aid starving Africans into a Fellini-esque photo op, underscored what the Pentagon had been saying for years: that the press simply could not discipline itself, that reporters would blithely endanger the safety of American troops for the sake of journalistic drama. (p. 215)

It was not one of the media's finer days.

David Hackworth (1992) of *Newsweek* wrote, "to lurch from thought control to no control is plain stupid. When the press corps beats the Marine Corps to the beach, everyone loses" (p. 33). The Pentagon wanted full coverage of Somalia so no controls were placed on the press, and what resulted was a confused circus. There are those, however, who suspect that the Pentagon deliberately orchestrated the fiasco to make the media look bad.

The situation in Somalia raised the question of whether the media, by its heavy barrage of pictures and stories of starving Somalis, pushed President Bush to send troops on their humanitarian mission. The answer is unclear, but Bush did react by committing U.S. armed forces to a limited and supposedly doable assignment of famine relief. (On the other hand, despite horrific pictures of death, destruction, and "ethnic cleansing" from Bosnia, the United States refused for many months to get involved militarily.)

When the Somalia assignment expanded in the early Clinton administration to include warlord hunting, it provoked a devastating firefight in the streets of Mogadishu. When 18 U.S. soldiers were killed and the pictures of a dead U.S. soldier being dragged through the street was shown on U.S. television, the American public was unprepared to accept casualties when vital U.S. interests were not at stake. The White House soon announced the United States was getting out of Somalia. So it was said that television pictures got the Marines into Somalia and more pictures got them abruptly out.

James Hoge (1994), editor of *Foreign Affairs*, commented:

> From its understanding of Vietnam came the military's subsequent emphasis on quick solutions, limited media access and selective release of smart weapons imagery. The public, however, will not remain dazzled when interventions become difficult. As in Vietnam, public attitudes ultimately hinge

on questions about the rightness, purpose and costs of policy—not television images. (p. 139)

The "peaceful" landing in Haiti in September 1994 provided more perspective on military and media relations. When it appeared that a full-scale military invasion to oust the military rulers would take place, U.S. media were planning the most minutely documented war coverage ever. Several hundred reporters and photographers from television networks, newspapers, and magazines were already in Haiti, with the most advanced equipment ever brought to a war zone. The Pentagon had promised more cooperation than ever, and journalists said they would not be relying on the military for primary access.

However, White House and Pentagon officials, in a meeting with television representatives asked for a broadcast blackout of 8 hours. The Clinton Administration also wanted to restrict reporters to their hotels until military commanders gave them permission to go to the fighting. In this case, a press and military showdown was averted when U.S. forces landed without incident in Haiti.

Nor were there any frictions between press and military in Bosnia when NATO imposed a military truce and thousands of U.S. and NATO peacekeeping troops occupied that troubled land in late 1995. There the Pentagon policy was to encourage friendly relations with reporters and broadcasters. GIs carried a 16-page guide to Bosnia with a section devoted to "Meeting the Media," which instructed a soldier that he or she "can be an excellent unofficial spokesperson."

NATO'S AERIAL WAR AGAINST YUGOSLAVIA

After NATO bombs started falling on Serbia and Kosovo in 1999, military relations with the press deteriorated abruptly. Critics said the lack of detailed after-action reports—routinely provided in past conflicts—had made it impossible to assess NATO's claims that they were steadily dismantling Milosevic's war-making powers. At both the Pentagon and at NATO headquarters in Brussels, spokesmen stubbornly refused to provide specific information about bombing sorties. These policies were considered even less forthcoming than in the Gulf War, which the press had considered overly restrictive. Of course, NATO had its reasons: the need to hold the somewhat reluctant NATO alliance together and the need to retain the support of American public opinion for the military action. But most journalists covering the war were highly critical.

Yet, of course, the war was reported and, in some basic ways, differently than any previous battlefield coverage. After being forced to watch 78 days of bombing through the lenses of official video cameras, some 2,700 journalists had a chance to see for themselves when NATO troops rolled into Kosovo in June. Even though military censors blocked specific information, satellite communications enabled reporters from Brussels to Kukes, Albania, and other points, to triangulate information more easily than in previous conflicts.

According to editors, the key device for putting together information into coherent stories was the satellite telephone and, more broadly, satellite communications. Just as CNN's 24-hour cable TV service first caught on in the Gulf War, the satellite uplink was the information medium for the air war. "Instantaneous communication has changed things," said Andrew Rosenthal, then foreign editor of the *New York Times*. He continued, "The ability of a reporter on the Macedonian border to call a reporter on the Albanian border or to call a reporter in Brussels or Washington instantly made a huge difference. Newspapers were able to put together groups of reporters to do joint efforts in a way that was previously impossible" (cited in Barringer, 1999, p. C1).

For television, the same satellite technology allowed a profusion of images to be transmitted at great speed. When the vivid images were of the fate of Kosovar refugees or fleeing Serbian troops, the emotional impact of television was great indeed. Some thought such reportage helped justify the humanitarian aspects of the hostilities and convinced otherwise dubious viewers to support the NATO effort.

The expanded role for the Internet and cable television news meant there were far more outlets for instantaneous reporting and analysis. CNN, MSNBC, and Fox News Channel also offered loud and compelling debates about the conflict, even though much of it was discounted by critics as lacking in serious depth and context. For the first time, the Internet was a player in war reporting, providing a plethora of Web sites presenting war issues and some information from diverse angles: Serb, Albanian, Republican, Democratic, and ranging from the depth of BBC to the fervid nationalism of Belgrade news outlets.

As a result, some observers thought that the sum total of these trends amounted to sharper, speedier coverage. David Halberstam said, "Despite all the restrictions and just God-awful limitations and dangers, there were enough different people in different places to give you the dimensions you needed" (cited in Barringer, 1999, p. C1).

Even though CNN had more competition this time—BBC World, MSNBC, Fox—than in the Gulf War, the Atlanta cable network emerged from the Yugoslav conflict in a much enhanced international role for its news dissemination as a global 24-hour cable news channel. During the Gulf War, some 10 million households outside the United States had access to CNN. In the Yugoslav conflict, that number jumped to 150 million households.

The air war in Yugoslavia demonstrated that the democracies of America and NATO are still unwilling to be candid and forthcoming with reliable information to their own peoples when engaged in hostile actions against other states. As in the Gulf War, the Pentagon gave misleading and exaggerated accounts of the effectiveness of the aerial campaign over Kosovo. Joint Chiefs Chairman General Henry Shelton claimed that NATO's air forces had killed "around 120 tanks" "about 220 armored personnel carriers" and "up to 450 artillery and mortar pieces." But months later, *Newsweek*, quoting a suppressed Air Force report, reported on May 15, 2000 that the number of targets verifiably destroyed was a tiny fraction of those claimed: 14 tanks, not 120; 18 personnel carriers, not 220; and 20 artillery pieces, not 450. Out of the 744 "confirmed" strikes by NATO pilots during the war, the Air Force investigators later found evidence of just 58.

Yet, despite such deceptions, the events surrounding the air war also showed that today's news organizations can still get much of the news out if they pursue the story with vigor and imagination and make full use of the varied tools of communications technology.

THE WAR IN AFGHANISTAN

During the opening weeks of the Afghan war against the Taliban regime and Al Quaeda, almost all significant information was released by the Pentagon far from the battlefield and much of it was considered dated and vague. Defense Secretary, Donald Rumsfeld, following the practices of the first Gulf war, set up restrictive policies on the release of news, saying that the nature of the war on terrorism made the constraints necessary. Several times, Rumsfeld said that federal officials who leaked information may be in violation of federal law. A poll done at the time found that half of the respondents said the military should have more control over war news than the news media have.

Because reporters could not accompany the military units into the remote combat zones, reporters early in the war had to do what they did in Cambodia decades earlier: strike out on their own. As a result, the Afghan war was very dangerous for reporters. In the first days, eight correspondents were killed—more fatalities than the U.S. Special Forces had suffered at that time. One reporter said that we know less but we are more of a target. Yet some excellent reporting was done by correspondents who reported directly back to the United States by satellite phones. And as the war went better, the Pentagon became less restrictive of the press and permitted reporters to relay the good news to the American public.

THE WAR AGAINST SADDAM'S IRAQ

The invasion of Iraq and the toppling of the Saddam Hussein's regime was quickly accomplished by coalition forces—mostly American and some British—in the spring of 2003. Millions watched the most heavily televised war in history. As in the 1991 Iraq war, hundreds of journalists and photographers were in theater and used their new and refined communication gadgets—video phones, cell phones, e-mail, and Internet—to flood the world with words and images.

Combat journalism has changed as has warfare itself changed. Technology has markedly altered how wars are waged and for how long. The reporters use new tools to gather news and send it much faster than ever to their audiences. In Iraq, the typical television war correspondent found he needed this essential carry-along gear that weighed about 76 pounds: a digital video camera, 5 lbs.; microphones, cables, and batteries, 10 lbs.; camera tripod, 10 lbs.; 2 satellite phones, 20 lbs. each; laptop computer, 6 lbs.; and night scope lens, 5 lbs.

Reporters in Iraq were comfortable with their technology as never before. Television reporters carried hand-held video cameras and print journalists have traded their 70 pound satellite phones of the 1991 war for handy models that can be held up to their ear. High-speed Internet lines in the desert meant that journalists could make a connection almost anywhere. One reporter said that today's digital devices enable a reporter to provide a more intimate and multifaceted view of the war than would have been possible before. The high quality and diverse nature of the reporting reflected this.

But the most important policy innovation of this war was the Pentagon's unexpected decision to let journalists be "embedded" with the military units fighting their way across Iraq. For the first time since World War II and on a scale never seen in military history, some 600 journalists, photographers, and television crew members—about 100 of them from foreign and international news organizations, including the Arab network Al Jazeera, had access to troops in combat. Embedding was the greatest innovation (and improvement) in press/military relations in many years. The results of the experiment were generally positive. The American public had a front row seat during the invasion with embedded journalists providing a steady stream of news reports, anecdotes, human interest stories along with dramatic and vivid video and photos.

One observer, Rem Rieder (2003), commented:

> Now that the fighting has stopped, it's clear that the great embedding experiment was a home run as far as the news media—and the American people—are concerned. Six hundred journalists had a first-hand view of the combat. That's a far cry from the first Gulf war when reporters were at the mercy of government briefers and that misbegotten press pool. (p. 60)

But there were negative aspects to embedding. Some saw the reporters as tools of the military—only turning out good news. And it was dangerous duty—several correspondents were killed, including David Bloom of NBC News and Michael Kelly, editor of *Atlantic Monthly*. A total of 13 reporters were killed in Iraq in 2003.

Another important broadcast dimension of the war was the role of transnational satellite networks in the Arab world. They became major sources of information for Arabs and were in effect challenging the hegemony of the American and British media. Al Jazeera, a 24-hour Qatar-based news channel, reached more than 45 million people, broadcasting a view of the conflict very different from, say, CNN or BBC World. Al Jazeera and other Arab broadcasters were accused by the West of airing propaganda but millions of Arabs were for the first time getting news and views that differed from those heard on their own closed media systems.

How good was the televised reporting of the war? At their best, reporters managed to humanize the war without becoming cheerleaders for the military. News organizations went to great expense to provide thorough coverage.

But critics questioned how clear and complete the coverage was. One journalist said the war was too big a canvas to capture on the small screen of television. Yet at the same time, there was so much television coverage that viewers sometimes became confused. The effectiveness of television was limited by the limitations of the medium itself—the mismatch between images and words. Vivid pictures from one fixed position in a battle of no great consequence could overwhelm any context provided by voice-over correspondent. Embedded reporters could not report visually a key aspect of the ground war—that incessant bombing attacks had attrited Iraqi ground forces before battles began. And sometimes, reporters were too downbeat about the war's early setbacks.

After the fall of Baghdad, the war changed into another and unexpected phase—an episodic and persistent guerrilla war waged against the occupying forces. Attacks against American forces took a steady toll of American soldiers. The better media maintained full coverage of the confused and disheartening affairs in Iraq throughout 2003, even though the attention of cable news and the public's interest seemed to veer off to cover "celebrity justice" stories.

CONCLUSION

All too often, though, in recent times, the U.S. press has been inhibited or even barred from fully covering wars on which it has historically and traditionally reported. Despite the popularity of the Pentagon's embedding of journalists during the Iraq war, there no real indications that the White House and Congress would act to further extend access to war news. This is important because the U.S. Supreme Court has ruled that the press, in order to inform the public, has a First Amendment right to be in those places that "historically" and "traditionally" it has had the right to cover, such as trials and town meetings. The Court has also ruled that the press has a First Amendment right to be present at all "public" events. Certainly a military action by American forces lasting more than several hours or a full-scale war is a public event.

The press has no right to report sensitive military information that could aid an enemy and would not want to do so, but it does have a right to be there to keep a watchful eye on the military, just as it does at a criminal trial. No modern war has been fought as quickly and effectively and with as few allied casualties as by the American-led forces in the two wars with Iraq, although we know now that much unflattering and negative news was kept from the public.

And when wars are unsuccessful, as they sometimes are, with incompetent leadership, confused tactics, and unnecessary casualties, it is essential that the press, as independent representatives of the public and of the soldiers, be there to report what has occurred. The citizens of Iraq had no independent press reporting to them about the military disasters and political incompetence that led to the battlefield deaths of thousands of their young men—a basic difference between a democracy and a dictatorship.

The Supreme Court is unlikely to come to the defense of the U.S. press in this matter. Perhaps the best hope of the press is to protest and lobby until a significant portion of the public supports their right to know. In the 1991 Gulf War, the U.S. news media and their owners did not complain loudly and vehemently enough about the pool and censorship restrictions before the bombs started dropping. Nor has the press expressed much concern about NATO's news restrictions. A sitting president like George W. Bush or Bill Clinton is not likely to modify such restrictions of free expression in wartime until forced to by political pressure.

Ironically, the greatly expanded capability of global television to report instantly on a modern war provides another rationale for governments to control and censor war news. Yet when American or European journalists are denied access to war news, the rest of the world is denied access as well.

News and Comment on the Internet

Like some raging computer virus, the Net seems to be devouring the media culture, shattering the usual definitions of news and eclipsing more traditional subjects. The so-called old media are invading this brave new world with near-revolutionary fervor, fueling a growth industry that might be called e-news.

—Howard Kurtz

The blogging revolution undermines media tyrants.

—Andrew Sullivan

Internet news is rapidly becoming a rival and partner of print and broadcast news. Most of the online news sources are, in fact, tied to broadcasters, magazines, and newspapers. News on the Internet is a moving target and we can only offer a snapshot of this "bird on the wing." Everything about the Internet and the World Wide Web, it has been said, is about the future—and the future has been arriving faster than anyone predicted.

The relevance of the Internet for journalism and the news business has been apparent for some time. Publishers, broadcasters, and journalists were early adopters of this explosive information revolution. However, neither they, nor anyone else, seem to know just where this brave new world of communication is headed. (A few years ago, few had even foreseen the potential of the Internet itself.)

Certainly no consensus exists as to how much journalism will be changed by the Internet, but no one doubts that change is happening. The future of cyberspace itself is murky and yet exciting. Newspaper publishers and other media managers worry about how they can fit into the changing scene and still prosper. Concerned journalists wonder as well how the traditional values and standards of good journalism can survive in the turbulent world of the Internet. Internet news has a strong future but is quite unlikely to replace either print or broadcast news.

A newspaper is, of course, a business enterprise and must survive in the marketplace. At a time when some publishers were downsizing staffs and trimming costs to increase profitability, many other newspapers (and broadcasters) were investing heavily in the new electronic or interactive journalism. Although no one seems to know when they will make real money on the Web, the Internet system is on the verge of becoming a mass news medium itself.

In 1994, there were 20 newspapers online—that is, with electronic editions; by mid-1999, there were 4,925 worldwide, 2,799 of them in the United States. The numbers keep going up and the Web sites have been carrying more and more news as well as comment, opinion, and rumor. The media conglomerates as well as cable and network broadcasters are in hot competition with print media for the proliferating Internet viewers.

Currently, some of the most popular and widely used Web sites carrying news are MSNBC.com; CNN.com; ABCNews.com; USAToday.com; NYTimes.com; Washingtonpost.com; BBC.CO.UK.com; LATimes.com; Foxnews.com; and APBnews.com. For important breaking news stories, these are the sites concerned Americans turn to for reliable news and comment.

However, Internet journalism (and the "old media") have been greatly influenced by the so-called "bloggers." In the strict sense, a blogger is someone's online record of the Web sites he or she visits. Blogger is a contraction of "Web logger." Web loggers have been called one-person Internet blabbermouths who pop off to anyone who will listen. They criticize each other but some of the best take on, sometimes unfairly, the big newspapers and networks. They provide a kind of instant feedback loop for media corporations. Some equate them with the more lively editorial pages of earlier times. Web loggers are having an important impact on the "old media" as well as on public opinion over salient political and social issues.

Bloggers have been given credit for (a) helping to topple Senator Trent Lott and *The New York Times* editor, Howell Raines, from their high offices; (b) for helping to organize and coordinate protests over the Iraq War; (c) for forcing mighty CBS to back down from showing a controversial docudrama about Ronald Reagan; and (d) for boosting the presidential hopes of Howard Dean with both followers and cash contributions. No doubt about it—bloggers can turn out the partisans; CBS received 90,000 e-mails protesting the Reagan television drama and the FCC received 520,000 comments, mostly from people opposed to lifting limits on television license ownerships. These campaigns have utilized e-mails and cell phones as well as the Internet.

Bloggers write personal online diaries and commentaries with the best of them weighing in on hot-button issues. They often report news items that national media miss or suppress and also provide links to other bloggers with something to say. Anyone can be a blogger and no one is in charge. Although there are a multitude of them, few can make a living out of blogging. However, two bloggers who have are veteran journalist Mickey Kaus, whose "Kausfiles" is carried on Slate, the online magazine, and Andrew Sullivan, a former editor of *New Republic*, who reportedly pulled in $79,000 during a 1-week pledge drive. His conservative Web site received over 1.6 million visits during 1 month

Most Web logs are produced by individuals with a passion for a particular subject. But after some hesitation, some print and broadcast media have joined in with their own.

Here is a sampling: *ABC News* publishes a blog, The Note, for political junkies; FoxNews.com publishes ten blogs; MSNBC.com puts out six; and *The Wall Street Journal* publishes Best of the Web, by James Taranto.

For those who just want to read *about* journalism on the Internet, *Brill's Content*, (now defunct) recommended the following sites: 1. Jim Romenesko's Media News (poynter.org/mediagossip); 2. Arts and Letters Daily (cybereditions.com\aldaily); 3. Salon Media (salon.com/media); 4. Online Journalism Review (ojr.org); 5. Feed Daily (feedmag.com); and 6. Slate.com. (Best of the Web, 2000, p. 68).

PROFITS AND LOSSES

For the news media, two basic uncertainties persist about interactive journalism:

> First, will the public pay for electronic news on a medium where information, after a basic user's fee, is free? Second, will advertising displayed on Web pages "sell" and lead to profitable results on such an anarchic medium?

Hence, the media's rush to online services can be seen as driven by both fear and greed. The fear comes from the threat to the newspapers' advertising base, especially classified advertisements. The computer provides point-and-click technology, the ease of getting answers quickly, and this is complete with pictures and sound from great amounts of electronic information. Greed is stimulated by the possibility of large sums to be made when a profitable "model" is developed that counts and categorizes every visitor to a Web site. Internet publishing could then be a profitable marriage of newspapers' advertising bases with franchise strengths. Publishers also hope to attract the younger Internet users who no longer read newspapers.

Internet journalism has been producing a lot of red ink but recently there have been signs that a small but diverse range of journalistic sites have begun to turn a profit or are quite near to it. But most sites still lose money and no business model has emerged that so far seems to offer a key to success. Success may depend on a combination of approaches: banner and classified advertising, as well as subscriptions for niche publications and electronic commerce. Some observers are betting on subscriptions and the fact that the idea that everything on the Internet should be free is starting to die. Most quality Internet-based news sites will in time have to be supported by subscription fees and will have ads. *The Wall Street Journal* has led the way by charging an annual fee for access to its online version of the paper. In 2003, its online readership was over 400,000.

RAPIDLY EXPANDING USE OF INTERNET

So far, the numbers of potential users of interactive news media are still small compared with total newspaper readership but the numbers are growing fast. Kohut (2000) reported that numerous recent polls have shown the public's appetite for Internet news and information is growing rapidly. At the end of 1999, half of the American public had access to the Internet, up from about 40% just a year before and from 23% just 3 years ago. About two in three of those people say they go online for news at least once a week. About 12% say they read the news online every day. (Only 6% reported doing so in April 1998.)

For many Americans, these news sites have become primary sources of information. Eleven percent of adults said in an October 1999 survey that they mostly rely on the Internet for national and international news (That figure was 6% the previous January.) The findings are more impressive among key demographic groups. Among college graduates, under 50, Kohut (2000) found that 23% said they principally depend on the Internet for national and international news, rivaling the percentage who said this about network TV news (26%), radio (27%), and local TV (21%). Only cable news (32%) and newspapers (46%) scored better in this important demographic category. So for that influential segment, the Internet is already a mass medium.

Now the downside. There is some evidence so far that the Internet may not be a great boon to civic engagement. Some surveys show people use the

Internet for information that interests only themselves rather than to seek out general enlightenment. Thirty-eight percent go online for updates on stock quotes and sports scores, 41% to follow up on news they had heard about what interests them, and 44% are motivated by the ability to search the news for a particular topic. Considerably fewer (29%) say that they go online for general news updates or to keep informed about the day's events. Kohut (2000) cautions that trends may be slow to emerge because the news habits of Internet newcomers evolve slowly. It takes time for people to understand how to use the Internet to suit their own individual needs. And at any given time, there are a lot of newcomers trying to work it out.

Another study, done at Stanford, found that the Internet is leading to a rapid shift away from the "old" media. The study reported that 60% of regular Internet users said they reduced their television viewing, and one-third said they spent less time reading newspapers. The study found that 55% of Americans have access to the Internet and of these, 36% said they were online 5 hours per week. Over all, the study found the Internet is causing many Americans to spend less time with family and friends, less time shopping in stores, and more time working at home after hours, thus creating a broad new wave of social isolation in the United States, raising the specter of an atomized world without human contact or emotion. Similar concerns were expressed when television first became pervasive. (Markoff, 2000)

THE INTERNET AS THE NEXT MASS MEDIUM?

The Web incorporates many elements of various print and electronic media that have preceded it; computers can be used to send and receive text, sound, still images, and video clips. Yet for all its versatility, the Web is not expected to replace its media predecessors but to take a place alongside them as a social, cultural, and economic force in its own right. The history of mass communication has taught us that new media do not replace old media, but instead supplement and complement them; radio did not replace newspapers and television did not replace radio or the movies.

The Web's complementary role is already evident: Along with the steadily increasing numbers of newspapers and magazines with Web sites, many radio stations and all the major television networks have Web sites, publicizing and providing additional information about their programs and performers. One of the big players is NBC, which with its partner, Microsoft, puts out the top-rated Msnbc.com site—an elaborate online version of MSNBC, its 24-hour cable news channel. So NBC's various news outlets—*NBC Evening News* with Tom Brokaw, and the *Today Show* on broadcast television, MSNBC and CNBC on cable, and Msnbc.com online all share content as well as anchors and reporters and mutually publicize and promote each other.

Another recent trend is for the media to provide "portals" rather than just Web sites for their online publications. When the *Boston Globe* created Boston.com in 1995, it did more than create a Web site for the paper, instead it started a regional online site and invited all other Boston media to become a part of it. A "portal" becomes a starting point for computer users when they surf and it guides them to a wide variety of services. (Portals are not new; *Yahoo* and *Lycos* are well-known examples.) The idea is that if a portal offers enough services in a single place, its online audience will grow, convincing advertisers to buy more space. The strategy is that the newspaper would be the first stop on everyone's electronic journey into a metropolitan area. The shift to portals suggests a change in news media strategy: to be successful, online newspapers must be more than merely newspapers online.

JOURNALISM CAREERS ONLINE

Interactive journalism is already developing a new generation of young journalists who are attracted to online jobs for the money, opportunity, excitement, and a way to avoid unpaid internships and small-town newspaper jobs. The *Chicago Tribune*, for example, has a staff of 20 who work exclusively for the Internet edition—writing stories, taking pictures, using video cameras, and even creating digital pages. The young people entering the uncertain world of digital journalism now are the ones who will bring about important changes later. The older generation of journalists, who wonder whether it is really journalism, have been much slower to recognize the changes that are coming.

Some reporters are in demand often because of their expertise with computers and the Internet that they have learned on their jobs. Simon (1999) commented:

> Sometimes we fail to appreciate the pace at which technology has been changing our jobs. Think for a moment: palm-sized computers provide features useful to news gathering that were not available on the most powerful laptops just five years ago. With a well-organized laptop and a good Internet connection, a reporter in virtually any part of the world has access to the same information—whether from his own archived files or another database—as someone in the newsroom. With digital cameras, photographers file their shots through e-mail so quickly that an editor can look at the image and, before the event is

over, call back on a cell phone to request a different angle. It is in computer-assisted reporting where the real revolution is taking place, not only on the big analytical projects but also in nuts-and- bolts reporting. New tools and techniques have made it possible for journalists to dig up vital information on deadline, to quickly add depth and context. (p. 19)

Without question, print journalists have benefited immensely from the Internet. A 1999 survey of managing editors and business editors found that 73% said they went online at least once a day, compared with 48% in 1998. In 1994, only 17% went online daily. The study also found changing trends on how print journalists use the Internet. In 1999, the most popular use was research, displacing e-mail, although both were up from 1998. Ninety percent of respondents used the Internet to research articles or as a research source, up from 74% in 1998. Some 83% used e-mail, up from 80% in 1998. Half of the respondents used the Internet to search for ideas for articles, up from 30% in 1998 (Fass, 2000).

CHALLENGES TO PRESS FREEDOM

Only 25 years after its development, the personal computer's potential as a medium for ideas, information, and news flowing freely around the globe was being recognized. At the same time, the virtual press was already facing serious legal challenges over what could and could not be transmitted over computer networks. Legal restrictions, imposed here or abroad, could very well prevent the personal computer from reaching its full potential.

The sweeping communications bill passed by Congress in February 1996 banned pornography over computer networks and set penalties for those convicted of distributing indecent material to minors. Civil liberties groups quickly vowed a court battle over the provisions that would block the free flow of material over computer networks. Congressional committees debating the communications bill rejected the idea that the Internet is the electronic equivalent of the printing press and thus should enjoy the full free-speech protections of the First Amendment. Instead, Congress opted to regard the Internet as a broadcast medium, subject to Government regulation and eligible for only some of the Constitutional rights given to newspapers.

The irony is that the same words, printed on ink and paper are fully protected by the First Amendment, but once those words go on the Internet and become bits traveling in packets over wires and fibers, they lose their protection. But the protection returns when the words are reprinted on paper.

The potential erosion of free speech is due in part to sincere efforts to protect children from pornography being transmitted over the Internet. Despite the existence of current laws punishing those who make and distribute child pornography in any medium, some saw the opportunity in this new medium to banish words and images that heretofore had been considered indecent but not illegal expression. At about the same time, CompuServe voluntarily denied its 4 million subscribers access to over 200 newsgroups, because a prosecutor in Germany found them offensive and had threatened legal action. Many technologies already exist to let parents restrict areas of the Internet and online services that children can visit. But these are only partial solutions. Some advocates of the Internet fear the possibility that this freest and most open of all media may be restricted to carrying ideas and information only suitable for children. It may be years and many hard-fought legal battles before guidelines defining legal protections for the Internet are firmly established.

However, a major advance for free speech occurred in June 1997 when the U.S. Supreme Court declared unconstitutional the Communications Decency Act, which made it a crime to send or display "indecent" material online in a way available to minors. The unanimous decision was the Court's first effort to extend First Amendment principles into cyberspace. The court held that speech on the Internet is entitled to the highest level of First Amendment protection, similar to that given to newspapers and books. This is in contrast to more limited First Amendment rights accorded to expression on broadcast and cable television, where the court has tolerated a wide amount of government regulation.

This decision was not the final word. But the decision bodes well for the future of the Internet as a purveyor of serious news and information on what is being recognized as the most participatory marketplace of mass expression the world has yet seen.

Yet another setback did come in June 2003, when the U.S. Supreme Court upheld a federal law that requires public libraries to install antipornography filters on all computers providing Internet access as a condition of continuing to receive federal subsidies and grants. The intent of the law was to prevent children from viewing pornography online but the effect was to deny adults the ability to see a substantial amount of information online.

INTERNET VERSUS FOREIGN AUTOCRATS

The potential of the Internet as a technology of freedom has been demonstrated in recent years by clashes between computer users and authoritarian regimes in Serbia, Singapore, and China.

In Belgrade, President Slobadan Milosevic, faced with large antigovernment demonstrations, forced the last of the independent media, the station Radio B92, off the air and thus set off a technological revolt in December 1996. Tens of thousands of students, professors, professionals, and journalists connected their computers to Internet Web sites around the world. B92 soon began digital broadcasts in Serbo-Croatian and English over audio Internet links, and its Web site took over the reporting of the protests that had been triggered by annulled elections.

Milosevic quickly backed off, and the radio station was soon back on the air, but the event showed the protesters the potential for bypassing government transmitters, news agencies, and television studios to get their message out across Serbia and abroad. (In the 1999 bombing war over Serbia and Kosovo, the Internet played a significant role as an alternative to official government propaganda.)

On the other side of the world, the small, affluent, and authoritarian nation of Singapore believes it can control the technologies of freedom that threaten its one-party rule. To control television, satellites dishes have been banned and the country has been wired for cable television, which enables the government to screen out objectionable material. Controlling cyberspace will be harder, but Singapore is trying. Use of the Internet was encouraged by equipping schools with computers and urging Singaporeans to link up with the computer network by dialing a local telephone number. Thus, the government is able to monitor use of the Internet that goes through the local servers. Singapore has already blocked material it considers pornographic. Local officials concede that some users can bypass this system by dialing into the Internet through foreign phone systems. In the future, however, Singapore is not expected to be able to maintain controls over the flow of electronic information.

The People's Republic of China has also been trying to regulate and monitor the Internet, which has been used by human rights groups to communicate with dissidents within China. In January 2000, the Chinese government issued stern new regulations intended to control the release of information on the Internet, underscoring the love-hate relationship between the government and cyberspace. The new regulations specifically govern the posting and dissemination of *state secrets*—a vague term relating to information the government has not sanctioned. The regulations may have little direct impact because other laws already cover such situations. Enforcement would be difficult as China now has over 250 million cell phones and 78 million Internet users, plus many Internet cafes and free e-mail services. However, a computer technician recently was given

2 years in prison for providing 30,000 Chinese e-mail addresses to dissidents overseas.

RUMORS AND CONSPIRACY THEORIES

One of the strongest arguments for increasing the presence of serious journalism on the Internet concerns the wild rumors and unfounded conspiracy theories that often fly through cyberspace in an age of easy global communication. Often mainstream media reports are distorted and gross assumptions are made about the government's capacity for malevolence; and on occasion, some stories and theories are just fabricated.

When TWA Flight 800 exploded off Long Island in July 1996, killing everyone on board, investigators focused on three possible causes: a bomb, mechanical failure, or a terrorist missile. Within 36 hours after the disaster, a message posted on an Internet discussion site suggested a darker possibility: "Did the Navy do it? It is interesting how much evidence there is that it was hit by a missile." Within days, numerous Internet writers speculated that the jet was downed by accidental friendly fire from a U.S. Navy ship on a training cruise. Such a blunder, according to the evolving theory, was quickly covered up by a conspiracy involving U.S. investigators, the military, and President Clinton. Although it was weak, the rumor hung around despite official efforts to discredit it.

Four months later, the theory gained new life when Pierre Salinger, a veteran journalist and former spokesman for President John Kennedy, told an audience in France that he had a document showing that Flight 800 had been shot down by the Navy. Because of Salinger's reputation, the theory once again bounced around the news media, particularly on television news. The story had a familiar ring to it, so CNN called Salinger and confirmed that Salinger's document was a printout of the Internet message posted anonymously 4 months earlier.

What formerly was considered just gossip takes on a new credibility when it appears on the Internet. Clifford Stoll, an Internet critic, said

Gossip's been blessed by the computer and sprinkled with techno holy water. The gossip that comes across the Internet comes in precisely the same format as does professional news, Wall Street reports, and other important factual information. (cited in Wald, 1996, p. 5)

Net watchers say that such wild, unfounded rumors and conspiracy theories can run into the hundreds at any one time.

Obviously, the news media can play an important role by providing reliable, disinterested, and professionally sound news and information to counter and shoot down some of the wild rumors or just plain gossip on the Internet.

In conclusion, one thing that can be said with some certainty about the future of journalism on the Internet is that more changes and innovations are coming fast. But for many millions, the Internet has already taken its place as a *news* medium.

CHAPTER

13

Educating Journalists

By maintaining close relations between journalism and liberal arts, the [journalism] faculty hopes that the students will not only come to see how much the exercise of their technique depends on content but will habitually employ their humanistic knowledge in their journalistic exercises.

—David P. Host

Journalism has been taught at a number of colleges and universities for about 100 years. Willard G. Bleyer began teaching a journalism course at the University of Wisconsin in 1905, and his scholarly interests later greatly influenced the field. The country's first separate School of Journalism, with newspaperman Walter Williams as dean, began in 1908 at the University of Missouri. The Pulitzer School of Journalism at Columbia University, backed with a $2 million gift from the *New York World* publisher, enrolled its first class in 1912.

There was a widespread belief that the nation's newspapers could be improved and elevated if the journalists themselves were better educated as well as more ethical and public-spirited. Some impetus for journalism education certainly came from public revulsion toward the sensationalism and excesses of yellow journalism, which was so prominent at the time. The growth of journalism education has been steady and at times explosive, especially since broadening its curriculum to include radio and television, advertising, public relations, plus communication theory and processes. As such, the field has paralleled and mirrored the growth of mass communication in general.

THE INFLUENCE OF WILLARD BLEYER

Journalism education generally had its beginnings in English departments with an emphasis on techniques courses—reporting, news writing, editing, design, and photography—often taught by former journalists. Among the pioneer teachers, perhaps the most influential was Willard Bleyer of Wisconsin, who was an English professor from a family of Milwaukee newspapermen. Bleyer advocated integrating journalism education with the social sciences, and, through his own research on journalism history, he provided an example and impetus for scholarly research about journalism.

In 1906, he laid out a junior–senior curriculum of course work in economics, political science, history, English, and journalism; he subsequently added sociology, psychology, and the natural sciences. He took journalism out of the humanities into social studies; in time, the new field followed his lead. He specified a 4-year bachelor's program of courses that would be one-fourth journalism and three-fourths social sciences and humanities. This became the model for many journalism programs and decades later became the basic command of accreditation of journalism programs, of which Bleyer was an early advocate.

Bleyer gave high priority to the reporting of public affairs, was often critical of press performance, and advocated academic study and research about the press and its interaction with politics and society. Besides techniques courses, Bleyer stressed the study of journalism history, legal aspects, ethics, and professional concerns.

Like most of his colleagues, Bleyer thought journalism should be taught by teachers with professional newspaper experience; however, he wanted them to be scholars as well. During the period of 1925 to 1935, he attracted a number of former journalists to do graduate work at Wisconsin. Some took masters degrees, but others earned a doctorate degree in a social science discipline, often political science, combined with a double minor in journalism. A partial list of Bleyer's graduate students who later greatly influenced programs at other universities included Chilton Bush of Stanford, Ralph Casey of Minnesota, Ralph Nafziger of Minnesota and Wisconsin, Robert Desmond of California–Berkeley, Kenneth Olson and Curtis MacDougall of Northwestern, Fred Siebert of Illinois and Michigan State, Henry Ladd Smith of Washington, Ray Nixon of Emory and Minnesota, Neil Plummer of Kentucky, Blair Converse of Iowa State, Roy French of Southern California, H. H. Herbert of Oklahoma, Fred Merwin of Rutgers, Hillier Kreighbaum of New York University, and others.

Bleyer believed in internships for students and that credits should be given for practical experience, as on a college newspaper. He was active as well in establishing a professional organization of teachers and scholarly publications such as *Journalism Quarterly.*

The focus on newspapers dominated journalism education through the 1940s at leading schools such as Missouri, Columbia, Northwestern, Minnesota, Wisconsin, Illinois, Iowa, Marquette, and others. But important changes were taking place in "J schools" as radio and television emerged as major news and entertainment media. More courses and, in time, sequences of courses were offered on radio news, television news, and on broadcasting production techniques.

Speech departments, also offshoots of English departments, became involved in the preparation of students for careers in broadcasting. In some universities, the speech or communication arts departments were merged with the journalism programs; on some campuses, they were kept separate.

Concurrently, more and more journalism programs were offering courses in advertising and public relations. Here, too, courses proliferated, with some schools offering sequences in both specialties. Even separate departments of advertising appeared. Obviously, advertising and public relations were distinct from journalism, giving rise increasingly to the term, *mass communication,* to describe this new amalgam of college courses on newspapers, radio, television, magazines, advertising, PR, and an increasing involvement with the study of communication itself.

The Bleyer model of journalism education was particularly influenced by this closely related field—the study of communication, a new academic discipline in American higher education. Wilbur Schramm, who taught at Iowa, Illinois, and Stanford, was the leading scholar in communication studies and is credited with inventing as well as popularizing the field through his prolific writings as well as passing on the word to his graduate students.

The earlier strands of communication study are found in various social sciences. *Communication* can be defined as the study of mass media and other institutions dedicated to persuasion, communication processes and effects, audience studies, information interpretation, and interpersonal communication. Yet, it was more, because communication is one of the few fundamental processes through which virtually any social event can be portrayed. The field grew enormously because its perspective proved a useful one for perceiving society.

Rogers and Chaffee (1994) made a persuasive case that communication study found a lasting home in the branch of journalism education identified with Willard Bleyer and his proteges, Ralph Casey, Chilton Bush, Ralph

Nafziger, and Fred Seibert, all administrators as well as scholars, whose journalism programs developed major components of communication studies, especially at the graduate level.

The universities also produced the new PhDs who staffed the next generation of journalism and (mass) communication faculties from the 1950s onward. Increasingly, graduate work was concerned with communication theory whereas undergraduate courses stressed pre-professional training for careers in news media, advertising, and PR.

By the 1960s, many of the former journalism departments and schools had been transformed and acquired new names such as School of Journalism and Mass Communication, Department of Communication, School of Communications, College of Communication Arts, and other variations. Some did not change their names; at Missouri, it was (and is still) the School of Journalism and at Columbia University, the Graduate School of Journalism.

EDUCATION FOR JOURNALISM
AND MASS COMMUNICATION TODAY

By the end of the century, about 150,000 students were studying for bachelor's degrees in journalism and mass communication at over 400 four-year institutions. Teaching these students were over 5,000 full-time faculty and about 4,000 part-time faculty members, often from local media. Journalism education has indeed become a giant academic enterprise, yet a somewhat amorphous one, with great variations in quality, size, and focus. (Becker, 1999)

Today, there are some excellent programs and others that can only be described as marginal and weak. (Becker's [1999] surveys do not include another flock of related programs, some with such names as Speech Communications, Communication Arts, or Media Studies, which have come out of the speech departments and study aspects of communication as well.)

A variety of journalism and mass communications-related subjects is taught in today's universities. In the Department of Journalism at the University of Texas' College of Communication, sequences (related courses) are offered in broadcast news, magazine journalism, news and public affairs reporting, public relations, photojournalism, media skills, and media studies. The University of Florida, which granted 584 undergraduate degrees in 1998 and has a regular faculty of around 60 full-time instructors, grants separate bachelor of science degrees in advertising, journalism, PR, and telecommunication, as well as masters and doctoral degrees in mass communication.

By whatever name, journalism and mass communication study is not a discipline in the sense that political science and history are but a rather loose interdisciplinary field covering a wide range of subjects somehow related to public communication.

The various research and teaching interests of today's faculties are reflected in the names of the divisions or interest groups within their professional organization, the Association for Education in Journalism and Mass Communication (AEJMC)—advertising, communication technology and policy, communication theory and method, history, international communication, law, magazine, mass communication and society, media management and economics, minorities and communication, newspaper, public relations, qualitative study, radio–television journalism, scholastic journalism (high school), and visual communication. In addition, there are other interest groups on gays, lesbians, and family diversity, media and disability, religion and media, and civic journalism.

BACK TO EDUCATION FOR JOURNALISM

Journalism education, in the narrow sense of pre-professional training and education for careers on newspapers, broadcast news, news services, magazines, or other publications, has become a diminishing portion of what goes on in today's academic programs, just as news operations are a small fraction what goes on at the giant media conglomerates.

A high-school graduate intent on a career in news journalism usually has three options. First, look carefully at the journalism programs offered at well-regarded universities and select one that fits your needs; pick your courses carefully, work on the college newspaper, and try to get an internship or two while still in school. A second option is to obtain a bachelor of arts degree in a social science and then go on for a professional masters degree in journalism at, say, Columbia, University of California–Berkeley, or Northwestern. Finally, the would-be journalist can obtain a good college education and perhaps work on a college paper. After graduation, look for a news job. Graduates of Ivy League and Big Ten universities who lack journalism degrees often have been hired on the national media in the east.

There are several advantages to studying journalism in college. Clearly, it is a path to a news career that many thousands of professional journalists have followed. A student learns about the field—its relevant history, legal controls on the press, ethical and social concerns—and also acquires some basic skills of reporting, writing, and editing news. In most programs, the student also studies social science courses relevant to journalism—history, political science, economics, and sociology. One pitfall for some students is spending too much time on techniques courses—how to run a video camera or radio broadcast gadgets—to the neglect of substantive courses that develop critical and informed thinking. Many journalism teachers believe that a university degree should prepare a student for lifelong learning and not just for the first few weeks on a job; in other words, for a career and not a vocation.

Should a student interested in journalism take communication theory courses in college? Yes and no. Communication and media studies, it has been argued, have very little to do with the practice of journalism. On the other hand, many top communication professors had newspaper or magazine backgrounds, scholars such as Wilbur Schramm, Paul Deutschmann, Ralph Nafziger, John McNelly, and Philip Meyer.

CONTROVERSIES AND PROBLEMS

The evolution from small, newspaper-oriented departments of journalism to larger schools, and even colleges of journalism and mass communication has engendered a number of controversies, some long-standing and unresolved. Some journalism professors as well as newspaper executives have been suspicious of academic research, especially the more theoretical communication variety, feeling with some justification that it has little to do with the news media or the training of tomorrow's journalists and in, fact, impedes the process.

This controversy been around a long time; 40 or more years ago, it was characterized as the "green eyeshades," who thought journalism could only be learned on the job or from ex-journalists versus the "chi squares," the college teachers who measured and counted phenomena but could not teach a student how to cover a police beat or write a good lead. More and more, the professors on journalism faculties doing the most research usually have PhDs in communication and have lacked significant professional media experience. Yet these professors or their teaching assistants have been teaching undergrads how to report and write the news.

This controversy surfaced again in a report of a year-long survey by Betty Medsger (1996), a former journalism teacher and ex-*Washington Post* reporter. Medsger argued that journalism schools need a major overhaul, including changes in the curricula and the credentials that they require of new faculty hires. Medsger found that journalism students are being trained by people with doctorates but little or no experience as reporters or editors. She also reported that journalism courses are giving way to generic communication courses, a trend opposed by news professionals and many journalism educators. The increased emphasis on communication theory at the expense of basic reporting and writing skills has been accompanied by the elimination of journalism as a stand-alone major at some schools.

Some journalism educators agreed with the Medsger report but noted that a number of schools have resisted the trend and have continued to emphasize news reporting and writing "from the sidewalk up." More than half of the journalism educators that Medsger polled reported the number of students intending to become journalists was declining. Most students were heading instead for a related field such as advertising and public relations.

Low beginning salaries for journalists was certainly part of the problem. She cited an annual survey on job recruiting on the Michigan State University campus as evidence. There the starting journalist's average salary of $20,154 in 1996 was the lowest of any college-educated workers entering the workforce. However, it should be added that journalism salaries tend to increase quickly with experience.

By November 2003, the job picture had clearly improved and the median salary for bachelor's degree recipients was $26,000. But this average salary did not compare favorably to salaries earned by other liberal arts graduates. Moreover, the job market for journalism graduates continued to be depressed in 2002 and 2003.

Journalism schools cannot be blamed for low starting salaries. Instead, the responsibility lies with the news media themselves who place so little value on their new hires and make so little effort to attract the best and brightest of college graduates. It is a reflection on our society's values that a Washington media star can make twice as much money for one public appearance than a new reporter can earn in a year.

In general, financial support for journalism education by major media organizations has, with a few exceptions, been tentative and reluctant. Still, over the years there have been some major benefactors: particularly, the philanthropic foundations associated with Gannett, Knight–Ridder, Dow Jones Newspaper Fund, Cox Newspapers and others.

DECLINE AND FALL OF THE BLEYER MODEL

The model of journalism education forged by Willard Bleyer and followed by so many universities is clearly in decline, particularly at the major universities where it once flourished. A number of reasons account for this shift.

First, there were changes in higher education. Before World War II, universities were primarily concerned with teaching, which journalism departments stressed. Since then, we have seen the rise of the research university and the primacy of research over undergraduate teaching. The better the college or university, the greater the rewards—higher salaries, research grants, research leaves, named professorships, lighter teaching loads—go to professors who can win grants and get their research published.

To keep abreast of this trend, universities and even smaller colleges have placed high priority on hiring new faculty with doctorates. In journalism education, this has meant hiring PhDs in communication or other social sciences. Significant professional media experience—5 years or more—is no longer a prerequisite and in fact may be considered a drawback because those years might have been better spent doing advanced graduate work.

It is ironic that at the universities where Bleyer's proteges had the greatest influence—Stanford, Wisconsin, Minnesota, Michigan State, and Illinois—have produced many of the scholars and PhDs who have rejected or downplayed Bleyer's ideas about the importance of preparing young people for news careers.

Further, the research university has often been dubious of any kind of professional training at the undergraduate level whether it be in journalism, social work, or library science. For this reason, California–Berkeley, Columbia, and Michigan have provided journalism training only at the master's degree level. The Ivy League universities have never taught undergraduate journalism. The University of Pennsylvania's Annenberg School has focused on communication studies. Big Ten universities with their "land-grant tradition" of public service were early leaders in journalism education because of a perceived need to provide trained graduates for a state's dailies and weeklies.

In today's research-oriented universities, journalism faculties are expected to do more than teach beginning reporting classes. In fact, in some schools, these basic courses are often taught by teaching assistants with little or no media experience. Most professors prefer to teach substantive or theoretical courses, or better yet, seminars for graduate students that relate to their own research specializations.

Today, the faculties of a number of well-known schools and departments of journalism and communication are really collections of diverse social-science scholars, each with his or her own research interests and priorities. For example, the excellent journalism faculty at the University of Wisconsin–Madison pursues such diverse scholarly interests as history of media and popular culture, communication theory, communication of science news, feminist studies relating to Africa, media in developing countries, history of motion pictures and movie censorship, economics of newspaper publishing, communications law, and problems of misleading advertising, among others. Understandably, this talented faculty, as do others, lacks both the professional background and apparently much interest in preparing undergraduate students for jobs with the news media.

ACCOMPLISHMENTS
OF JOURNALISM/COMMUNICATION EDUCATION

What then has the field of journalism and communications education accomplished in the past 100 years? In short, a great deal. Literally thousands of would-be journalists and communicators have been prepared for careers in news and other related fields of advertising, PR, specialized publications, and so forth. Some editors believe that those who study journalism in college tend to be more committed to the field as a career than those who enter it casually. Lists of distinguished journalists and public communicators can be compiled, for example, from the journalism alumni of Missouri, Columbia, and Minnesota over the years. (Much the same can be said of students who studied advertising and PR.)

Of course, anyone is free to enter and practice journalism. No license or certification is needed; the First Amendment prohibits that. However, a century of journalism education deserves credit for establishing the precept that anyone in journalism or media occupations should have a college education or better, a masters degree.

In the specific field of journalism, many useful textbooks, monographs, and journal articles, including a great deal of press analysis and criticism have been written by journalism faculties. Much of this work on the history, legal aspects, social, political, and economic aspects of journalism has found its way into journalism courses as well as everyday journalistic practices. Many of the numerous books and articles by practicing journalists and broadcasters also are used in journalism courses and reading rooms. A careful look at the impressive *Mass Media Bibliography: Reference, Research, and Reading,* by Eleanor Blum and Frances Wilhoit (1988), with its 1,200 annotations, gives an idea of what has been accomplished and covers all fields except communication law.

Research by journalism and communication professors has contributed substantially as well to a long list of pressing public issues, such as the effects of television on children, improved public-opinion polling, media relationships with politics, and a variety of legal issues such as pornography, access to government news, free press and fair trial, privacy, and so on.

A bibliography of the books, monographs, textbooks, and major journal and magazine articles produced in the past 40 years by the faculties of the leading 24 journalism faculties would be impressive.

In the much broader realm of mass communication and communication studies and research, similar contributions by faculty members have added to our knowledge of persuasive communication, including advertising, PR, public opinion, and propaganda, as well as other facets of communication processes and effects. The academic study of communication, as described earlier, also has had interactions and mutual benefits from like-minded scholars in political science, sociology, history, economics, and education. The field of international communications studies has had global impact in Europe, Asia, and Africa due to work done by American scholars in journalism schools. In fact, the American concepts of journalism education and communication research have been widely emulated in many nations.

Journalism and communications programs have helped, too, to educate the public—the consumers of mass media—to be better informed and more critical of the media. Many non-journalism students in colleges, as well as journalism dropouts, have taken journalism courses, such as introduction to mass communication or mass communications and society. Of course, it will take far more than this to build a critical and concerned public at a time when young people are reading less and paying less attention to the news media.

MID-CAREER EDUCATION FOR JOURNALISTS

Mid-career working journalists who wish to broaden their expertise into new areas have ample opportunities to return to college for specialized study. At least 20 such programs have been available, including the John S. Knight Fellowships at Stanford, Michigan Journalism Fellows at Ann Arbor, Fellowships in Law for Journalists at Yale, the National Arts Journalism Program Fellowships at Northwestern, and the progenitor, the Nieman Journalism Fellowships at Harvard since the 1930s. Participating journalists as of 2000 were well remunerated: At Stanford they got a $40,000 stipend and benefits; at Michigan, they got a $30,000 stipend, plus tuition and a travel allowance.

Surprisingly, applications for these programs have been dropping off in recent years, yet such programs certainly have had an impact on journalism. For example, the Knight Center for Specialized Journalism at the University of Maryland offered intensive week-long seminars on science, technology, business, economics, law, and social issues. More than 950 journalists from some 250 news organizations, both print and broadcast, have attended the 43 courses since 1988.

Another major center for external training for working journalists is the highly regarded Poynter Institute for Media Studies at St. Petersburg,

Florida. Since 1988, for example, *The Washington Post* has sent 84 staff members to intensive writing and editing seminars at Poynter. Training conferences are also offered by the National Institute for Computer-Assisted Reporting and Investigative Reporters & Editors. NICAR's national conference in Boston in 1999 drew 560 journalists and its week-long "boot camps," held mainly at the University of Missouri, have led 752 journalists through statistics and databases since 1994.

CONCLUSIONS AND COMMENTS

Education for both journalism and the broader area of mass communication has both considerable strengths and dismaying weaknesses. The outside critics, for example, fail to understand its research and other contributions of the academy; on the other hand, many professors arrogantly ignore the real concerns of news media about the way students are being prepared to enter the field. Perhaps, we need fewer and better schools of journalism, yet the same thing can be said about law schools, business schools, and schools of social work. Some downsizing seems to be going on with several universities and others are re-evaluating and modifying their journalism and mass-communication programs. Gene Roberts, former managing editor of *The New York Times* has a good perspective because he teaches journalism at the University of Maryland. Roberts sees no problem with the disappearance of some programs as long as an adequate number of good ones remain. He stated:

The country probably needs 30 or 40 or 50—some reasonable number of journalism schools that are really good at what they do.... They should emphasize writing but also emphasize enough of a history of journalism that people really emerge with some sense of where we've been and how we developed as newspapers—and that is missing even more than writing. (cited in Kees, 1996)

Important as that view is, the field is changing rapidly, and the academic community can play a helpful role in dealing with the challenges and opportunities presented by online publications and other innovations in public communication. Change, after all, is what journalism and education for journalism are all about. At the same time, I personally regret the decline in the teaching of journalism as such.

More than any other sequence such as advertising, PR, communication, or media studies, journalism has the greatest claim on being a profession. By objectively and dispassionately gathering all the important news of the day and making it available to the public, journalism performs an essential public service for our democracy and our society.

14

Conclusion: Journalism at a Time of Change

In this question, therefore, there is no medium between servitude and license; in order to enjoy the inestimable benefits that the liberty of the press ensures, it is necessary to submit to the inevitable evils that it creates.

—Alexis De Tocqueville (1835)

For journalism in America today, the news has been both encouraging and dispiriting. At its very best, during a time of crisis or a momentous event, the news media can do a marvelous job of telling the news thoroughly, yet quickly, then following up with needed interpretation and explanation to inform and reassure the public. For example, on the day of the death of China's top leader, Deng Xiaoping, *The New York Times* provided five full pages of news and informed analysis. Several days later, *Newsweek* published a 25-page special report, "China After Deng," written by 11 experts. Such thorough coverage of major news events is not unusual. The well-reported 9/11 terrorist attacks on the United States may have been the press's finest days but the revived interest in serious journalism dissipated as the immediate dangers receded.

Much of the media resumed their bad habits. And even the best news media, when caught up with a riveting but essentially trivial story that may combine varying elements of celebrity, sex, crime, or scandal (preferably all four) can compete vigorously and persistently with the bottom-feeding tabloids for tidbits of scandal. The long-running saga of O. J. Simpson and the death of Princess Diana were only glaring examples of occasional journalistic excesses. This kind of journalism has at times turned much of the public against the news media and damaged the credibility of serious news media.

REASONS FOR CONCERN

This book has been concerned about the fate of serious news and public information at a time when our vast popular culture apparatus has engulfed legitimate journalism into a churning melange of entertainment, celebrity, sensation, self-help, and merchandising—most of which is driven by corporate entities devoted to advertising, promotion, PR, marketing, and above all, a healthy bottom line. Much of the time, the day's news menu seems dull and routine and, at such times, news media have sought out frivolous stories or gossip that may intrigue the public. Reporters are always alert for the good story that will appeal to a wide swath of readers or listeners—regardless of the story's significance. The history of journalism reminds us that newspapers and journalists concerned with reporting significant news have always been a minority. And yet the great news media—as exemplified by *The New York Times, The Wall Street Journal,* and *The Washington Post*—are essential to American public life.

Further, since the time of Gutenberg, the press has always had its critics and enemies, beginning with kings and other autocrats who ruthlessly controlled the printing press for centuries. Yet today, a widespread feeling exists that serious journalism is in trouble, not because of a threat of censorship, but because the news itself—accurate and informative—has become a diminishing portion of what Americans glean daily from their television sets, newspapers, magazines, radios, and computers. Further, news as public knowledge too often seems all wrapped up in a glitzy package of entertainment and diversion. News has too often become trivialized and even on the best media, opinions and assertions have often crowded out carefully recorded factual information.

Equally distressing is the trend that a smaller portion of Americans, especially young people, are paying attention to news from any medium in their reach. Serious news about the public sector and the world beyond our borders does not seem as important and compelling to the public anymore. Polls show that fewer Americans are paying attention to the news—whether on broadcasts or in print. Even if the media provided more serious news, it is questionable whether the public would pay more attention.

There is ample evidence as well that much of the public holds the press in diminished regard and when asked, expresses irritation and animosity toward newspeople. Journalists as a whole are not trusted by the public and are equated in their ethical standards with lawyers, elected officials, and corporate officers—all with self-serving interests. The public views journalists as part of the political elite, not their independent representatives.

Television news, with its tremendous power to inform, educate, and influence public opinion, has largely failed to report much significant news beyond providing an erratic headline service. Among the print media, a few of the national publications still do a competent job of reporting a comparatively wide range of news developments, but news coverage in many daily newspapers is often bland, unimaginative, and incomplete.

Probably the principal concern the news media face, then, is the increasing intermixing of news with entertainment in various forms—gossip and scandal, promotion of pop culture products (movies, television programs, etc.), publicity about celebrities, and eye-catching self-help features on personal health, and so forth.

Neal Gabler (1998) expands on this in *Life the Movie: How Entertainment Conquered Reality,* (1998) and argues that entertainment values have come to dominate the mass media as well as personal conduct. The headline stories of recent years—the O. J. Simpson trial, the bombing of the federal building in Oklahoma City, President Clinton's alleged dalliances, and thousands of other episodes that life generates—these are the new blockbusters that preoccupy the traditional media and dominate the national conversation for weeks, sometimes months or even years at a time while ordinary entertainments quickly fade and the day's serious news is ignored.

Public affairs journalism—the life blood of democracy—has been particularly trivialized and corrupted. Top-of-the-head opinions and predictions, whether on television talk shows or in signed columns or even in news stories, have often replaced careful reporting and cautious interpretation, particularly during political campaigns. Journalists see a deterioration of their professional standards. Highly paid celebrity journalists are perceived by the public as cynical, arrogant, and out of touch with the needs and interests of the average citizen.

Another cause for concern has been the persistent trend toward larger media conglomerates primarily concerned with providing entertainment and diversion for a mass public. News organizations within such behemoths represent a small part of those diverse companies whose main concern is to make profits for their stockholders.

The corporate mentality of these mega-corporations seems at odds with vigorous efforts to aggressively report the news and defend freedom of the press, as did *The Washington Post* during its confrontations with the Nixon White House in the Watergate and Pentagon Papers affairs. The majority of the biggest and best news organizations are controlled by these large corporations that seem to put profitability ahead of public service. Further, corporate journalism, with some exceptions, seems less able or willing to counter or question the overwhelming influence of great corporations on public policy here and abroad.

But all the media, big and small, have been under increased economic pressures to be more profitable. For many hard-pressed newspapers, this has meant cutting staff and trimming news coverage to maximize the return to stockholders and investors. For broadcast news on the television networks, audience share and profitability have higher priority than adequately covering the news from Washington and overseas.

WHAT IS TO BE DONE?

Here are several modest suggestions for reversing some of the discouraging trends discussed throughout this book.

First, most critics believe an immediate challenge is somehow to restore the well- known fire wall that separated news from entertainment and sensation in most responsible news organizations. Editors and broadcast producers in the national media need to make their own news decisions, stand by their standards and values, and forgo chasing after scandalous or titillating stories that surface in the mixed media. Television news—both broadcast and cable, as well as *Time* and *Newsweek,* seem to be seriously corrupted by this scramble for competitive advantage. Change will not be easy because much of the public seems conditioned to equate news with diversion and entertainment. (Another fire wall, the one separating the editorial and business sides of a news organization, has also been breached at times and is a further reason for concern.)

Second, the news business must find ways to improve the stature of journalists, whose public image has become so badly tarnished. To do this, the news media must improve their performance and do their own reporting. Political journalists must work to be again viewed as reliable, objective, and dispassionate news gatherers, rather then highly visible and opinionated performers. The task of winning back the public's respect and admiration for journalists will be a difficult one, because, alas, the majority of us want to be entertained by the news media, not challenged to think seriously about salient public issues.

The public must understand that there is a real difference between a journalist carefully reporting and explaining an important and complex story and a well-paid television celebrity interviewing a rock star or entertainment personality on a television news magazine show. One is a public servant and the other is a quasi-entertainer.

Journalism has some, but not much, claim to being a profession such as law, medicine, or the clergy. The principal virtue that good journalism does have is that, like recognized professions, journalism does provide an essential public service: the reporting and presentation of important news or public knowledge in a disinterested and objective manner. When journalism is practiced in that manner—and eschews the temptations to pontificate, mislead, sensationalize, or entertain—the press merits the unusual protection it enjoys under the First Amendment that "Congress shall make no law ... abridging freedom of speech or of the press."

Another prerequisite of an emerging profession that journalism may some day become is the practice of monitoring and criticizing its own errant colleagues. In an open system of free expression, no journalist can be or should be coerced or restrained by government or by any private source, but, on the other hand, no journalist or news medium is immune from incisive, scalding criticism or censure from their peers or the public.

As mentioned, a real strength of U.S. journalism is the longtime and still-common practice of criticism of press performance from within the ranks of journalists. Such exchanges are healthy and evidence indicates that some egregious conduct has been modified. In recent years, some prominent journalists are avoiding conflicts of interest by steering clear of the lecture circuit and irresponsible television talk shows.

Media criticism may be inhibited, of course, by the complications and practices of multimedia corporate giants. Will *Time* magazine critically report on Time Warner's control of cable channels or AOL's Internet policies? Will NBC News ever look into General Electric's dealings with the U.S. government? Not likely. Despite such problems, more diversity still exists among U.S. news media than in any other democracy.

In the final analysis, *diversity*—the dissemination of news from as many different sources and different facets as possible—may be the most important value to cherish. The media, as well as the public and the courts, must ensure that the public will continue to have a variety of sources of information and opinions from which to choose. When diversity disappears, in its place come orthodoxy and conformity.

Third, the news media must broaden and expand their audiences for serious news, particularly among younger readers and viewers. Newspapers and news itself is often viewed as obsolete or irrelevant among the 50 million who make up the 15 to 30 age group in America. Each new generation tends to read more news as it gets older but still reads less than the previous generation.

News organizations are well aware of the problem but are not having much success in dealing with it. In general, most agree that news content must be more relevant to the needs and interests of young people. Partly, of course, this is an education problem; many in the current generation do not read much and lack the general knowledge of modern history required to absorb and make sense of significant news. Schools must do a better job of educating our youth in national and world history.

In an open, democratic society, members of the public have an obligation to keep themselves informed, to be discerning and skeptical users of the media, and to demand and reward substance and relevance from the news media.

The growth of interactive newspapers on the Internet offers the potential of creating more news consumers among computer users who are mostly younger people.

Fourth, the Internet and other communication innovations have already greatly impacted on journalism and will probably play a crucial role in redefining the future directions and format of news. One editor, Rem Rieder (2003), believes the Internet needs the traditional values of journalism—news judgment, accuracy, fairness, and context—to make sense out of the tremendous volumes of information, much of it inaccurate, tendentious, and misleading that is available to computer users.

As the Internet matures, journalistic skills and values should play a key role. The onrush of raw data, including much garbage and misinformation, will require validators, that is, trusted editors and other experts, to separate the wheat from the chaff. The Internet will require interpretation and context, hence a need for individual, online judges to tell the surfers what it all means. Nonetheless, no one knows just how important a role journalism will play in cyberspace or how, in time, journalism itself will be transformed. Adapting to the Internet and the new mixed media culture are perhaps the greatest challenges to journalism in the years just ahead.

Fifth, another priority for journalism is to restore and expand the importance of world news on the news agenda. It is ironic that at a time when the big players—Murdoch, Time Warner, Disney, and NBC—are all expanding their international operations and seeking foreign markets, the news media they own, as well as the public, are paying much less attention to the world outside our borders.

Two of America's best newspapers, *The Washington Post* and *The Los Angeles Times,* rose to prominence in the 1970s, in part, by expanding their corps of foreign correspondents and carrying much more authoritative news from overseas. Attention to world affairs seems a litmus test of quality journalism but too few other publications have emulated those two dailies.

America's pivotal role in the world today requires greater attention to world affairs. Yet television news, news magazines, and many daily newspapers have been moving away from public affairs news and instead, featuring more self-help and personalized news on health, self-improvement, or whatever story *du jour* might appeal to a large audience. Similar to what is found in women's magazines, this soft news has the effect of pushing aside other more pressing news.

Despite the shortcomings of today's journalism and the low esteem in which many journalists are held, there are reasons for hope and encouragement. The U.S. press still is the freest and most unfettered press in the world and enjoys the most constitutional protection. The values and standards of good journalism and press freedom are firmly established in the hearts and minds of thousands of working journalists, even if lacking in some of their corporate bosses. There are probably more talented and capable journalists now working in America than any time in our history. Most news organizations are financially sound and make money. Americans like to criticize journalists, just as they do politicians and football coaches, but all of us are dependent on the press to know what is happening in our communities and the world. We need the news to know what there is to criticize about the news.

Good journalism has a way of being there when we need it most. During times of national crisis in the previous century—World War I, the Great Depression, World War II, the Korean and Vietnam wars, the civil rights struggle, and the Cold War—Americans have struggled to understand these momentous events and were largely able to do so because they had access to independent and reliable information from their newspapers, radio, and television stations. Today, many Americans are confused by the war on terrorism and really don't understand what it means or portends. We are all dependent on the press for fuller understanding as the intricate story unfolds over future years.

The importance and need of good journalism has not decreased in our society; if anything, we need it more than ever. Take a careful look at any of several leading publications—*The Washington Post, The Wall Street Journal,* or *The New York Times*—and glance at the headlines or tune in NPR's *All Things Considered* and you will be reminded of how important a free flow of reliable public knowledge is to our personal well-being and to the welfare of the republic.

Good journalism does matter.

References

A changing profession. (2003, May) *American Journalism Review, 25*, 9.

Adelson, A. (1994, May 9). More radio stations drop coverage of local news. *The New York Times*, p. C8.

America's best newspapers. (1999, November/December) *Columbia Journalism Review,* 14–16.

Arnett, P. (1998, November). Goodbye world. *American Journalism Review,* 51–67.

ASNE Poll (1998, December 28). Another glum portrait of American journalists. *The New York Times*, p. C6.

Associated Press v. United States, 326 U.S. 1 (1945).

Auletta, K. (1995a, March 6). The race for a global network. *The New Yorker,* 53–54, 79–83.

Auletta, K. (1995b, November 27). The wages of synergy. *The New Yorker,* 8–9.

Auletta, K. (1996, July 29). No honeymoon, no marriage. *The New Yorker,* 29.

Bagdikian, B. (1992). *The media monopoly* (4th ed.). Boston: Beacon Press.

Barringer, F. (1999, June 21). A new war drew on new methods for covering it. *The New York Times*, p. C1.

Bartlett, J., & Kaplan, J. (1992). *Bartlett's familiar quotations.* (16th ed.). Boston; Little, Brown.

Becker, L. (1999) Enrollment and degrees awarded continue 5-year growth trends. *Journalism & Mass Communication Educator, 54*, 3, 5–22.

Best of the Media 2000 (2000, April). *Brill's Content,* 68.

Blasi, V. (1977). The checking value in first amendment theory. *American Bar Foundation Research*
Journal 3, 521–649.

Blum, E., & Wilhoit, F. (1988). *Mass Media bibliography: Reference, research, and reading.* Urbana: University of Illinois Press.

Brandenburg v. Ohio, 395 U.S. 444 (1969).

Brill, S. (1999, July/August). War gets the Monica treatment. *Brill's Content,* 84–95.

Browne, M. (1991, March 3). The military vs. the press. *The New York Times*, p. 45.

Colors of mendacity. (1996, July 19). *The New York Times*, p. A14.

Dennis, E. (1992). Comment on the survey. *Intermedia,* 20, 31, 33, 36.

Diamond, E. (1993). *Behind the Times: Inside the New York Times.* New York: Villard Books.

Dunbar, R. (1996). *Grooming, gossip, and the evolution of language.* Cambridge, MA: Harvard University Press.

Emerson, T. (1966). *Toward a general theory of the first amendment.* New York: Vintage Books.

Emerson, T. (1985). Foreword. In P. Lahav (Ed.), *Press law in modern democracies.* (pp. xi–xiii). New York: Longman.

Emery, M., Emery, E., & Roberts, N. (1996). *The press and America* (8th ed.). Boston: Allyn & Bacon.

Fabricant, G. (1996a, July 20). Murdoch's world from a to z. *The New York Times,* p. C7.

Fabricant, G. (1996b, July 29). Murdoch bets heavily on a global vision. *The New York Times,* p. C1.

Fakhreddine, J. (2003, January 13) News that travels well. *The New York Times,* p. A27.

Fallows, J. (1996). *Breaking the news.* New York: Pantheon.

Fass, A. (2000, March 20). Journalists among the online crowd. *The New York Times,* p. C14.

Fibich, L. (1995). Under siege. *American Journalism Review, 17,* 16–23.

Fibison, M. (1996). Washington Post's Broder aims at media dishonesty, "punditocracy." *Murphy Reporter, 43,* 1–2.

Fleeson, L. (2003, October/November) Bureau of missing bureaus. *American Journalism Review, 32–39.*

Frankel, M. (1994, November 27). The shroud. *The New York Times Magazine,* 42–43.

Frankel, M. (1995, December 17). The murder broadcasting system. *The New York Times Magazine,* 46–47.

Gabler, N. (1994). *Winchell: Gossip, power, and the cult of celebrity.* New York: Knopf.

Gabler, N. (1998). *Life the movie: How entertainment conquered reality.* New York: Knopf.

Gabler, N. (2003, January 9) The world still watches America. *The New York Times,* p. A27.

Getler, M. (1991, March 25–31). The gulf war "good news" policy is a dangerous precedent. *The Washington Post National Weekly Edition,* p. 24.

Geyer, G. A. (1996, April). *Who killed the foreign correspondent?* Presented at the Red Smith Lecture in Journalism, University of Notre Dame, South Bend, Indiana.

Glaberson, W. (1994, October 9). The new press criticism: News as the enemy of hope. *The New York Times,* sec. 4, p. 1.

Glaberson, W. (1995, July 30). The press: bought and sold and gray all over. *The New York Times,* sec. 4, p. 1.

Glass, A. (1992, August 18). The last of an era. *Wisconsin State Journal,* p. 1C.

Goldberg, B. (2002). *Bias.* New York: Perennial.

Goodman, W. (1995, June 16). In Jackson romp, echoes of two mergers. *The New York Times,* p. B1.

Grossman, L. (1998, September/October). The death of radio reporting: Will TV be next? *Columbia Journalism Review,* 61.

Gunther, G. (1994). *Learned Hand: The man and the judge.* New York: Knopf.

Gunther, M. (1995, October). All in the family. *American Journalism Review, 17,* 36–41.

Hachten, W. (1999). *The world news prism* (5th ed.). Ames: Iowa State University Press.

Hachten, W., & Scotton, J. (2002). *The world news prism* (6th ed.). Ames: Iowa State Press.

Hackworth, D. (1992, December 21). Learning how to cover a war. *Newsweek,* 33.

Hand, L. (1945). *Associated Press v. United States,* F. Supp. 362, 372.

Harwood, R. (1995, June). Are journalists elitists? *American Journalism Review, 17,* 27–29.

Herbers, J., & McCartney, J. (1999, April). The new Washington merry-go-round. *American Journalism Review, 20,* 50–56.

Hess, S. (1994, April). The cheaper solution. *American Journalism Review, 16,* 28–29.

Hess, S. (1996). *International news and foreign correspondents.* Washington, DC: Brookings Institution.

Hickey, N. (1996, November/December). Over there. *Columbia Journalism Review,* 53–54.

Hoge, J. (1994, July/August). Media pervasiveness. *Foreign Affairs, 73,* 136–144.

Johnston, D. H. (1979). *Journalism and the media.* New York: Barnes & Noble.

Kees, B. (1996, July). Some universities begin to rewrite the story of journalism education. *Freedom Forum,* 4–8.

Kimball, P. (1994). *Downsizing the news: Network cutbacks in the nation's capital.* Washington, DC: Woodrow Wilson Center/Johns Hopkins.

Kohut, A. (2000, January/February). Internet users are on the rise, but public affairs interest isn't. *Columbia Journalism Review,* 68–69.

Kolbert, E. (1995, October 15). Robert MacNeil gives a thoughtful goodbye. *The New York Times,* p. H39.

Kovach, B. (1996, August 3). Big deals, with journalism thrown in. *The New York Times,* p. A17.

Kovach, B., & Rosenstiel, T. (1999), *Warp speed: America in the age of mixed media.* New York: Century Foundation Press.

Kurtz, H. (1993). *Media circus.* New York: Times Books.

Kurtz, H. (1996). *Hot air: All talk, all the time.* New York: Times Books.

Kurtz, H. (1998, March/April). The erosion of values. *Columbia Journalism Review,* 44–47.

Lasswell, H. (1971).The structure and function of communication in society. In W. Schramm & D. Roberts, (Eds.), *The process and effects of mass communication* (pp. 84–99). Urbana: University of Illinois Press.

Margolick, D. (1994, October 24). The Enquirer required reading in the Simpson case. *The New York Times,* p. 6.

Markoff, J. (2000, February 16). A newer, lonelier crowd emerges in Internet study. *The New York Times,* p. A1.

Masses Publishing Co. v. Patten, 224 Fed. 535 (S.D.N.Y. 1917).

Medsger, B. (April 1996). Winds of change: Whither journalism education? *Freedom Forum,* 10–15.

Miami Herald v. Tornillo, 418 U.S. 241 (1974).

Mifflin, L. (1996a, March 1). For Rather, technology has drawbacks, too. *The New York Times,* p. C5.

Mifflin. L. (1996b, May 13). Media. *The New York Times,* p. C5.

Mifflin, L. (1998, March 22) An old hand's view of TV news. *The New York Times,* p. C5.

Moeller, S. (1999) *Compassion fatigue: How the media sell disease, famine, war and death.* London: Routledge.

Morton, J. (1995, October). Farewell to more family dynasties. *American Journalism Review, 17,* 67–69.

Morton, J.(2003, June/July) Less of a loss. *American Journalism Review,* p. 68.

Mott, F. L. (1947). *American journalism.* New York: Macmillan.

Near v. Minnesota, 283 U.S. 697 (1931).

New York Times v. United States, 403 U.S. 713 (1971).

New York Times v. Sullivan, 376 U.S. 270 (1964).

Nieman poll finds decline in media quality (1995, Fall). *Nieman Reports,* 38–39.

Nunberg, G. (2003, November 9) It's not just the media. These days everyone is biased. *The New York Times,* p. 44.

Pember, D. R. (1992). *Mass media in America* (6th ed.). New York: Macmillan.

Peterson, I. (1996a, January 12). Media. *The New York Times,* p. C7.

Peterson, I. (1996b, September 9). Media. *New York Times,* p. C5.

Peterson, I. (1996c, August 19). *USA Today.* The fast food of dailies, is expanding menu. *The New York Times,* pp. C1, C8.

Peterson, I. (1997, May 19). Rethinking the news. *The New York Times,* p. C1.

Pew Research Center for the People and the Press (1996, May). *TV news viewership declines.* Washington, DC: Author.

Pew Research Center for the People and the Press (1997, April). *The Times-Mirror news interest index 1989–1995*. Washington, DC: Author.

Pew Research Center for the People and the Press (2003, July 13). *Public little concerned with NY Times problems*. Washington, DC: Author.

Phillips, K. (1996, January 28). Bad news. *New York Times Book Review,* 8.

Prato, L. (1996, September). Still tuning to radio news. *American Journalism Review, 18,* 52.

Rafferty, K. (1975). *That's what they said about the press*. New York: Vantage Press.

Red Lion v. FCC, 395 U.S. 367 (1969).

Remnick, D. (1995, September 18). Last of the red hots. *New Yorker,* 76–83.

Rich, F. (1994, October 24). He got the poop on America. *New York Times Book Review,* 1, 31–33.

Rich, F. (1996, May 18). Media amok. *The New York Times,* p. 15.

Rieder, R. (1996, September). Primary values. *American Journalism Review, 18,* 6.

Rieder, R. (2003 May/June) In the zone. *American Journalism Review,* p. 6.

Rogers, E., & Chaffee, S. (1994, December). Communication and journalism from "Daddy" Bleyer to Wilbur Schramm: A palimpsest. *Journalism Monographs, 148,* 1–9.

Rosenstiel, T. (1994, August 22 & 29). The myth of CNN. *The New Republic, 211,* 27–33.

Rothstein, E. (1996, August 26). Anxiety in the land of gargoyles and giants. *The New York Times,* p. B1.

Rottenberg, D. (1994, May). "And that's the way it is." *American Journalism Review, 16,* 34–37.

Rutten, T. (2003, June 6). *Information superhighway carries Raines to his exit, Los Angeles Times* online edition.

Schell, J. (1996, August). The uncertain leviathan. *Atlantic, 278,* 70–78.

Schudson, M. (1995). *The power of news*. Cambridge, MA: Harvard University Press.

Schuster, S. (1988, May/June). Foreign competition hits the press. *Columbia Journalism Review,* 45.

Self-censorship at CBS. (1995, November 12). *The New York Times,* p. 14E.

Shafer, J. (2003, July 16) The Washington Post grand plan to give it away. *Slate.*

Shepard, A. (1999, February). White noise. *American Journalism Review,* 20–25.

Shaw, D. (1994, Spring). Surrender of the gatekeepers. *Nieman Reports,* 3–5.

Simon, J. (1999, March/April). We're all nerds now. *Columbia Journalism Review,* 19–27.

Soifer, A. (1985). Freedom of the press in the United States. In P. Lahav (Ed.), *Press law in modern democracies* (pp. 79–133). New York: Longman.

Stepp, C. S. (1995, October). The thrill is gone. *American Journalism Review, 18,* 15–19.

Stewart, J. (1999, July 4). Consider the sources. *New York Times Book Review,* p. 8.

Strentz, H., & Keel, V. (1995). North America. In J. Merrill (Ed.), *Global journalism* (pp. 355–394). White Plains, NY: Longman.

Tipson, F. (1999, August) Goods move. People move. Ideas move. And culture changes. *National Geographic,* 12.

Waxman, S. (1999, November 9). Los Angeles' troubled Times. *The Washington Post,* p. C1.

Who gets paid what. (1999, May) *Brill's Content,* 84–95.

Witcover, J. (1998, March/April). Where we went wrong. *Columbia Journalism Review,* 19–25.

Wald, M. (1996, November 10). Cyber-mice that roar, implausibly. *The New York Times,* p. 5.

Walsh, K. L. (1996). *Feeding the beast.* New York: Random House.

Zane, J. P. (1996, September 29) Liz's love life! Oprah's diet! Dole's foreign policy! *The New York Times,* sec. 4, p. 2.

Author Index

Subject Index